Street Smart Internet Marketing

Street Smart Internet Marketing

Tips, Tools, Tactics &
Techniques to Market
Your Product, Service,
Business or Ideas Online

Justin Michie

Published by Performance Marketing Group Inc.

ISBN: 1-4243-1963-3
ISBN-13:   978-1-4243-1963-3

Notes to the Reader:

While the author and publisher of this book have made reasonable efforts to ensure the accuracy and timeliness of the information contained herein, the author and publisher assume no liability with respect to loss or damage caused, or alleged to be caused, by any reliance on any information contained herein and disclaim any and all warranties, expressed or implied, as to the accuracy or reliability of said information. The publisher and the author make no representations or warranties with respect to the accuracy or completeness of the contents of this work and specifically disclaim all warranties. The advice and strategies contained herein may not be suitable for every situation. It is the complete responsibility of the reader to ensure they are adhering to all local, regional and national laws.

This publication is designed to provide accurate and authoritative information in regard to the subject matter covered. It is sold with the understanding that neither the author nor the publisher is engaged in rendering professional services. If legal, accounting, medical, psychological, or any other expert assistance is required, the services of a competent professional should be sought.

The words contained in this text which are believed to be trademarked, service marked, or to otherwise hold proprietary rights have been designated as such by the use of initial capitalization. Inclusion, exclusion, or definition of a word or term is not intended to affect, or to express judgment upon the validity of legal status of any proprietary right which may be claimed for a specific word or term.

The fact that an organization or website is referred to in this work as a citation and/or potential source of further information does not mean that the author or publisher endorses the information the organization or website may provide or the recommendations it may make. Further, readers should be aware that the websites listed in this work may have changed or disappeared between when this work was written and when it is read.

Success in any business is a result of hard work, time, effort and a variety of other factors. No express or implied guarantees of income or spillover are made by reading this work, or by joining and/or purchasing any program(s) recommended within this work. Individual results may vary.

Printed in Canada
Simultaneously published in the United States

10 9 8 7 6 5 4 3 2 1

Dedicated to my wife, Christine,
my children Kaylin and Ty,
my Mom, and my entire family,
who have been exceptionally supportive
throughout this entire process.

MEMBERS ONLY WEBSITE

While researching for this book, I came across countless links that did not work, or sites that had simply changed direction since their links were published. That's the nature of the internet. It is constantly evolving and changing, faster than any other medium on the planet, and something that's there one day, may not be the next. Therefore, don't be surprised if you go to a link in this book, and it's no longer there, or not what it's supposed to be.

For that reason, I have created a special membership site for readers of this book, so you'll always have access to the most up-to-date information available. You don't need to provide any additional information, not even your email address.

Simply go to www.ssim.biz and login using the username: "ssim" and password: "member"

Besides up to date website links, products and services that I recommend, I'll also post all kinds of other information including free ebooks, articles, tips, techniques, current trends etc. that can assist you in building your online empire.

Finally, I must ask that you don't share this username and password with your friends, as it is specifically for people that read this book, and I don't want to be responsible for misguided use of the information provided.

Contents

Section 2
What You Need to Know About Websites

Section 3
Email Marketing Secrets

Section 4
Search Engine Optimization

Section 5
Low Cost Website Promotion

Section 6
Joint Venture and Affiliate Marketing

Section 7
The Conclusion

i

Introduction

You may not realize it yet, but the book you're holding in your hands has the potential to dramatically change your life – forever. Once you open your mind to the possibility that you can live very comfortably working only a few hours a day, a few days a week, from the comfort of your own home, life as you presently know it will cease to exist.

But there's a catch; you will actually need to apply some of the techniques and strategies you'll read about and adapt them to your business and/or life. You can't just read this book and expect miracles to happen. They won't.

As you're reading I encourage you to highlight important topics, make notes in the margins and dog ear the pages. Keep this book in your office or by your desk and use it as a reference guide whenever you can.

As a business owner and entrepreneur I have spent thousands upon thousands of dollars educating myself with some of the top marketing and business growth experts in the world. There's nothing stopping you from doing this as well, and I recommend that you do. The only downside is that it costs a lot of money, and takes a ton of time. If you can afford to, go nuts. But if you can't, the purchase and study of this book is the next best thing.

While I was writing this book I struggled with whether I should have it published traditionally, sell it as an ebook, or sell it as a complete internet marketing course. As a book, it sells for $19.95, as an ebook it would have sold for $197, or as a complete internet marketing course for $497. As you can probably guess I opted for the traditionally published book. Want to know why?

Writing a book isn't a good way to make a lot of money. After all is said and done, you only make a few dollars per book after almost a year's hard work. When you're an experienced successful marketer, it's not directly worth it to write a book for the money. In the time it's taken me to write this book, I could have made many times more money through other, less time consuming methods. For me, there are two reasons to write a book: you either write to gain prestige, or because you want to help people increase the quality of their life. To be brutally honest, I've written this book for both reasons. I want to help you become more successful and increase your quality of life both, personally and financially, and I'll also take any glamour that comes with being an optimistically slightly successful author.

Also, by publishing a $20 book, it allows me to reach a far bigger market. Not everyone can afford $497 for a home study course, or even $197 for an ebook, but almost everyone can afford $19.95; in fact you can't afford to not afford $19.95.

Money Talk

As you read this book, you might notice that I talk a lot about increasing the amount of money you make. Although the concepts in this book focus on growing your business to ultimately make you more money, I want to recognize that making money is not the most important part of life. Friends and family are, and they should always come first. The reason I focus on making money online (besides the fact that this is what the book is about), is that having money allows you to live life the way it was meant to be lived. And that increases the quality of your life and ultimately the lives of those around you.

Some people say that money doesn't buy happiness and it doesn't. You can't go to your local corner store and say "I'd like to buy $100 worth of happiness please." However, if you have enough money, it allows you to do a lot things that can ultimately make you happier.

In fact, even a study by Macleans (a Canadian magazine) found that people with more money are actually happier. Think about it: not worrying about paying your bills, being able to go on vacation whenever you feel like it, buying what you want, driving the car of your choice and living life the way you want while still having the same family/friend relationships… How could you not be happier?

When you have money, you don't worry about it; in fact you don't even think about it that much. It's just always there, like the air we breathe - you never really give much thought to it; unless of course, it's not there. You don't waste time wondering about if you can make next months rent or mortgage payment. Trust me, I've been there, and it's no fun sitting down scraping together dollars to make sure there is enough money in your account so your payment doesn't bounce.

My Story

I had an expensive car, I had a big house, I'd go on vacation to fancy resorts; my friends and neighbors thought I was successful, but the truth was, I could barely pay my bills. I was in over my head. Creditors were calling me on the phone everyday. Credit cards were being cancelled; I had to take out a second mortgage on my house, a loan on my car, borrow money from family and friends… I was merely days away from bankruptcy. It wasn't because my business wasn't going well, it was going well. But not well enough to pay off the half million dollars of debt I had accumulated at the age of twenty-two! When I was twenty, I had $0 debt; in fact I actually had a little money in the bank.

You might be asking yourself "How do you go from 0 to -$500,000 in less than two years?" It's quite simple really: make a bad (expensive) business decision, take a risk you shouldn't take, and think you know it all, as many young people do…

So, I sold my house, sold my business assets, paid some of my debts, and moved across the country to start over. I am entrepreneurial by nature, and could not stand working for anyone else. I have never had a real job, and this was definitely not the time to start. Since I liked the theory of internet marketing, and had some experience with it since I had used it to successfully market my offline businesses, I reached a life changing decision: I would become an internet marketer.

Why I Love Internet Marketing

The reason is really quite simple: it's so darn convenient. The thing that drives me absolutely crazy about the internet is the ultimate freedom it affords. It gives me complete control of my life. I don't need to ask my boss if I want to take a few days off. I work when I want, not when I need to. I don't need to work late, unless I want to. I have lots more free time to spend with my wife and kids. My job does not control my life, my life controls my job.

I don't need much office space. I don't need any, or many employees. I don't need a storefront. I don't need to store/keep inventory. And with a laptop and an internet connection, I can work from anywhere in the world.

THE INTERNET = ULTIMATE FREEDOM

The other thing I love about the internet is that it makes it extremely easy to make money. You just test and track things until you find something that sells, then you test some more until you sell more. The more testing you do, they more selling you'll do and the more money you'll make.

Not that I want to be boastful, but if I choose to, I could work a couple of hours a day, a few days a week, and live better than most of the population. Why? The reason is simple: The internet is an automatic money making machine. You set it up, get it started and: it sells for you, it processes transactions, it even delivers the goods - and you don't even need to lift a finger.

Compared with socially accepted traditional businesses, internet marketing takes little time, little money, and is the ultimate low risk investment with potential for the creation of enormous amounts of income. Think about how much would it cost to:

- Open, staff and run a small store? $100,000 +
- Start and run a carpet cleaning service? $25,000 +
- Design, create and sell a physical product? $10,000 +

More importantly, how much does it cost to make money on the internet? The real, honest-to-God answer is: as much or as little as you like. Literally, in less than twenty four hours you could be making money marketing on the internet, without so much as spending a penny. But you must know how, and that's what this book is designed to help you with.

The theory for making money on the internet is really quite simple:

1. Have a product or service to sell
2. Create a website
3. Drive traffic to your website
4. Sell them your product or service

In theory it's a walk in the park, but there are so many variables to consider throughout the process that it actually becomes very complicated. But that's why you bought this book, isn't it? The concepts I discuss are so amazing that they literally allow you to make truckloads of money 24 hours a day, 7 days a week, 365 days a year, while you sleep, eat or watch TV in your underwear.

You'll probably notice that I mention and/or recommend a lot of ways to do things throughout this book, as well as some websites, products and services that I use or have used. I just wanted to note that the methods and strategies I recommend are not the only ways to do things, but it's what works best for me and a lot of other people, that have made a lot of money doing things the way we do them. Of course, you're always more than welcome to try things out your own way, or use different products and services if you like.

Furthermore, time is our most valuable asset, so I am not going to waste yours. You'll find that throughout this book, I will be as direct as I can and get straight to the point. I don't believe in sugar coating anything. If you can't take a little constructive criticism, then in all honestly you probably shouldn't be reading this book. I will do my best to accurately tell you how it is, without any hype, fluff or filler in only as many words as I need and none extra.

Now that that's out of the way, what you are about to read are some of the most closely guarded and powerful marketing concepts for making money marketing on the internet, period. I should warn you though, that the power and potential of the information I'm about to share with you may cause as many sleepless nights for you as they have for me. It may be a little overwhelming, and your mind might countlessly wander through the unlimited potential as mine did. When you're ready, turn the page and let's get started.

Section I

Electronic Marketing

I

What Exactly is Internet Marketing?

When you walk into a room full of strangers, you are judged in the first few seconds. People notice what you look like, how you dress, how you carry yourself, even what color your eyes are. They quickly determine whether you are someone that they may be interested in communicating with, or if they should pass you by. Marketing is no different; if your campaign doesn't have something that shouts out "Hey, this is for you!" most people will quickly move onto something else.

So, what exactly is marketing? If you go to a search engine like Google and type in the word "marketing" you'll get well over a billion hits. With that many people claiming to know something about marketing, it can undoubtedly be difficult to understand what exactly marketing is. Similarly, if you ask a dozen people to define marketing, chances are you'll get a dozen different answers.

If you are in any business, whether it is home based, or you have a corporation with a hundred employees or more, when it comes down to it, no matter what your business is, "You are in the marketing business!" The reason is simple: if no one knew about your business, how long could you remain in business? How would people find out about your business? Bottom line - how would you make any money? This is why marketing is so important and a skill that we cannot afford to live without. We all possess some amount of marketing ability; however, those who utilize and spend the time to grow their skills will greatly improve the quality of their business, and ultimately their life.

Marketing is everywhere; it is all around us, on the TV, in the newspapers, on the internet and at the shopping mall. None of these circumstances exist by accident. They all are a result of marketing. In a recent study by the Yankelovich Partners, it was found that the average person encounters 3,000 ads every day, 7 days a week, 365 days a year. That is over a million marketing messages a year, which is known as the clutter factor. How do you compete with everyone else in a society that is mostly run by mega corporations with millions of dollars in their marketing budget? You don't. Marketing does not need to be expensive; in fact it can cost you little or no money at all, especially on the internet. It does however, need to be clear, clever, creative, well planned out, and most importantly, it must work.

Selling

Marketing is often confused with advertising or even worse selling. Many people even see the words as synonymous. A study suggests that the word "selling" triggers negative thoughts in the minds of about 95% of people. Most of us try to avoid negative situations, and therefore (many without ever realizing it) steer clear of anything that has something to do with selling, and more importantly, marketing. Realistically, that is not good for business.

When you think of selling, what is the first thought that enters your mind? For many, it is that of a used car salesman, a door to door vacuum cleaner salesperson, a life insurance broker or something of a similar sort. How many people like used car salesmen? What do they dislike about them? Are they too pushy, too smooth, do they talk too much?

Believe it or not, selling is a very important skill and something that when used properly can greatly enhance the quality of your life. However, you don't need to sell like a used car salesman - there are many different ways to sell. You need to find out what works best for whatever you may be selling, whether it is a particular product, service, or used cars. Used car salesmen sell the way they sell because that is what works best for them, and yields the highest results.

Selling is everywhere: When you apply for a job, you must first sell yourself on paper through your resume, and if you're lucky (or should I say skilled) enough, you get a chance to sell yourself in person through an interview. All other qualifications being equal, the applicant who has the best sales skills will surely always get the job.

The two most basic and important aspects of selling are the features and the benefits. What's more important, the feature or the benefit? Well, features are great, but if they don't apply to, or interest the customer then what good are they? For example, suppose you were shopping for a cell phone for use only in the case of an emergency, and the sales person at the store is going through a list of its features; the internet and email capability, the built in GPS, the fact that it can not only take pictures, but video as well, you can store 10 gazillion phone numbers yada, yada, yada. All these features are nice to have, but in reality what good are they if you will never need to use them? How do they benefit you? If they don't - then why should you care about them?

Features describe your product. Benefits are what your customers get when they use your product. When you talk about your product, you are doing "feature" selling. When you talk about results, you are "benefits" selling.

For example, when airlines want to sell you airline tickets to Hawaii, how do they do it? Do they describe the kind of aircraft you'll be flying in? Do they brag about the in-flight meals? Do they boast about the leg room? Or do they show you pictures of palm trees, sand and sun? Palm trees are benefits. Leg room is a feature. You'll get more people to Hawaii with palm trees.

Features are for the head. Benefits are for the heart. Features are about logic. Benefits are about emotion. Emotion will always outsell logic ten-to-one. Logic may be an important part of the sale... but only after you have engaged their emotion.

In essence, selling is the ability to describe the benefits of a product or service, as to make people eager to buy. Most people fail at selling for one reason: they simply don't ask for, or close the sale! The ultimate salesperson is one who can get customers to desire a product or service without even realizing that they are being sold to. Imagine what could you do with skills like that?

Advertising

Advertising is only part of a much bigger and more important marketing plan, but it happens to be the most common form of marketing and what most people automatically think of when they hear the term marketing.

Advertising is the promotional material that companies use to communicate their product or service. Some examples of advertising include, newspaper and magazine ads, TV and radio commercials, trade show booths, trade publications, direct mail, promo clothing, brochures, business cards, newsletters, internet and emails ads, and the list goes on.

One of the many goals of advertising is to successfully and effectively reach the largest number of people for the least amount of money. You need to carefully balance cost and effectiveness as different types of advertising have very different returns on investments (ROIs). Though, you might not want to necessarily utilize the type with the highest rate of return, as they usually cost the most upfront. For instance, direct mail can cost about a dollar a piece (postage, printing costs, and handling), whereas radio and TV can cost pennies a person. Direct mail will yield a much higher conversion rate than TV, but you need to look at the total cost involved in relation to the total sales and profits.

There are two general categories of advertising: direct and indirect. Direct advertising has by far the highest return rate, however it can cost significantly more than other types of advertising. The main reason that direct advertising is so effective is that only people who are already at least slightly interested in your product or service receive your material. Essentially, when using direct advertising you would send your material directly to a specific individual or business. You can either use your own mailing list made up of past customers, or you can buy or trade lists from other companies in a similar, but non-competing businesses.

Indirect advertising is made up of everything else, newspapers and magazines, TV and radio, trade shows and conventions, promotional products, billboards, infomercials and indirect mail just to name a few. Indirect advertising is called so because you do not send your promotional material directly to a specific customer as you do in direct advertising. In most cases of indirect advertising, you utilize a third party medium to get your message to the consumer. Your ads usually reach a very large audience, of which only a very small part are actually likely prospects. The more specific you get in the medium you use the better the return will be. For example, if you placed a TV commercial on a random television station at a random time, would you be reaching your target audience? Probably not. But if you carefully researched who watches what, and when they watch it, then placed your ad on a specific station at a specific time, you would have a much better chance of reaching your target audience.

Since direct and indirect advertising both have their pros and cons, how can you possibly decide what type of advertising to use for your business? Let me give you a hint. Direct advertising is the most effective and also the most expensive – right? Wrong! Ever heard of email? Direct email marketing costs almost nothing to use, and can be very effective when used properly.

But email is not nearly as effective as direct mail right? Right - it was found that people are ten times more likely to respond to a letter than email. So what do you do? Gather information and keep in touch (weekly newsletter/report) by email, then follow periodically by mail to only those you know are interested in what you have to offer. Sending something in the mail periodically also helps to build credibility as your customers actually have something physical that represents you, as opposed a faceless, virtual online email.

Marketing Defined

So now that we know what selling and advertising are, what exactly is marketing? Let me get right to the point: Marketing is the business activity of presenting products or services to potential customers in such a way as to make them eager to buy. It is everything and anything you do that brings a prospect to desire your product or service. Everything really means everything. It is in everything that you broadcast to the world. It is how you present yourself. It's how you dress, how you perform. Anything you send or put out into public. Absolutely anything that you do that influences people to want to do business with you.

Marketing is all of the activities that ensure the products and services we want are available to us at a place that is convenient to us for a price we are willing to pay. Therefore, a product's characteristics, its distribution and price are all tailored for a particular group of people and marketing communication keeps us informed. In my opinion:

Marketing is the single most important skill that an individual or group of individuals can possess!

This about that for a second... marketing is everywhere and one of the things that makes the world go round. Once you understand just how powerful marketing is for you and your business, it has the potential to completely transform your life.

Marketing on the Internet

The internet offers us an amazing new world of interconnectivity, and with that, a new way to interactively communicate with prospects and customers. Marketing on the internet gives you an unprecedented opportunity to communicate your message to millions of potential customers, for little or no money.

Internet marketing first began in the early 1990s as simple, text-based websites that offered product information. It has now evolved into complete automated online businesses with potentially unlimited possibilities. The actual term "internet marketing" however, is somewhat slippery and can mean different things to different people. Internet marketing is essentially everything that you do, both online and offline, to influence people to buy your product or service from an online medium such as a website. It is an all-inclusive term for marketing products and/or services online – and like many all-inclusive or umbrella terms, internet marketing includes many different aspects such as: search engine optimization, pay-per-click, paid-inclusion, directory submissions, linking campaigns, online press releases, website copywriting, website design strategies, online promotions, reciprocal linking, email marketing, online yellow pages, banner ads, email campaigns, newsletters and ezines, and more recently blogging and RSS feeds, just to name a few.

According to "The Changing Face of Advertising in the Digital Age" from Parks Associates, by 2010 spending on the internet will account for 10% of the total ad dollars spent in the United States.

The goals of internet marketing and traditional marketing are essentially the same - ultimately the common purpose is to present your product or service to the consumer in such a way as to desire them to buy it. Internet marketing is really based on the concepts of traditional marketing methods, but geared to the internet, a more modern marketing medium.

If you do a search in your favorite search engine for "internet marketing" take notice that the vast majority of ads (not listings) associated with internet marketing are focused on helping websites get more hits or traffic. Is bringing in web traffic what constitutes the definition of internet marketing? Not really. While traffic to a website is just as important as traffic to any retail store, it is only a part of internet marketing, albeit a important part. It isn't necessarily the amount of traffic that you should be concerned about, but the percentage of the traffic which you turn into sales; and how big the average sale is. Once you get the kinks worked out and are converting the largest possible percentage of visitors into customers, you can focus on getting more traffic to your site. If you haven't done everything possible to convert the traffic you are already getting into sales, you're only wasting your time and money on generating new traffic.

In some industries, the internet has lowered the cost of entry so that entrepreneurs, many times from a home office, can compete competitively with larger companies. While the cost of operating a physical business (such as a store) is steadily increasing every year due to the high cost of real estate, marketing and employees, the price to start an online business is declining due to cheaper domain registration, web hosting, shopping cart software, web and graphic design among other things. A few years ago it might have cost you four or five hundred dollars to get started on the internet; now you can start for next to nothing at all.

Marketing on the internet also gives you an unprecedented opportunity to communicate your message to millions of potential customers, for a very small amount of money and time when compared to that of traditional marketing. Along with a highly effective way to market your business, products or services, the internet has brought us a slew of new terminology, new techniques, and new twists in implementing marketing strategies and processes.

The reasons for marketing on the internet are quite simple:

Marketing on the internet allows you to get more done, in less time with less money.

That's exactly why I started marketing on the internet. I used it to market my offline businesses online because I didn't have a lot of extra money. When I started out, I was the marketing director, corporate executive, general manager, employee trainer, custodian, secretary, laborer and so on, so my time was somewhat limited. The internet was my solution. For a small amount of money, and not too much of my time, I could market by way of the internet, 24hrs a day to a very large segment (comparatively speaking) of my target market. In just two years my startup business was taking enough business away from the larger million-dollar marketing budget companies that it forced them to downsize. The funny thing is, they could never figure out where I came from or how I did it. That's because they didn't understand they true power of the internet... and until then, neither did I.

Benefits of Internet Marketing

The internet has become a part of most families household and daily routines. It gives people the ability to shop online, bank online, communicate quickly and effectively, and find out anything about everything, all from the comfort of their own home. There are thousands of businesses that solely rely on the internet to make money. If the internet were to suddenly dissappear ovenight, millions of people would be out of work. It's that big.

Consumer Benefits

Consumers love the internet for any number of reasons. They can browse products or services, 24hrs a day, 7 days a week. Not only can they use the internet at any time to browse products, they can also compare brands, prices and buy goods and services without having to face a single sales person with just a few clicks of the mouse.

That means no sales pitch, no emotional persuasion, no driving to the store and fighting for a parking space, and no battling crowds. Buying on the internet is quick, private and convenient. Oh yeah, it's also usually cheaper to buy something, pay for shipping/handling and get it delivered to their door.

The internet also provides them with a wealth of information at their fingertips which they could find nowhere else, not even an enormous library. They also have the ability to communicate, not only in words, but in pictures, audio and video as well.

Business Benefits

More and more businesses are turning to the internet for a variety reasons, most of which revolve on saving time, money and having easy access to their target markets. Nearly a billion people today have the ability to connect to the internet, which literally gives you access to more people than any other single medium on the planet. In addition, Forrester Research estimates that by 2010, online sales are expected to reach $329 billion in the United States alone.

Internet marketing is so popular that there are entire businesses dedicated to teaching people how to market on the internet.

Perhaps the biggest business benefit to marketing on the internet is the money that it saves. It has a very low cost of entry, which in turn lowers the risk, and has the possibility of huge success. If you wanted to open a retail store, it might cost a minimum of a couple hundred thousand dollars. It only costs a few hundred dollars, and even less in some cases to open an online store.

The other place that internet marketing saves money is in the advertising department. If you printed up a catalogue of your products and mailed it to 1,000 people, it might cost you $10,000 for design, printing and postage. If you distributed your catalogue via the internet it might cost you a few hundred dollars. What's more, what if you wanted to add new products, correct an error, or remove something you no longer carry? In the physical world, you might need to redesign, reprint, and re-mail the catalogue every year or so which would cost another $10,000. On the internet, it's still only a few hundred dollars, if that.

Another very compelling benefit of the internet is that it allows the marketer to inexpensively and effectively reach an unprecedented number of people anytime of day, any day of the week. Not only are you able to reach new customers, but you are also able to interact with them. By doing this, you are able to better understand their needs, wants and buying habits. It doesn't make any difference if they're in North America, or Australia. The internet destroys limitations of geography. Your website is always open and people can browse it at their convenience.

Some of the main benefits to marketing and doing business on the internet include the following:

- Unlimited worldwide market
- Extremely low entry cost
- Excellent ROI
- Saves money
- Saves time
- It's mostly automated
- It is open 24/7
- You don't need many or any employees
- Work from home if you choose
- Testing and tracking is a piece of cake
- Easily get surveys, suggestions, orders and more from customers electronically
- Cost effective distribution of your materials, whether customers are down the street or worldwide

On the internet, it's important to note that the surfer has all the power. If they don't like the site they're visiting, literally, in the push of a button they can be somewhere else, looking at someone else's advertising.

The rest of this book will show you the best practices and most effective methods to market your product, service, business, ideas or interests by the way of the internet. Let's turn the page to get started!

2

What Do I Market – A Product or a Service?

When you break it right down to the basics, for your business to make money you must either sell a product or offer some kind of service. When your neighbor wakes up in the morning, showers, has a bite to eat and goes to work, they are getting paid for a service which they are providing to their employer.

In service based businesses such as consulting, construction, factories or web design, there is a finite amount of work that can be done based upon the time that's available to do the work. There is absolutely nothing wrong with providing a service, however (pay attention, this statement could change your way of thinking forever): **In a service based business you are limited to the number of hours you and/or your employees can work each day.** You are essentially getting paid for your time and if you can't work more hours, how can you double, triple or quadruple how much money you make?

In a product based business, the amount of money you can make is only limited by how many products you can sell. Since it's not a relatively significant amount of extra work to sell 100 or 10,000 products, there is no cap on your income. Products can often be produced fairly quickly with a low number of man hours in comparison to that of a service based business. The main constricting limit is how quickly you can sell. If you can sell it, then there's someone who can produce it just as quickly.

Consider this for a moment: How much extra time does it take to produce a television ad series for a local TV station, versus a national network? It would and should probably take a little extra time (maybe double, triple or even ten times the time) because the ads need to be of a higher standard and more testing should be done. But the time difference in not at all comparable to the impact the ad could have. A local station may have 10,000 people who view your ad in the allotted time, while a national network might have 10 million. For only a few times more work, you could have a 1,000x increase in sales, if your conversion rate remained similar. I know that doesn't take into account the money aspect, but that's for a reason: there's no cap on how much money you can have, but there is a cap on how many hours are in a day.

So then, what is the best possible type of business to have, service based, or product based? That's easy, in a service based business you are limited by how quickly you can train and hire employees, and how many hours those employees can work. Sure, you could probably do well, and eventually earn an above average income, but is that enough? Is that what you want? Is that the best you can do? If it is, then fine; if it isn't, then keep reading.

If you want to make a lot of money in a relatively short period of time, you *need* to go with a product based business. A product based business can grow as quickly as you can sell – the sky really is the limit. Though, whatever type of product you sell, it is important that it can be very quickly and easily reproduced.

I don't want you to misinterpret what I'm saying; I'm not telling you to call it quits if you have a service based business. I'm just very politely letting you know that you might possibly want to consider making a small change here or there, **if you want to be hugely successful, quickly!** That doesn't mean going out and starting something new tomorrow, but it does mean looking at your business in a new way. If you're strictly service based, find and add a product that you customers could use.

For example, if you own a hair salon, start selling hair care and related products at your salon. Um, yeah, don't most salons already do that? Of course they do, the ones that don't are no longer in business. What else could you do?

Offer a free consultation to your customers on what hair care products are right for them; then sign them up for a monthly subscription and deliver the products right to their door. Start up a website and do the same thing online. Write an ebook on how to care for your hair like the stars, then sell it online.

You could even design your own line of hair care products to sell in your salon, distribute to other salons and/or sell online. Get your customers email addresses and send out a weekly newsletter with on hair care tips, tricks and techniques, and maybe a coupon or two. The possibilities are endless. What can you do with your business?

In a product based business you basically have two options: You can sell a lot of a cheap product or you can sell a little of a very expensive product. I have a relative of mine who sells yachts, very expensive yachts with prices starting at a half a million dollars. How many yachts do you think he has to sell to make a decent living? Not very many: only one or two a year.

I also have a friend that sells toothbrushes. At an average wholesale price of less than $1, how many does he need to sell to stay afloat? Say he makes $0.20 for every toothbrush he sells, how many would he need to sell to make an income of only $50,000? That's right, a quarter of a million toothbrushes. What do you think would be easier: selling one or two luxury yachts to a very specific target market, or selling hundreds of thousands of toothbrushes to everyone? (Ok, you caught me, I don't really have a friend that sells toothbrushes – but you get the picture). What do you think is more enjoyable, begging big corporations to buy your toothbrushes, or sailing a luxury yacht around to exotic boat shows only when you feel like it? How would you rather spend your time and your life?

Now that we've decided that a product based business it the best way to go, what kind of product should you ideally sell? Well, let's look at some examples.

George has designed a revolutionary new garden gadget that he sells for $100. George primarily markets his product on TV through infomercials and the home shopping channels. George's costs are broken down on the next page:

Manufacturing Costs	*$40*
Marketing Costs	*$20*
Administrative Costs	*$ 5*
Storage & Distribution	*$ 3*
Packaging Cost	*$ 2*
Total Costs	*$70*

Net Profit → $100 - $70 =   *$30*

Therefore George makes 30% net profit for every item he sells. Let's check out another example:

Meghan has developed a six CD audio set on how to write a book and get it published, that she sells via her website, magazine classified ads and trade shows. Her costs are as follows:

Manufacturing Costs	$ 6
Marketing Costs	$18
Administrative Costs	$ 3
Storage & Distribution	$ 1
Packaging Cost	$ 2
Total Costs	$30

Net Profit → $100 - $30 = $70

Why does Meghan make 70% net profit, and George only makes 30%? Why does Meghan make almost two and a half times that of George? Let me tell you: Megan is selling one of the hottest commodities available on the market today: **INFORMATION**. What's so good about information you ask? Well, for more info on information, check out the next chapter.

3

The Best Business in the World: Information Marketing

Information marketing is as simple as it sounds; the marketing of information. Some people also refer to information marketing as infopreneuring (entrepreneur who sells information). Information marketing or infopreneuring is undoubtedly the most exciting and lucrative business in the world. Here's why:

- Unlimited worldwide market
- Easy to research
- Easy to create
- Easy and cheap to test
- Easy and cheap to produce
- Low cost start-up
- High perceived value → high mark up → high profit margin
- Mobility - operate from anywhere in the world
- You don't need any or many employees
- Work from home if you choose
- Make money 24/7
- Automation of sales and distribution process
- Cost effective marketing

To continue with the examples from last chapter, let's take a look at an automated web based information business.

Heather has written a 250 page ebook, which she sells for $100, on how to immigrate to the United States. She markets, sells and distributes her ebook exclusively via the internet (website, email, joint ventures etc.) Her costs are outlined below:

Manufacturing Costs $ 0
Marketing Costs $ 4

Administrative Costs	*$ 1*
Storage & Distribution	*$ 0*
Packaging Cost	*$ 0*
Total Costs	*$ 5*
Net Profit → $100 - $5 =	*$ 95*

This example not only shows how lucrative information marketing is, but also the beauty of doing everything (marketing, distribution, production, packaging, sending) via the internet. As you may notice, there is very little operational and production costs. The bulk of the business expense lies in the marketing department, exactly where it should be.

If you have an expertise in anything, sell it - it has a market value and you can easily turn your story into money. Turn your specialized knowledge into something that the average person in your target market can use.

The serious money is in providing specialized information, that is properly packaged, and can be quickly and easily accessed, to create fast results.

Let me give you a little example of why I like information marketing so much:

Traditional job: work, get paid, work, get paid, work, get paid

Information marketing: work, get paid, paid, paid, paid, paid…

When you create an information product you only need to work once to create it and you keep getting paid over and over. This book, for example will continue to sell over and over for the next three-to-five years, and I don't need to rewrite it each time I sell a copy. But that's what you, your neighbour, friend or family member are doing each time you or they go to work. You work; then get paid for your time, and if you want to make any more money you need to work again. To me it seems silly that people would choose to live this way. You have no real freedom, no real flexibility and quite often your boss has more control of your life than you do. That's not living, and there's no reason life needs to be that way.

Most people have jobs for any one of three reasons: they need money, it offers stability, or they really like what they do. Even if you love your job, nobody says that you can't do anything else with your life.

With information marketing there is zero or very little risk. You can start very small in your free time and create a short 40-50 page ebook. If you only spend only an hour a day, in about a month you could be selling and making money with your first information product. Find out more in Chapter 31 on page 245.

Information is everywhere, and with the widespread use of the internet, the amount of information at our fingertips has never been so great. That's exactly the problem with information – there is so much of it that most of us don't know what to do with it all, or where to start. That's where you as an information marketer come in.

The problem faced by many is not a lack of information or ideas, but a lack of information that is packaged properly. Believe it or not, there are thousands of people that are looking for the information and expertise that you have. There are mountains and mountains of information out there, so much so that as Robert Allen puts it, "we are drowning in data." The problem is that most of the information is in its raw form. It needs to be refined and transformed into something that is actually useable. Your job as an information marketer is to refine the mountains of raw data into specialized knowledge, then present it in a way the consumer can easily assimilate and use quickly.

I was watching TV the other night, and Donald Trump was on with Conan O'Brien because he had just come out with a new information product, which he was promoting. The reason that it struck me is because even a multi-billionaire like Donald Trump knows just how important information is, and how much money he can make from it.

The 3 Steps to Sell Information

There are three main steps to selling information, and with a little practice (and sometimes a little help) it's something anyone can do.

Step #1 - Research

The first step in selling information is the research or gathering step. If you know a lot about something or have a core expertise, a good part (but not all) of your research may lie in determining that the information you have is something other people want. In the upcoming paragraphs, we'll discuss how you research, discover, acquire and/or organize your ideas.

What do you know that we don't? Or who do you know that knows something that the rest of us need or want to know? You don't need to spend years becoming an expert in something. You do however need to borrow, license, acquire or rent the expertise from someone. If you don't have an expertise that you can write or speak about, the easiest way to go about finding someone who does is to look for an expert who is under marketed. Then ask them if they would consider letting you repackage their information and take it to the marketplace. Negotiate a way to split the profits that will be mutually beneficial; then they're happy, you're happy and you'll both have more money in the bank. Here's an example:

You go to a PTA meeting at your kid's school there's this guy there speaking on how to influence your children to form good study habits. He really seems to know what he's talking about and is selling an under-priced Saturday seminar on the subject. You could approach him with an offer to either market for him on a commission based basis, or better yet, take his information and repackage it in the form of a self help book, ebook, audio or video disc, or anything else for that matter, then split the profits with him.

No matter whether you yourself are the expert, or you are using someone else's expertise, proper research is essential. No matter how much you know, or how great your expertise, you need to be able to back what you have to say up with facts, studies and real world examples. Take some time to make sure that what you're saying is correct and can be verified. Nothing ruins your credibility more than when a customer catches you saying something that is not true. If they catch you just once, how can they know that everything else you say is correct? Check, and double-check the facts before you put anything to print.

There's been a saying that's been floating around for quite a while; it goes like this: "Copying from one or two books is plagiarism, but copying from many is research." That doesn't mean to copy anything word for word, or to take other's ideas and call them your own. But it does mean that you can learn from the experience of others, form your own conclusions, then put them to print, audio or video. Take any non-fiction book for example; most of the concepts and ideas in the book have surfaced somewhere, sometime in the past; everything is not by any means a completely new idea or concept. The key is how you package them. How you put them together into something that is concise and easy to apply and understand.

I believe it was Jay Abraham who said *"All the notes had already been discovered long before Mozart came along."* It's not the notes that are important, but how they are packaged together (into a song) that matters. Information is much the same, you can take the same information, repackage it into something that is easier to understand and implement and you have a whole new product. It's a simple concept called repurposing or repackaging information. An ebook could easily become an audio CD set, or a home study guide.

In conclusion, make sure you take the time to produce quality work, and that means researching your information. Be sure others back up what you have to say, as a mistake can be drastically costly to you or your business. Don't forget that once you publish your information, there's no taking it back -- it's out there forever.

Researching the Market

Before you even start creating an information product, or make a deal with an expert to use his or her expertise, you need to research the market. An easy way to do this is to look for other people that are selling similar information. If there isn't anyone selling it, there's probably a good reason – there's no market for it. That doesn't mean there's no one who wants your information, it just means no one wants to pay for it, or not enough people want to pay for it to make it profitable. It would be very rare that you come across a category of information no one else has tapped, and in my opinion you're better off with something that is tried and true than something new. There's no reason to try and reinvent the wheel.

Determine who your potential customers are and then determine their needs, wants, and expectations; figure out if there is a demand for your product. Get their opinions about it. Find out how they would like it packaged (book, audio CD) and how much they would be willing to pay for it. Then take a look at who your competitors are and how well they are doing. Find out what they're doing, how they work, then do it better. It's as simple as that.

While market research may appear to be a tedious, time-consuming process, it is often necessary if you want to be successful. It is an invaluable tool that can save you time, effort and money.

Step #2 – Packaging

Packaging isn't limited to fancy graphics and showy slogans on the package of your product. Packaging is how your information is organized, including the form you sell it in, at what price, and how easy it is to use. The main goal of packaging is to make sure that your product is desirable to the consumer. That means everything from choosing the right format for selling your information, to making sure that it is organized in a fashion that is easy to understand and simple to implement.

These are the three steps which are essential to proper packaging:

1.   How you physically package it

2.   The way you organize the materials
3.   Selecting the best price to sell your information for

Packaging Information

This isn't what color or type of packaging you should use, but the format that you use. The format is the medium which you convey your information through. This could be anything from an ebook, to a DVD, to hosting a live seminar.

Perhaps one of the most important aspects of information marketing is how the information is packaged, or put together into a format that is easy to follow, can be quickly accessed, and can achieve fast results. That is what makes the information that you have to offer so much better then that of all the other information floating around out there. There is tons of raw information swarming all around us. But most of us don't have the time to sit down and decipher it into something that is easy to understand, and easy to use. Not only do you need to provide the information, but you must provide the tools for the user of the information to integrate it into his or her business and/or life.

There are tons of different ways you can package your information. Thirteen of the more popular packaging techniques are listed below.

1.   Publish a book or article
2.   Host a seminar
3.   Become a public speaker
4.   Host a teleseminar
5.   Publish a newsletter or ezine
6.   Create a computer program or educational game
7.   Produce a television program or infomercial (informative commercial)
8.   Become a consultant
9.   Teach or train
10. Publish a magazine or newspaper
11. Become a talk show host
12. Create a product (how to course, audio CDs, video etc.)
13. License your information

Put yourself in the shoes of your target audience. What format of information would you want most? What would work best for your needs and lifestyle? Don't stop at just one format though. If you start with an ebook, put it on CD. If you have a home study course, teach it in a seminar or teleseminar. Start with one format, then branch out and expand. Different people like different formats. Some people might like a home study course, then to go to a seminar and learn that way, then listen to audio CDs in their car as a refresher. Give some choice, but not too much or people will put off making a decision.

Organizing Your Materials

The big thing about organization in general is the fact that it keeps things neat and tidy and puts them in a place where you can easily find and use them. When you're organizing information the goal is much the same. A good information product must be:

- Organized

- Simplified
- Systematized
- Personalized
- Interactive
- Ready to use, on demand, instantly

Most people don't have the time to spend studying and reorganizing the readily available data into something that fits their unique circumstances. They want something they can use now, which is easy to understand and provides fast results. And the best part is, they're willing to pay for it.

To illustrate this, let's say you own a late model car that requires lots of love (think maintenance and repairs) to keep it running in tip top shape. You may have a decent knowledge of how cars work and enjoy working on yours, but you don't know absolutely everything about everything, and might need a little guidance once on a while. When you need help, you have a few options:

1. Ask a friend or acquaintance for help who might possibly know something you don't.

2. Plop yourself down in front of your computer and plough through webpage after webpage in an attempt to find something helpful (and correct) on the internet.

3. Or, you buy a readily available book for $29.95 at your local book bookstore that explains everything you'll ever need to know.

Do you spend the $30 for the book, waste countless hours researching for credible information on the internet, or ask a friend who might know? Since I value my time, the choice for me is easy; I spend $30 for the book. Research shows that most other people feel the same way. Why? The book gives you access to immediate, credible, specialized information that you can quickly act on.

Price

A well-thought-out marketing strategy takes into consideration not only the marketing factors, but also pricing strategies. While it's always important to make a profit, if the market won't bear such a high price, it's better to lower your profit margin than not do any business at all. You may actually be able to make more money with a lower price than you will with a higher one. Make sure your marketing plan combines marketing and pricing.

Also be sure your price is fair and competitive with the marketplace. If your price isn't right, people will pass you by without even giving you a chance. Above all, always be sure you test different price points adequately to determine which will make you the most money, not get the most sales.

Step #3 - Marketing

When you're selling anything, marketing is the absolute most important skill to have. If you wanted, you could market junk with right marketing campaign (not that you would want to). Since this entire book is on internet marketing, we won't go into too much detail here on how to market your product, the rest of the book will cover that. We'll just cover some of the basics that apply to information marketing.

Marketing information can be both harder and/or easier than marketing other types of more physical products. If you're trying to convince people that they need the information you have to offer, it can be quite a chore to actually persuade them to purchase it; especially with all the free information floating around on the internet. However, simply find the right audience that knows the true power of properly packaged information and the impact that it can have on their lives and their business. If you find the right market and they'll be begging you to sell them anything they can buy.

When selling any type of product online, including information, there are four routes you can take:

1.   You can create **your own product** from scratch (write an ebook).

2.   You can join an **affiliate program** and sell products that have been created by other people and earn a commission from every sale you do.

3.   You can join a **multilevel marketing** (or network marketing) program.

4.   You can acquire **resell rights** for products already created by other people and earn 100% of the profits.

Option 1 is a must do, eventually. However, if you're itching to get started immediately, you don't always want to wait to get a product put together.

Option 2 is great for a quick start, except that you're working on commission, and someone else is gaining a new customer, and ultimately the majority of the profits from your hard work.

Option 3 is a good choice only if you're a natural networker. If you don't like networking, this probably isn't the best choice for you.

Option 4 is another good choice; all you need to do is find someone who is willing to grant you resale rights to their product. The only downside is that you must have enough money upfront to purchase the rights.

For the purpose of this chapter, we're going to concentrate on option 1; and touch on options 3 and 4. Towards then end of the book (Chapter 34 and 35), there's two full chapters on option 2 - affiliate marketing.

Option 1 – Creating Your Own Info Product

Creating your own information product is a must and a great add-on if you already own a small (or large) business. The rewards of creating your own product are a definite advantage. Not only do you get to share your own, or someone else's expertise, but by doing so you get to help improve your customer's quality of life. The best part is that you keep all the money you make - you don't split it with anyone else, nor do you work for a commission. You get all the money, along with the recognition of having your own product that you created.

There are no real new or totally unique human needs or wants. They have been the same for a long time: money, self esteem, sex, health, relationships, beauty and greed. Your information should tap into one of these universal wants or needs:

"How to Earn an Extra $50,000 - $100,000!"

"Stay in Shape Exercising Only 10 Minutes, 3 Days a Week"

"How to Have the Best Sex of Your Life"

If you already have an established email list or database of prospects or customers, one of the easiest ways to find out what they want is to ask them. Are you trying to sell them what they want or what you think they need? Find out what information is vital to them and how they want that information packaged. How much information do they really want? How much are they willing to pay for it? You would do well to ask these questions to a representative of your list before you ever put your fingers to the keyboard. If you don't have a database, get one. Find out how in Chapter 19.

You can also discover who else is already providing information to your target market. Who are the top information providers in your field? Who are the best? The biggest? The most expensive? Sign up for their email list. Let their salespeople sell you. Become a customer. Get their product. Rip it apart. What makes it so special? Is it a matter of design? Is it the marketing? Find out their strengths. Probe for weaknesses. Observe what other startups are doing. Are they gaining market share? If they are, what are they doing to draw away customers from the big boys?

If your list is already buying info products from someone else, here are a few questions to ask:

What do they like and/or dislike about your competitor's product?

What would they add to your competitor's product to make it perfect?

What would they remove from your competitor's product that is not necessary?

If they could design it exactly the way they wanted, how would they do it?

Ask questions, find out what they do and how they do it. Then, the best way to distinguish the information you are offering from your competitors is your competitive advantage. Make sure your information product is:

- Faster to implement
- Cheaper
- Simpler
- More efficient
- Prettier
- More secure (longer, stronger guarantee)
- Has more features, benefits to the consumer
- Better value
- Better design
- Advertised more
- Better advertised

- More easily available

These are the things people look for and the more you can do better than your competitor, the larger your competitive advantage and your list of very satisfied customers. Always remember, when you're selling anything, you're not selling a product - you're selling the results it produces.

Above all, don't forget to position your product properly. Remember, people are lazy. If they have a choice between easy and hard they'll take easy every single time. If they have a choice between fast and slow, they'll take fast every single time. If they have a choice between simple and complicated, they'll take simple every single time.

Option 3 – Multilevel Marketing

Multilevel marketing is no small thing... by the early nineties, more than 100 billion dollars worth of products and services had been moved because of it. Multilevel marketing (MLM), also known as "network" or "referral" marketing, offers you a commission for the products you sell and also for the sales of those you recruit or refer to the program. Multilevel marketing isn't for everyone. If you're not a natural networker, or even a little on the shy side, it probably isn't the best choice for you.

Here's how it works: After making an initial investment, you receive the marketing materials and/or products necessary to sell start selling. In many cases, the products are nutritional or healthcare related including vitamins and weight loss supplements. Every time you sell something you get a commission, as does the person who recruited or referred you. In addition to selling the product, you need to refer or recruit others to the program, and then you'll earn money from what is sold by people you've recruited into the program. In fact, multilevel marketing probably puts more emphasis on the recruiting part than the selling part. The more people you bring into the program, the more money you're likely to earn through their commissions.

If you've done any looking into home based businesses and even if you haven't, you've probably read articles and news programs warning you to stay away from multilevel marketing programs. While it's true that many of the multilevel marketing opportunities aren't really what the promise to be, not every multilevel marketing opportunity is a scam. What the news programs and articles warn you against is not really multilevel marketing, but a pyramid scheme. Pyramid schemes focus only on recruiting distributors, not selling a substantive product to make money. The new participants pay a fee to participate and hope to profit by recruiting others into the system. No products ever really get sold as they're just a front for the pyramid scheme, so as to appear as a legitimate MLM business. Most areas have laws banning pyramid schemes that pay commissions for recruitment, not sales of products. However, most MLM companies still typically structure their payment plan so that recruiting is more profitable than selling. With the right company, multilevel marketing is a legitimate, moral way to make money.

The thing about MLM is that is almost always requires you to make an initial investment, and often even a more substantial investment for additional training or marketing materials. The most successful companies usually have the most advanced educational programs which cover everything from marketing and sales, to leadership and money management.

The failure rate with multilevel marketing is very high. The main reason being that most people give up after a month or two because they haven't made the fortune they thought they would. It usually takes longer than that for the sales and commissions to start to roll in at a significant rate. If joining an MLM program, you need to first make the decision as to whether it is worth it to work hard for possibly a long period of time without much of anything to show for it.

Some MLM companies have opportunity meetings or training seminars. The hidden agenda is usually to get you hyped up and purchase an advanced training package, or additional materials. Don't ever sign a contract at one of these high pressure events. Insist on taking your time to think over any decisions. Talk it over with your spouse or a knowledgeable friend or peer first to be sure you're making the right decision.

One last consideration before you decide to get into MLM is that many people see it as a scam. Because of this, you might have trouble recruiting others to join you in the program, and thus making a financially rewarding go of it. If you are interested in investing in a multilevel marketing program, you'd be well advised to research the company and product thoroughly. Do some research on the net first and check with the Better Business Bureau. There are a lot of scams out there, and if you're not careful, you could become part of one of them.

Option 4 – Resell Rights

Have you every bought or looked into buying a cheap ebook? If you have, you probably know that a lot of them come with some kind of resell or resale rights. These cheap $10, $20 or $30 ebooks are all over the internet and provide pages and pages of words often with little actual content. I know because I own thousands of these ebooks with so called resell rights and most of them are junk. The only reason authors sell them with resell rights is so they can justify charging more. When I talk about making money with resell rights, this generally is not what I'm talking about.

Needless to say resell rights come in many forms and sizes. They can come in large packages of many products that are bundled together and offered for an almost suspiciously low price (junk), or they can be offered as a single product for thousands of dollars. If you're looking for a way to make money with resell rights, you want to make sure you purchase something that actually has value, which means it will cost more than a few dollars.

Resell rights have different restrictions, limitations and allow you to do different things, so as always, be sure to read the terms and conditions.

Basic resell rights often only give you the right to sell the product and don't offer much other flexibility. You usually cannot claim the product is your own and you do not have permission to offer the resell rights to anyone else. Sometimes you can change the affiliate links to your own, other times you need to leave things exactly as they are. Basic rights are usually the cheapest to purchase, so it can be a good way to get started.

Some of the conditions or restrictions to look for are as follows:

- The price(s) you can sell the product for.
- Can it be given away as a bonus?
- Can it be given away for free?
- Can it be modified in any way?
- Can you change the affiliate links to your own?

- Are there any conditions for distributing the product on membership and auction sites?

Master resell rights often include a web or sales page with the product. They give you the right to resell the product and allow you the right to sell the resell rights to your customers as well. However, that is typically as far as it goes; your customers cannot sell the resell rights for the product to their customers. While master resell rights usually do not allow you to alter the product, they quite often allow you to replace the affiliate links with your own, and usually offer more flexibility in terms of how you distribute the product including pricing.

If you're buying the resell rights to software make sure you know the product well enough to deal with any troubleshooting inquiries. Some software rights sellers are prepared to deal with inquiries themselves which is a definite advantage for you. Software may also come with a FAQ or troubleshooting webpage or link to the manufacturer's webpage that you can use.

There are also two types of resell rights that may be referred to as private label rights. The first type is where you are given resell rights for a finished product and you are allowed to put your name on it as the author or creator. This is usually for information or software products.

The second type of private label rights is known as source code rights. The product may or may not be ready to sell. Sometimes it is raw material that you can use to produce a finished product such as information for an ebook that needs to be organized, or the source code for a software product. With the source code rights you can change the product in any way you want. You can add your name as the author, put in your links, add, remove or change the content, or even split it into several products.

Most often with both types of private label rights you are able to sell resell rights and even master resell rights. Most private label rights packages also come with a webpage, sales letters, graphics and other ads that you can use to sell the product. If you are buying private label rights you are also able to edit the product. This is especially important if you are buying rights for software. Private label rights are usually priced in the hundreds or thousands of dollars range, however they offer you more flexibility and the opportunity to make a lot more money than you could with basic or master resell rights.

As always, take time to do market research before purchasing the resell rights to anything. Make sure there are people who actually want the product and are willing to pay for it. Find out how many other people have bought the resell rights, so you know how many competitors you have. How do they market the product? And are they successful?

4

Internet Marketing Terminology

If you're fairly new to the internet you may be overwhelmed by the ton of technical information that's available, especially when it comes to internet marketing. There are many new and very different terms that were coined specifically for the internet marketing world. Some are confusing and some are simple. Some are simple but sound confusing. This chapter is designed to give you an idea of what they are, what they mean and how they relate to you doing business online.

Conversion Rate

One of the most common marketing terms whether it be online or offline is the conversion rate. The conversion rate usually refers to the number of prospects that convert to a sale. On the internet the conversion rate refers to percentage of website visitors who take the desired action. The desired action can take many forms including sales of products or services, newsletter subscriptions, membership registrations, downloads, or any other action that you want your visitor to take.

If 4 visitors out of every hundred to your website purchase a product from you, then your conversion rate would be 4% (4/100).

A high conversion rate depends on several factors, all of which must be at least satisfactory to yield the desired results: the quality of the visitor, the attractiveness of the offer, and the ease of the process.

1. The quality of the visitors depends primarily on how they get to your site. How targeted are your ads, search engine listings and other links to your site? How interested are your visitors when they arrive at your site? Again, this is a case of quality over quantity, especially if you're paying for each lead. All other factors being equal, your conversion rate is directly proportional to the quality of visitors you receive – the higher the quality of visitors, the higher the conversion rate and vice versa.

2. The attractiveness of the offer includes the value proposition and how well it is presented. The attractiveness is influenced by several factors:

    - What is the offer?
    - How much does it cost?
    - What is the perceived value to the visitor?
    - How well is it presented?

3. The visitor's ease of completing the desired action is dependent on site usability which includes ease of navigation, access to additional information, page load time, payment methods accepted and so on. The easier you make it for them, the higher your conversion rate will be.

Small, impulse items typically have a higher conversion rate than large, "I'll shop around before I make a decision" items. The easiest way to increase your conversion rate is to test different variables in your advertising. This could be the headline of an ad, or the price of a product. Find what yields the highest possible results and then test another variable. It goes without saying that the better the conversion rate, the more sales you'll do, and the more money you'll make.

Impressions

An impression is a single instance of an ad being displayed on a webpage. The acronym CPM refers to the Cost Per Mila (Spanish term) meaning cost per 1,000 impressions.

For example $10 CPM is $10 per 1,000 impressions, or $0.01 per impression. Therefore 10,000 impressions purchased at $10 per CPM would be 10,000 impressions x $0.01 per impression, or $100 total.

Click-through Rate

Another factor that will help determine the number of sales you do is the click-through rate (CTR) of any online advertising with a direct link to your website. The click-through rate (CTR) is the average number of click-throughs on your ads per hundred ad impressions (or ad views), expressed as a percentage.

To give a quick example, if your banner was shown on a webpage 1,000 times, and 27 people clicked on your banner, your CTR would be 2.7% (27 clicks / 1,000 impressions), meaning that for every hundred people who see your banner, 2.7 will click on it.

A high click-through rate does not necessarily assure a good conversion rate - the two rates may even share an inverse relationship. An advertisement geared towards curiosity clicks will result in fewer sales percentage-wise, than an advertisement geared towards qualified clicks.

The CTR measures immediate response to an ad, but not an overall response because it doesn't account for the people who saw the ad, then visited the site at a later date. An exception involves ads that display no identifiable information about the destination site (such as a web link); where in these cases the click-through rate equals the overall rate. With a steady click-through rate and conversion rate, the math is simple: the more visitors you get to your site, the more sales you'll do. More sales = more money.

Cost and Payment per Click-through

The terms payment per click-through (PPC) and cost per click-through (CPC) are sometimes used interchangeably. The difference is that PPC indicates payment based on click-throughs so you only pay for every click-through that you receive; while CPC indicates measurement of how much it costs you on a per-click basis when you're paying per impression.

For example, consider a campaign where payment is based on impressions, not clicks. Impressions are sold for $10 CPM and you get a CTR of 5%.

1,000 impressions x 5% CTR = 50 click-throughs

$10 CPM / 50 click-throughs = $0.20 per click

Therefore your cost per click-through (CPC) is $0.20.

On the other hand, you could have an ad campaign where you pay a predetermined amount of $0.25 for every click-through to your website. If you receive 100 click-throughs you pay 100 x $0.25 or $25. Your CPC is $0.25.

Paying per click is seen by some as a compromise between paying per impression and paying per action. When paying per impression, the advertiser assumes the risk that the traffic generated by the publisher may be of low quality. When getting paid for actions, the publisher assumes the risk of a low conversion rate on the advertiser's sales page. With PPC the advertiser does not need to worry about low quality website traffic since users actually have qualified themselves by clicking on the ad showing interest, and the publisher does not have to worry about a low conversion rate on the advertisers site. Pay per click is a middle ground and what most advertisers prefer to use. I generally don't pay for impressions (unless it's a super great deal) as it's not usually worth the cost and it drastically lowers the overall conversion rate of my website.

Payment per Action

Payment per action (PPA), sometimes also referred to as payment per sale (PPS), is an online advertising payment model in which payment is based solely on qualifying actions such as sales, registrations or signups.

The actions defined in a payment per action agreement relate directly to some type of conversion, with sales, registrations and signups being the most common. This does not include deals based solely on clicks, which are referred to specifically as cost per click (CPC).

The PPA model is at the other end of the spectrum from the cost-per-impressions model (CPM), with the cost-per-click model somewhere in the middle. In a PPA model, the publisher is taking most of the advertising risk because their commissions are dependant on a good conversion rate on the advertiser's website.

PPA advertising is essentially the same as an affiliate program. The publisher gets paid when the advertiser makes a sale or other qualifying action.

Commissions can either be percentage based or flat rates. The nice thing for the advertiser (you) is that you don't pay until you get paid. There will be much more on affiliate programs in towards the end of this book in Chapters 34 and 35.

Cost per Visitor

CPV is the amount that it costs you to get each visitor to your website. This is very useful to know, so you can determine exactly how much you should spend on advertising per visitor to keep the numbers positive.

If your conversion rate is 2% and your product sells for $100, for every 100 visitors you receive you make $200, (100 visitors x 2% conversion x $100). That means each visitor is worth $2 to you ($200/100 = $2) on the front-end. So you can spend up to $2 on advertising for every visitor you receive, and more if you have a strong back-end.

Cost per Sale

The cost per sale (CPS) in marketing terms is simply the amount it costs you in advertising to make each individual sale. Simply divide the promotional cost by the number of sales to calculate the CPS.

For example, if you spend $500 on a text ad campaign and you generate 10 sales from that campaign, your cost per sale is $50, ($500 / $10). If your product sells for $200 that's great - you make $150 from each sale, but if it sells for only $50, the text ad may not be worth it - unless you're using the $50 product as a loss leader to generate leads for future backend sales.

Here are some more terms that you should be familiar with:

Customer Acquisition Cost (CAC) – This is the amount that it costs you on average, in promotional, technical and other related costs to acquire each new customer.

Value per Visitor (VPV) – This is an average of how much each visitor to your site is worth in terms of sales.

If you have 100 visitors and 5 of them purchase a $100 product from you, then your VPV is $5, ((5 x $100) / 100 visitors).

Annual Customer Value (ACV) – This is how much each customer is worth to you on average, in sales each year.

Why is all this helpful?

Well, if it costs you $500 to acquire 100 new customers, then your CAC (customer acquisition cost) is $5 per customer. If your AVC (annual customer value) is $80, then it is well worth it to spend $5 acquiring each customer. If your goal is to acquire 500 new customers this year, then you'll need to budget $2,500, (500 x $5).
Alternatively, it might cost you $3 in acquisition costs for each name you add to your list. If your conversion rate of your list each time you send an email offer is 2%,

and you send 10 emails per year to an email list of 1,000 people, you would make 200 sales over the course of a year, (1,000 x 2% x 10 emails). If your average sale is $50, then that totals $10,000 in sales, or an average ACV of $10 per email, ((200 sales x $50/sale) / 1,000 people). Since it costs you only $3 for each email address and you make $10, you would make a total profit of $7 (not including developments, design, creation and other overhead costs) per email address.

There are other internet marketing terms such as search engine optimization that we will discuss in the rest of the book that are pertinent to the chapters they're discussed in, so I've saved them for then. The terms defined above are among the most common, especially when dealing with testing and tracking and should give you a good understanding, as well as the ability to get started. If you're unsure of any of the other marketing terms I've used throughout this book, check out the glossary starting on page 299 for more definitions.

So, how do you know how many people actually visit your webpage, where they come from and what they buy? You must track your results, which ends this chapter, and begins the next.

5

Tracking – Measuring Success

One of the greatest attributes of the internet is the ease of its ability to track and be tracked. You can't test properly if you don't track and you'll have a hard time knowing what works and what doesn't if you don't test. Tracking and analyzing traffic to your website can prove to be invaluable for serious website owners. If you want to improve your site and grow your business, there are certain things you need to know. That's why you need a stat tracker to monitor your web statistics. Chances are you will spend a lot of time, money and effort on your ads, and without tracking their performance, you will have no idea what's hot and what's not.

A stat tracker is a marketing tool that tracks particular things on a website including the number of click-throughs to a specific URL, sales ads conversion rates, ROI, where the visitors come from, where they live, what browsers they use and so on.

There are two main ways to monitor your stats: through the web logs generated by your hosting companies server, or through a third party tracking service.

There are also ad trackers and stat trackers. Ad trackers might track the success of a particular ad campaign, how many clicks and sales you received, where the visitors came from and so on. Stat trackers also have the ability to track ads, but they also track a variety of other options including where the visitors live, what browser and operating system they use, what search engines they came from (and for what keywords) and a whole bunch of other options.

Most web hosts offer web logs, but not all do, so check with your host, or look in the control panel of your hosting account. These logs contain important information such as the user's host or IP address, the file they requested and at what time and what URL they visited last. They are usually found in the control panel of your hosting account under "web logs" or "log stats" and can be interesting to look at, but are unnecessary if you use a proper statistics tracker.

Sometimes, the tracking in the stats area of your web hosting account counts every item on a webpage as a hit. If for example, your webpage had 3 graphics plus the HTML file, it would count as 4 hits. If a visitor visited 5 pages, with an average of 3 graphics each, it would count as 20 hits, ((3 graphics + 1 HTML page) x 5 pages), but there would only be one unique visitor. For this reason you need proper tracking software that counts unique visitors, along with the many other things it tracks that your web logs don't.

When I say unique visitors, I mean unique. If a visitor finds your webpage, moseys around for awhile then comes back a few hours later and looks around some more, they should only count as one unique visitor. A unique visit is a single computer connecting to your website. While each visitor may view several pages and travel throughout your site, they will only register once as unique (usually per 24 hour period).

I should note that some other things like web counters that track the number of visitors to a webpage, count one visitor every time the page is loaded, or when a new page is viewed. If you went to a website with one of these counters 3 times in a single day, it would count you as 3 visitors.

Simple Tracking Methods

URL Tracking

You can track your ads simply by adding some special coding to your URL. To code your URL, add a question mark followed by a special tracking code to the end of your web address. Your coded link will still open your webpage. Your code could look something like this:

www.yourdomain.com/?ad1

The text after the question mark should identify a specific ad. To view your results, you'll need to look at your web log files. Your code will be displayed within your log files beside your URL. Though, as mentioned this does not necessarily track unique visitors or any other pertinent information. It will count a visitor every time the link is clicked.

Relay Pages

Relay pages aren't used too often anymore. However, they are occasionally used by third party ad trackers. For example, some will give a unique web address that will track your ads results, then forward or relay the visitor to your website. Relay pages have a code on them that keeps track of each time it is loaded. The relay page (also known as a refresh page) then magically redirects the visitor to whichever page you like after a preset amount of time.

Types of Stat Trackers

There are two types of stat trackers you can use, three if you include the stats included with your hosting. I don't include them because they're not anywhere near sufficient. The first type is a stat tracking software that you can purchase, and install on your web server. The second is to use a third party tracking service.

Installing Tracking Software on Your Server

The big thing here is that you usually need your own dedicated server to install the software and you need to have some technical ability (or know someone who does) to install it. Instead of making a small monthly payment there is usually one larger upfront payment, which may or may not benefit you depending upon the amount of the payment. Perhaps the best part of installing actual software on your computer is the fact that there is no dependence on third parties, and they are slightly more discreet for users.

Many third party tracking companies charge you for each website you have, so if you buy a software license which allows you to use it on unlimited websites (or at least quite a few) it can be a more cost effective method, since they start at about $100.

Never, and I mean never, use a free ad tracking program or software. On the internet, when you're in business, free usually means bad for business. Besides the inadequacy of features, free tracking services might suddenly stop being free, or drop from the planet in the middle of a big campaign and render your links useless.

Third Party Tracking Service

With a third party provider, there is no installation required and no large upfront cost. Most third party providers charge a monthly membership fee, or sometimes ask you to pay annually at a discounted rate. You can usually be up and running in a matter of minutes. The tracking system is usually managed via a web-based control panel, and there are none of your hosting systems resources used.

A major disadvantage of third party trackers is your reliance on them. What happens if the tracker suddenly goes out of business or changes their link formats? In simple English, you're screwed; unless you use the right type of tracker.

If the tracker you use forwards, redirects or relays their tracking link (ex. www.thirdpartytracker.com/?ad12345ver67890) to your site, all the links in your advertising, articles, digital products and everything else linking to your website and affiliate programs that use the ad tracker won't work anymore if the tracker goes out of business, or changes their link code formats. One way to avoid this is to point your tracking links to your website, then redirect them to the third party tracking service you're using. That way, if there's a change, you can simply redirect your redirects and you're back in business.

However, there are other and better options. With the third party tracker that I use and most of the better (more expensive) ones, you just install a snippet of code on your website and it will track everything for you. If you want to track ads, you use a code like www.JustinMichie.com/?WSCam=code1&WSEvt=code2 so you're not reliant on the tracking company should they go out of business or change code formats. By using the code that starts with a question mark like above, it will always go to the main page of your website no matter what happens with the tracking service.

What Should You Be Tracking?

Although there are a multitude of aspects of your ad's performance that you should be tracking, there are some things are essential for you to know in order to judge whether your ad campaign is effective.

Some of the more common things tracked by web trackers include any number of the following:

- Visitors IP addresses
- Browser types

- Operating systems
- Date and time
- Referring URLs
- Visitors location (where they live)
- Total page views
- Common entry and exit pages
- Amount of data sent and requested
- Unique visitors
- Views per page
- Track visitors progress
- Split run testing results
- Return on investment
- Costs of campaigns
- Cost per click, sale, lead and action

Action Tracking

Most website owners bring people to their site for a reason. It might be to make a sale, to get them to join your mailing list or sign up for your affiliate program. A good stat tracker can record such actions and let you know the outcome of your visitors. For instance, you might get 100 visitors to the main page of your website, 27 of those to may go to your sales page, then 13 of them might venture on to the order form, and 4 might actually order. Some trackers can also calculate the time between visitor's visits, if they visit more than once and how long they spend on each page.

When you're testing variables, it's almost a necessity that you get this information. It's essential to calculate your return on investment and overall conversion rate for an ad campaign.

Full Site Tracking

Do you know the exact point in your sales process where your prospects stop paying attention? Do you know which of your pages result in sales and which pages lose sales? Are you losing sales because your order page isn't simple enough? These are just some of the questions that can be answered if your tracker can trace the complete path of a customer within your site. A good tracker should be able to do this. This is what sets average internet marketers apart from rich internet marketers: the quality and the ability of their testing and tracking.

Remote Site Tracking

Some trackers can even monitor what your visitors do when they leave your site. This can be helpful for tracking visitors that click through to an affiliate program of yours, so you can see if they sign up or if they get cold feet, and where they go when they leave the site.

Reports

Most trackers should be able to produce weekly or monthly reports that total all the information and give it to you in an easy to understand format such as charts and graphs.

Viewing Time

Which pages are visited most often and when? How long do your visitors stay on the page? Which pages of your site interest them most? By watching the stats that show which pages were most visited, you can understand what interests your visitors and customize your site more to their interests.

Which pages were visited least often? If you know this, you can consider changing your content on the least popular pages in your site. You might also want to consider re-optimizing these pages for search engines if you're not getting much traffic from them.

Top Entry Pages

The top entry page is the page that the most people enter your site from. Knowing where people enter your site and where they go next will enable you to promote sales, discounts, special offers and more where they will be seen most.

Top Exit Pages

The top exit page is the last page your visitors see before they leave your website. If you know what page this is, maybe you can do something about it to keep visitors on your site longer. The longer they stay, the more likely they are to buy. Maybe it's because you have an interesting link on this page that they click on and leave your site. If this is the case, consider opening a new browser window for all external links. That way they don't exit your site in the process of going to a new one.

Referral Sites

Each time someone visits a page of any site, their browser sends a referrer which allows you to track where they arrived at your site from. This can be used to analyze which sites are sending visitors your way, allowing you to track the effectiveness of promotions, advertising, search engines and more. I can't emphasize too strongly how critical it is to know which search engines and which keywords are motivating visitors to come to your site. If you're unaware of this information, you may change a keyword that brings in the bulk of your traffic and not know what happened.

You'll also be able to determine which search engines aren't sending you traffic and can try creating a custom optimized page geared just for them and see if it helps. For more on search engine optimization check out Chapters 23 – 25. You can also monitor how well your reciprocal links, classified ads, newsgroup signatures and other sites are working and how many visitors they get for your site.

Ad/stat trackers can be used in a variety of places including:

Newsletter ads	Traffic exchanges	Press releases
FFA sites	Auctions	Ebooks
Tell-a-friend forms	Email signature files	Reciprocal links
Article submission	Contests	Discussion lists
Newsgroups	Banner ads	Product downloads

Discussion boards	Safe lists	Search engines
Classified ads	Email campaigns	Popup ads

Several of the better tracking services are available at:

www.webstat.com
www.web-stat.com
www.adtrackz.com
www.webtrends.com

For a current list of the top stat/ad trackers and web analyzers, there's a good site that keeps fairly up-to-date at www.topadtrackers.com, or you can log in to the "members only" site for my current list.

Once you have learned the basics of ad tracking, you can use it to tweak your ad campaigns, do comparison testing and try out new advertising ideas on a small scale to test the waters before investing too much time or money on a full-fledged campaign.

I can't really overemphasize the importance of tracking the results of your advertising campaigns. If you don't track what your visitors are doing on your website, how many visitors came to your site through a particular ad campaign or how many visitors convert into buyers, you cannot be certain if a particular ad campaign is worth continuing or not.

6

Testing the Surf

On the internet, testing is a way of life. Testing is one of the things that sets the internet apart from any other marketing medium. The reason is that it is so absolutely easy and painless to test on the internet. Consider this:

If you want to place an ad in a print magazine, you can run what are referred to as split run tests. That means you put one ad (ad A) in half the magazines, and ad B (the same ad but with one variable changed) in the other half of the print run. Each ad would have a different phone number, or the same number with a different extension or promo code so the results can be tracked. A month or so after the ads come out, the results are tallied up and one ad is declared the winner. Let's say that ad B wins. Well, you then take ad B, change a different variable, then do another split run test. You get the results and the process repeats itself for as long as it takes for you to pull the highest conversion rate possible.

The problem is this: For the April issue of a magazine, the magazine publisher needs the ad copy by the end of January. The magazine is printed in the middle of February and hits the stands sometime in March. By the time you get your results, May is blossoming. The earliest issue you could get the next revised ads in (with different variables) would be August. Of course you can run different ads in between, but you won't have up-to-date results to go by.

Magazine ads are also very expensive to run. To give you an example, Time magazine currently costs $246,000 for a full color one page ad. Rolling Stone magazine is $138,260. I don't know about you, but I'm not going to blow that much dough on a single ad.

One of the major benefits of the internet is its testability: you can test pretty much everything and anything very easily, and more importantly, very cheaply. Proper testing allows you the ability to calculate the likelihood of success, before emailing your entire list, or broadcasting your website to thousands of people. This also reduces the chance of making a costly mistake.

The title you select, the words you use to market your information, the benefits your information offers and the way it is packaged will determine how successful you are. It's just a matter of discovering the right combination of message and media.

Comprehensive testing involves changing variables one-by-one in order to assess and measure relative success. The best elements to test are those that will have the greatest impact on your response rates.

If testing email subjects for example, only the subject would change. All other elements of the email, sales and order pages would remain identical, except for the variable that you are testing.

Here are some of the major variables you can test that have the greatest impact, in no particular order:

1. Headlines or sub-headlines
2. Lead or opening
3. Copy
4. Offer
5. Price
6. Design and color
7. P.S. or P.S.S
8. Subject - email
9. Payment plans
10. Guarantee
11. Bonuses
12. The email list (better to use your own list than buy, but if you are buying, test it first)

You can dramatically increase your sales simply by taking the time to test and track your results. Not only will it help you to determine what's working and what's not, but it will also enable you to focus your efforts only on the strategies that produce results.

When testing your marketing strategies, keep in mind, a strategy that produces results for one person may not produce results for you. There is no "set in stone" strategy that works for everyone. You must develop your own style and technique and test your results to determine what works for you.

Test until you find a mix of variables that yield the highest result, then test some more.

Some Basic Rules of Testing

1. Test only one thing at a time.
2. Always test a random sample from a mailing list.
3. Be sure you test a sufficient quantity to obtain reliable test results.
4. Always test all new offers, and test to refine old ones too.
5. Email your tests and the control at the same time on the same day.
6. Don't get too test happy – test those things that can have a meaningful impact first, before you test less relevant variables.
7. Minimize your risk and improve the reliability of your results, by using a proven list (your own opt-in list is best) to test new offers, formats and/or copy.

It's a Numbers Game

Email Testing

When you're sending out a test email, how many emails should you test to get a good grasp of what kind response you can expect to get from your overall list? Your test volume should be no less than the number you need to produce statistically reliable results. According to research by mathematicians, you need at least 39 responses to get statistically valid result, with a 90-95% probability of accuracy. The way they came up with this number is quite complicated, but it seems to work well and be fairly accurate. To give you an idea of what this means for your mailings, let's look at some examples of the minimum number of emails you should send:

Response Rate	Min. # of Emails to Send
1%	3,900
2%	1,950
3%	1,300
5%	780
10%	390
15%	260

So with a good email response rate of 5% to your own opt-in list, you would need to send a minimum of 780 emails to the control, and 780 emails to the test group to get the most statistically reliable probability of accuracy. Whatever number you choose, make sure it doesn't make up more than 25% of the total mailing list. This way, if the test doesn't go so well, you're not plum out of luck. A good rule is to always mail to a minimum of 1,000 people, or 5% of your list, whichever is greater.

Remember, when you're testing an email, you need to mail to a representative cross section of the list. I always take every Nth name (N being any number that will get you at least 1,000 emails, or 5% of your list), so my sample is as random as possible. Don't forget to mark the names you email to, so you don't mail to them again.

Even if you have a tried and true email that you have used, try changing something to see if you can register an improvement. **If you ever do a mailing without testing something, you are wasting an opportunity to make more money.**

The best things to test in an email besides the list (assuming you use your own), listed in order of impact are:

1. The subject
2. The headline
3. The offer (links to website, should include benefits, not price)
4. The lead / opening
5. The copy
6. The P.S.

The Direct Marketing Association has assigned values to several mailing elements (for direct mail, not email) along with possible percentage increases you could expect to receive by testing the variables listed below:

Tested Variable	Percent Increase in Conversion
Mailing list	100 – 1,000%
Package	50 – 300%
Offer	100 – 500%
Copy	10 – 300%
Timing	10 – 50%

Although these variables and their relative percentages are for direct email, you can expect comparable results when marketing by email. There are elements of an email for instance (like the subject) that might make a 2,000% difference. If they don't open the email, they won't buy, and something so simple can have a huge impact in the results you get.

Website Testing

Just like email testing, you need a certain number of responses to get a statistically accurate result. That means for each variable you test, you need a minimum amount of traffic to your website.

Before I learned of this mathematical statistical stuff, I would always make sure that I had at least 1,000 unique visitors pass through my site when I was testing something. It's enough traffic to generally get a good grasp of the difference that the variable I changed made. Not that I like to repeat myself, but here's the chart from page 45 again, except with the number of visitors you need to your site to get statistically accurate results:

Response Rate	Min. # of Web Visitors
1%	3,900
2%	1,950
3%	1,300
5%	780
10%	390
15%	260

As you can see, depending on your average response rate, you need a certain number of visitors. Some people may get 1,000 visitors in an hour or a day; for others it may take a week, or a month, or more. Here's the thing, even though I want to get 1,000 visitors to my site, I want to do it over an entire week or 7 day period. The reason is that depending on your target audience, there will buy differently on different days of the week. If I tried one variable on Sunday and then another on Monday, the results would be statistically invalid because two of my variables changed: the one I was testing and the day of the week.

What to Test

It really depends on what kind of website you have and what's on it. Test absolutely everything, starting with the things that will have the most significant impact.

One of the big things that needs to be tested on any website is the navigation system. Its placement and the way it is organized have a noticeable impact on how long visitors stay on your site. For that very reason, you should test it. First start by its organization, or what links (home, about us, contact us etc.) it links to, and then test placement. The top of the page works best for placement, followed by listing it down the left-hand side. Be sure you have the ability to monitor visitors from when they arrive at your site until they leave, so you can see how long they stay and how they navigate while they're surfing.

Another thing to test is your newsletter or opt-in mailing list signup form. I've found that the top left hand corner works best, then the top right. Popups and pop-overs can also work for the signup form as well. Try each out for a while and see what your signup conversion rate is and then use what works best.

Test the information in the body of the page. If your ultimate goal is to convert sales, put information on your products there. If you're holding a contest mention it there. If it's a sales page, try changing around the different elements of the sales copy including the lead and headlines.

Load time is another thing that needs to be tested. There are different programs that can do this for you, or you can simply divide the total page size, by a dialup modem speed. Simply take the page size in kb, and divide it by 4kb/s, which is the average dialup speed that most modem users get. If your webpage is 120kb divide that by 4kb/s (120kb / 4kb/s) = 30 seconds load time. If any of your webpages takes longer than this to load, find out why and shorten the load time to keep it under 30 seconds.

Other things to test on a webpage include the headlines, headers, background colors, fonts, color scheme, use and placement of graphics, sales ad copy and design and layout. Make it easy on yourself – test everything.

Although it's a different type of testing, test all of your links, autoresponders and other page elements to ensure they are functioning properly.

Banner Ads

Banner ads are starting to fade a little, but nonetheless are still a part of the web. Always make sure you keep track of the click-throughs you receive in relation to the number of impressions the banner gets, and follow it all the way through to tracking the click-through conversion rate. Most banner exchanges and ad agencies you advertise with will keep track of this for you, but not all do and it's always best to track your own results.

Change the variables in your banner to test each component individually over a finite period of time. For example, change the background color of the banner, or the wording slightly, such as from "save 10% off your purchase" to "save $10 on each purchase." Try testing static banners vs. animated, animated is almost always better, but not in all situations. Try using different buzzwords like "Free," "Act Now," "Click Here," and see what works best. You can also try testing completely different design formats and concepts. Keep track of the click-throughs and your desired results. Compare the two. You are aiming for an increase in both. When you find the best results, keep that banner for awhile, but continue testing.

Other Testing

Above anything and everything you do, test everything that has the remote possibility of being possible to test. Test different text ads, change the heading, change the visible link, change the copy. Try a different keyword here or there.

Test your search engine submissions. Submit a listing, see how it ranks, then see if you can do better. Try different online advertising techniques; if you test and track properly, you can easily determine your return on investment and find what works best for your market.

In the best of circumstances, your internet marketing experiences should be a continuous learning process conducted with the aim of achieving the best possible response and return on investment. Testing and tracking your marketing strategies is an essential part of doing business. By concentrating your efforts on strategies that produce results, you can not only increase your sales, but you'll also save yourself a great deal of time and money.

Section 2

What You Need to Know About Websites

7

Do You Need a Website?

So, should you have a website? Well for starters, it's next to impossible to make money online if you don't have a website. Sure you could try sending out emails, or even place ads on different sites advertising your product or service or redirecting to an affiliate link, but if someone wants more information or has a question, where do they go? Most people use the internet for one reason: convenience. If they need to disconnect their dialup connection to call you for more information, or get in their car and drive to your store, is that convenient? They'll simply move on to someone else who has a website, and can provide them with the instantaneous information they want. Furthermore, how can you build an email list without an opt-in form on your website?

That brings us back to our original question: should your business have a website? Even if your business is small and sells products or services you don't think can be sold online? Of course you should! If you have a business you *NEED* a website, period! It doesn't matter whether you're a one-man show or a 10,000 employee corporate giant; if you don't have a website, you're losing business to other companies that do. In this day and age, if you, your company, business or product isn't online, you're perceived to many as old-fashioned, not to mention the fact that you're missing out on a large percentage of your market share. Having a website is a marketing investment that, dollar-for-dollar has an exceptional ROI and is one of the fastest and least expensive ways to market whatever it is that you happen to be marketing.

And it's not just enough to have a website. Your site must be professional looking if you want to be taken seriously. Your website speaks volumes about your business and the way you do business and is often your first opportunity to make a good impression on potential customers. A website that looks as if it was designed by a barrel of colorblind monkeys can actually do your business more harm than good; so don't let your sister's, friend's, second cousin's, twelve year-old son design it.

One of the great things about the internet is that it has leveled the playing field when it comes to competing with the big boys. As mentioned, you have only one shot at making a good first impression. With a well designed and laid out site, you can project the image and professionalism of a much larger, million, or billion dollar company. The inverse is also true, if you happen to be part of a much larger million, or billion dollar company – your site must look the part. If it is badly designed and hard to navigate with a mistake here or there, it diminishes the image and credibility of your company.

Also, don't be so quick to dismiss your product as one that can't be sold online. Nowadays, there's very little that can't be sold over the internet. More than 250 million shoppers are now online, spending over 143 billion (yes billion) dollars a year, purchasing everything from books to computers to information to cars to real estate to jet airplanes to bald-head tattoo ad space. If you can imagine it, someone will figure out how to sell it online.

Don't get me wrong, I'm not saying you should spend all your efforts marketing over the internet (even if you are an internet based e-business), but at the very least you should have a strong web presence so customers, potential employees, business partners and perhaps even investors can quickly and easily find out more about your business and the products or services you have to offer.

Internet marketing research firms predict the number of online consumers will grow at a rate of thirty to fifty percent over the next few years. These numbers alone should be enough to persuade you that your business should be online.

Enough said. Since this book is about online marketing, we're not going to waste any more time on why you should have a website. Already having, or planning to have a site in the very near future is an implied prerequisite for reading this book.

8

Choosing a Domain Name

A domain name is a very important and much overlooked aspect of a great online marketing campaign. If you're an online marketer, the purpose of getting people to your website is to ultimately make money. If your domain name is too long (www.ThisIsMyLittleCornerOnTheWorldWideWeb.com), not applicable to your business (www.MyLittleBusiness.com) or just plain doesn't make sense (www.wuint&wykxtz.com) it's going to be enough of a challenge getting people to your website, let alone getting them to part with their hard-earned money.

Choosing a domain name might seem like a fairly simple task, but unfortunately it is not always a simple as you would like it to be. A domain name that matches your business or product name is very important because it is the first thing that people will try in their browser when trying to get to your website. It is also easier for your customers to remember and will be more likely tried than an obscure and hard to remember domain name.

Let's say you own a restaurant called "Appetizers." www.appetizers.com might seem like the logical choice of domain name... but what's the chance that it will be available? None - that's a small problem with the internet, most of the good domain names are already taken. So what if you already have an established business or product... you probably don't want to change the name of your product or business to suit an available domain name. There's a couple of things you can do; you might simply might want to try to buy the domain name from the current owner. Check out the whois information (www.who.is) for the domain and contact the owner to see if they may be willing to sell it. If they are, keep in mind that you will likely end up paying many times more than what it would of cost you to register it yourself. If they won't sell it to you, some other choices include: using a different extension (.net, .org, .biz, .ca, .us etc.), adding relevancy to the name (www.AppetizersRestaurant.com), or (www.Appetizers-Restaurant.com) where you add a hyphen and so on.

The KISS (Keep It Short and Simple or Keep it Simple Stupid) acronym applies applicably to domain names, as it does many other things in life. The more characters your domain name has, the greater the likelihood of a potential visitor making a typo and consequently not getting to your website. It's increasingly difficult to get short and meaningful domain names as they've been takes due to the explosive growth of the Internet Although it is unlikely you will be able to find a relevant three, four or even five letter dot com domain, you can still find or invent a catchy domain name with few letters and possibly a different extension.

If you can manage to get an acceptable short domain name, by all means go for it, if not you may need to try something a little longer like I did for this book (www.StreetSmartInternetMarketing.com). Short names are easier to type, easier to remember and are far less susceptible to typing mistakes. For example, www.search.com is easier to remember and less prone to typos than www.ClickHereToSearchTheInternet.com.

Aside from the obvious problem that people might not be able to remember a longer domain name, it would also be a chore typing them into a web browser, email program and so on. However, some people argue that a longer domain name is easier on the memory; "www.bbfsinc.com" is a sequence of unrelated letters that is difficult to remember and type correctly; whereas if we expand it to its long form, "www.BillyBobFishSupplies.com," your customers are more likely to remember the domain name. In reality, longer domain names are only easier to remember over a short one if the short one is not meaningful to the web user, or just plain does not make sense. Another advantage of a longer domain names are that they have more keywords in them, which can prove an advantage in some search engine listings. If you decide to go with a longer name, just remember, a domain name approaching 67 (the max allowed in a domain name) characters (or even half that), is much too long. An acceptable long name might be ten-to-thirty characters at the most. The rule that I use is to get the shortest domain name possible, with the most prestigous extension, that is the most meaningful combination of letters or words, as related to the content of the webpage.

It is also important to make sure your domain name is easy to say, and understand when being said. www.gr8marketingtips.com is a clever play on words, but if it is verbally referred how will the receiver know that there is an "8" hidden in there? Domain names that use numbers in place of letters, sound like other words, or that are difficult to pronounce (like some last names) are hard to remember, let alone type correctly. The last thing you want to do is have them go to your competitor's website at www.greatmarketingtips.com.

Also try to avoid using plural versions of names, as they can often be confused with the non-plural version which might be your competitor's site. If you can register both the plural and the non plural, do it.

Hyphenated Names

Should you get a hyphenated name? Here are a few things you may want to consider: It's easy to forget the hyphens when a customer is typing in your domain name and they may accidentally wind up somewhere else. Also, if your website is referred verbally, the person referring the site, or the person being referred the site might forget the hyphens and/or where they go. (which one is it? www.ThatComputer-Shop.com, www.That-ComputerShop.com, www.That-Computer-Shop.com, or www.ThatComputerShop.com?) Quite frankly hyphenated names are also a pain in the neck to type.

The only two real advantages to using a hypenated name is that they are more likely to be available and some search engines can distinguish the keywords contained in your domain name a little better, and thus return your site more prominently in search results. Personally, I prefer to avoid hyphenated names if possible, but it really depends on the domain name you want, it's availability, and your unique situation.

Dot Com? What Extension Do I Get?

What domain extension should you get? Do you want a .com, .net, .biz, .ca, .us, .info, .org? The answer is not as straightforward as you might think. A dot com name is the most prestigious and professional looking, but it is also the hardest to come by. One of the easiest ways to answer this question is to see what extensions are available for the domain name you want. If you choose a country specific extension (.ca, .us, .uk, .de etc.) some internet users may think that your business only caters to the specific country of origin that your domain name refers to. If your website or business caters to the local area, such as a consulting firm, a country specific domain would be acceptable, so the people in your country know that they're dealing with a local entity, which is often what they want. On the other hand, if your business caters to an international audience, and you have a country specific extension, be sure to mention your areas of business on your website.

Another school of thought finds that .net and .org extensions are actually quite acceptable domain names. For some, the ".org" extension actually describes the non-profit nature of their organization.

In my opinion it's extremely important to get a dot com, but if you can't, then you can consider some of the other alternatives. Dot com names are the best known extension, the most professional, most easily remembered and almost expected for a reputable business. Furthermore, if you type in a domain name into your browser without the extension, some browsers will assume it is a dot com and automatically try to find that site.

Something else to keep in mind is that some directories list websites alphabetically in their categories. "A" comes before "B", and "123" comes before "A," and so on. Some search engines also use alphabetical priority in their ranking formulas, although I wouldn't really let this affect my domain name choice.

Once you find a domain name that you like, you should consider purchasing variations on the name you've chosen to protect yourself against competitors. This not only includes different extensions, but different ways to write the same name. GoDaddy will actually give you a good deal on registering new extensions (.net, .org, .biz) when you purchase the initial name. They will also forward your variations to your regular domain name for free.

Registering a Domain Name

To check and see if a domain name is available, simply go to www.godaddy.com and type the name you want into the search box. If it's available, they'll let you know, and just follow the simple steps to register it. Keep in mind, that they'll try to upsell and cross-sell you all kinds of other stuff you don't need along the way. Just register the domain name with them, and nothing else. Godaddy doesn't register country specific names (except .us), so if you're looking for a .ca or .uk domain name, just do a search for ".ca domain name registar" or whatever you're looking for. I've seen some domain registars charge as much as $80/year to register a domain with them. With GoDaddy it costs about $8, or better yet, you can get it for free. Stay with me here. Once you've decided on your domain name, you have to purchase hosting space (next chapter). Many web hosts will actually register and keep renewing your domain name for you for free as long as you have a hosting account with them. The next chapter's on hosting, so keep reading.

9

Selecting a Web Host

If you have, or plan on having a website in the near future, you invariably need someone to host it for you. A web hosting company "hosts" or "stores" your website on their computer servers where it can be accessed through the internet by anyone with a connection. I just want to note that it is also possible to host your website yourself from your home or office computer. This gets quite technical, is fairly complicated, can cause all kinds of problems and quite frankly is not worth the effort it requires – so I'm not going to discuss it in this book.

Choosing a host for your website is no small decision. Once you commit to one, it can be difficult to move your business elsewhere – not to mention the damage that can be done to your business if you make the wrong choice. This makes it very important to get it right the first time. This chapter is designed to help you find out as much as possible about any prospective hosts before making that important decision.

Some companies will host your website for free, usually in return for putting their ads on your webpage, or having a popup ad every time someone views your site. Free sites are great for a small personal site to share with your friends and family, but are not at all suitable for business. If your business is using a free web hosting company many prospective customers will question your credibility, honesty and staying power, which ultimately affects their decision to buy. Most free sites also don't offer any of the extras (unless you pay for it and then it's not free) that a business site will need to operate properly.

Almost all hosting companies have more than one hosting plan available, which can vary from a few dollars a month for very basic hosting, to a few hundred dollars or more a month for a dedicated server. Always keep a lookout for hidden setup or activation fees charged by some companies. You shouldn't need to pay a fee, as setup is mostly automated and only sometimes involves a human for confirmation.

Some of the more important features to look for in a hosting company are outlined below in order of importance:

Customer Service

All web hosting companies have the ability to host your website - that is after all what they do. So what really sets apart one web hosting company from another? That's easy: it's the level of customer/technical service they offer.

With many online services customer service is lacking and it is very rare to actually get a real person on the phone. With any online business, most of your business in one way or another revolves around your website, and if it goes down, or has problems, it can have a huge impact. As such, great customer service is very important when deciding on a company to host your site.

Does the hosting company offer 24/7 technical support? If they don't, then don't give them your business. Believe me when I say this: You won't need technical help between 9am and 5pm Monday through Friday – you'll need it at 11:00pm on a Sunday, which also happens to be a holiday. A good way to test and see if the site's customer service is any good, is to send them an email and see how long it takes for them to reply. A reasonable response time is twelve hours or less, but with an above average hosting company it should really be two-to-four hours at most. If it takes them longer to respond, or if you don't receive a human response to your email then it's time to walk away.

Is their tech support by phone, email, or live chat? Although it is best if they offer all three forms, they are not all necessary. Live chat is better than email and phone is better than live chat, so don't just settle for email. It is not easy to get your problem across by email and it can take a long time to get the problem solved going back and forth. Find out if their technical staff are certified, qualified and competent enough to help you when you need assistance. Do they treat you with respect and are they willing to go the extra mile to make you a happy customer? If you can't answer yes to both of these questions, then this probably isn't the right company for you. Try asking the support staff a few technical questions of the type you anticipate you will be asking when you host with them. Then monitor how quickly and efficiently they respond.

Reliability or Uptime

How reliable are their servers? Computers do fail sometimes - I'm sure you've had your own experiences with that. However, if the computer server isn't working, customers can't view your website and if it is a first time customer, you may lose them forever. What is their uptime (time when the server is functional)? Nobody will have 100% uptime. If they advertise this, they're lying. Servers do occasionally go down and they also need maintenance and updating. The uptime of the server should be about 99% (or 99.9%) which means that the server should be working properly at least 99% of the time. Does the host guarantee this? I've used everything, including free hosting, cheap hosting and quality hosting, and it's more than worth the few extra bucks for a quality host.

Speed

The speed and reliability of your host's servers will depend on several factors, including their type of connection to the internet, bandwidth and the speed at which your webpage can be retrieved from the server's computer. Only choose a host with a full T3 connection (or better). The smaller and cheaper service providers often use a T1 connection. A T3 connection is actually made up of 28 T1 connections, and thus is 28 times faster, running at speeds of 45 Mbps. 45 Mbps is very fast - to help give you an idea of its speed, it is about 10,000 times faster than a typical dial up connection and about 50 times faster than a home high speed connection.

Redundancy

Now that you've established that they have a fast connection, what happens in the unfortunate event that the connection goes down? Do they have more than one connection to the internet in case one goes down? A good hosting company should have at least two different connections to the internet. If the weather knocks one out on a Saturday, you can't afford to wait till it is fixed on Monday. If they have at least two connections, if one goes down, can the other one adequately cover all their sites until the repair is made? At the absolute minimum they should have a T1 line for backup, but try to look for something faster than that.

Effective Bandwidth Management

In addition to having a fast connection to the internet, your host should be able to manage how its available bandwidth is used. As a guide, it should typically not use more than 50% of its bandwidth. That way if there is a large spike in visitors to your site, there won't be a problem covering it.

Backup and Security

If there is a system, network or power failure, the last thing you want is to lose your data or to have your website go down for a long period. Good hosts will have backup systems in place to guard against this. Most hosts will regularly back up your data (usually daily) in case of a failure of some kind. You don't want to waste time re-uploading all of your files. I had to do this once when I switched hosting companies, and it wasted about ten hours of my time to get everything working properly. This is something that is definitely an asset, but not absolutely necessary. You should always have a backup copy of your site and its information as a safeguard in case of a problem.

Besides backing up your data, the host should also have some kind of backup in case of a power failure. Make sure they have an uninterruptible power supply system (often referred to as "UPS") and/or a backup power generator available in case of emergencies. How long does it last for? Is it battery or fuel powered? One is not necessarily better than another, although batteries do run out and a fuel powered system will last as long as there is fuel to power it.

Also find out whether their server is secure, or they have a secure server available to process credit card transactions.

Features and Benefits

As well as checking out the reliability of the servers and hardware, you will also need to compare the features provided by the host and analyze the benefits they offer to you. When choosing a host, keep in mind your possible future needs and check out whether the host will be able to accommodate them.

Data Transfer (Bandwidth)

Data transfer (sometimes loosely referred to as "traffic" or "bandwidth") is the amount of data (bytes) being transferred from your site to the visitors computer when they browse your site. Some hosts offer free unlimited bandwidth to entice you to sign up with them but that is hardly the case. The host has to pay for bandwidth and if you consume a lot of it, they will usually not silently bear your costs.

There is a point where the "unlimited" has a limit. Don't find out the hard way and get stuck with an exorbitant bill for having "exceeded" the "unlimited bandwidth." Always look for details on how much traffic the package allows and how much extra it costs if you exceed the allotment. Usually you will find that they redefine "unlimited" to be limited in some way.

To give you a rough idea of the typical traffic requirements of a website, if your average page size is 50 kilobytes, and you receive 10,000 page views a month, your website uses 500 MB, (50 KB x 1 MB/1000 KB x 10,000 page views) of bandwidth per month. Always make sure that your hosting plan comes with at least twice as much bandwidth (preferably more though) than you actually need in case of increased traffic. Most hosts offer somewhere around 10-20 gigabytes, so unless you get millions of page views a month, or have lots of large downloads, bandwidth should not be too much of a problem for you.

Your traffic requirements will grow over time as your site becomes more well-known, so you will also need to check the hosts policy for overages (exceeding the bandwidth that comes with your hosting plan). Is there a published charge per GB over the allowed bandwidth? Is the charge made according to actual usage or are you expected to pre-pay for a potential overage? It is better not to go for hosts that expect you to prepay for overages, since it can be difficult to foresee when your site will exceed its bandwidth and by how much. Most hosts actually have real time stats which include the exact up to the minute bandwidth usage, so if you need to prepay for extra bandwidth, you'll be able to find out before you go over.

Storage Space

The amount of storage space is how much space your website takes up on the hosting company's computer. The more pages you have on your website, or the more graphics, audio or video you have, the more space you'll need. For the same reason as bandwidth, watch out for those "unlimited disk space" schemes. Most sites need less than 5 or 10 MB of web space, unless it is a media (audio, video, graphics) intensive site. Even though you may be tempted with 500 MB, or even 1,000 MB of space don't let that be too big a factor in your consideration when comparing with other web hosts. You'll probably never need that much, but it is nice to have just in case. The hosting company is also aware of that, which is why they feel free to offer you that as a means of enticing you to host there.

Stability

The last thing you want is for your host to go out of business. I had that happen once without warning and my site was down for a couple days until I could get everything updated and switched over. Luckily it was when the site was just starting out, so there wasn't too much lost business. Try to get some idea of how stable they are. Number of years in business is sometimes (not always, of course) a good indicator.

Shared or Dedicated Server?

A shared or virtual server is a computer server provided by your host that is shared between more than one user or website. A dedicated server is when one user gets the exclusive use of an entire computer server at the hosting company. Depending on your requirements, either a shared or dedicated server may work better for you. Shared servers are usually more than adequate for lower volume or entry-level sites that don't require any highly specialized software.

Dedicated servers are typically used in cases where there is a high level of traffic (well over a million hits a month), you have multiple websites, there is a strong need for security, or the user wishes to run their own customized software and applications rather than the standard ones supplied by the host. Unless you are very computer savvy, dedicated hosts require the help of someone who knows what they're doing to set up and get going.

Shared servers also usually have a shared IP address and dedicated servers have their own unique IP address, though you can usually pay extra for your own IP on a shared server. This is useful for sending bulk email... more on this later. It goes without saying that dedicated servers are more expensive than shared servers – typically costing about ten times more, but depending on your requirements, they may be well worth it.

Resellers?

Not all hosting companies own their own web servers. Some of them are actually resellers for another hosting company. The main disadvantage of using a reseller is the possibility that you are dealing with people who don't know much about the system they are selling and who take longer to help you (they have to send your tech support request to the actual hosting company who then needs to act on it). I generally don't recommend using a reseller, exactly for this reason; time is money and the longer it takes to get a problem fixed, the more sales you lose. The only real upside to a reseller is that they sometimes offer the same package as the actual hosting company at a slightly cheaper price.

Others' Reviews

You should make it a point to check out what others have to say about the web host. Do your own research, don't just rely on testimonials supplied by the host, they may be a little biased. Read reviews with a pinch of salt. Some glowing testimonials may come from people working for the web host itself, disguised as satisfied customers. Likewise, negative reviews of a particular host can sometimes come from unscrupulous competitors.

What is the quality and caliber of the sites currently served by this host? If they generally host high-caliber commercial clients, then they may be a better bet for you than if they mainly host small businesses with two or three page static websites. (There may be cost trade-offs here.)

A host may boast of its popularity or the fact that it hosts lots of websites. However, the most "popular" are not necessarily the best; they may just be the ones with the largest advertising budget. Indeed "popularity" can be a double-edged sword -- support resources may be more thinly spread and bandwidth may be squeezed as a result of the number of sites hosted. So don't go on numbers alone.

Get in touch with some of the host's existing customers and ask them what they really think of the service and reliability of their host.

How many clients does the host have? 1,000? 10,000? More? If they have a lot, they're probably doing something right. If it's only a few, find out why, or better yet, just move on.

Email, Autoresponders, POP3, Mail Forwarding

If you have your own site, you would probably want to have email addresses at your own domain, like info@yourdomain.com. Does the host provide this with the package? They should, but sadly not all hosts do. Does it allow you to have a catch-all email account that allows anyname@yourdomain.com to wind up being routed to you? Are autoresponders available? Can you retrieve your mail with your email software such as Outlook Express or Eudora? Can it be automatically forwarded to your current email address? These are all things to consider, some may be important to you and some may not. Any reputable host should offer all of the above.

Control Panel

The control panel is the software interface that allows you to manage different aspects of your web hosting account yourself, in an easy to use web-based interface. Typically, and at the very minimum, it should allow you to do things like add, delete and manage your email addresses, change passwords for your account, add, edit and delete files, check your web logs, manage redirects or sub-domains and much more. Do not go for a host where you need to go through their technical support each time you want to change a password or add a new email account. The internet is supposed to be easy and automated, if a web host doesn't operate this way, it's probably not the host you want. Go to www.cpanel.com for a demo of how a control panel should look and operate.

FTP Access

FTP, or File Transfer Protocol, is a way to upload files to your server. It is much quicker for uploading your web files than doing it by hand and almost all hosts will have it available. Just make sure your host does, as it will prove extremely useful if you have a large site or many websites.

Cost

While the price does matter, it is not the most important thing to look for by a long shot. You would probably be better off going with a more expensive company than a cheaper one. Which car would you rather drive, a BMW or a Buick? Both with get you from point "A" to point "B" but one will be a lot more comfortable to drive and less likely to break down. Web hosting is a very important part of any online business and if your host fails, or has many ups and downs, so does your business.

While everyone always tries to get the best deal possible, the amount you pay for web hosting is insignificant when compared to the impact that a bad choice could have on your business. Just remember this Spanish proverb:

"Lo barato sale caro"

The rough English translation is: The cheap comes out expensive. Think about it for a second, if one hosting company is $10/month and is average, and another company is $25/month, but is way above average, is the extra $15/month really worth it? To put it in perspective: If your website does only $200 in sales a day, and it goes down for one extra day a year with the cheaper company, you're losing $200 to save $180 on web hosting. And it's not only $200 that you're losing, what about the lifetime of value of the new customers? That's thousands more in future earnings to save $180. If, and only if two companies are equal in absolutely every respect, you can go for the cheaper one.

Most web hosts allow you to select an annual payment plan that gives you a cheaper rate than if you were to pay monthly. Some only allow you to pay annually – watch out for these sites, even though they may offer a guarantee, there may also a reason why they want your money up front. Investigate them thoroughly before committing for the long term.

To help give you a better idea of what it should cost you, I pay $22 a month, get 20 gigabytes of storage space, 800 gigabytes of data transfer, 999 email address and a host (pardon the pun) of other options. I also have a dedicated server and they run from $100 for the most basic system to $500 or more depending on your needs.

PHP, Perl, CGI-BIN Access, SSI, SSL, Htaccess, Telnet and More

These are some of the more complex and technical features; still you should really make sure you have them all available, even if they're not included in your plan. Note that some commercial hosts do not allow you to install PHP or CGI scripts without their approval. This is not desirable since it means you need to wait for them before you can implement a feature on your site. ".htaccess" is needed if you want to customize your error pages (error pages are pages that display when a user requests a non-existent page on your site, among other things) and a few other technical things. You will definitely need SSL if you plan to collect credit card information through your site. Telnet access is useful for certain things, including testing CGI scripts, maintaining databases and so on. Check to see if these facilities are included, if not ask if they are available.

If you are planning on doing any sort of business through your website, you will want to see if the host provides the features you need. This sometimes involves going with a higher priced package, or paying additional "add on" charges to your existing package. If you think you might ever need extras check to see if they are available, before you commit to the any hosting company.

After you've looked at some different web hosting companies and narrowed it down to a few who fit your needs both financially and in the services they provide, don't forget to check with some of their customers. Ask them about their general experiences with the host, including speed, reliability and customer service.

For your convenience, here is a list of some of the better hosting companies I've found that provide all the necessary features and then some:

www.startlogic.com
www.lunarpages.com
www.ipowerweb.com

This list is by no means exhaustive. For a more comprehensive and up-to-date list login to the "members only" website, using the details found at the beginning of this book.

Tech Talk - HTML

Although it is not necessary to know the technicalities of how the internet works, or how webpages are designed, it is helpful to have at least a basic understanding. So here's a little info on how the internet works:

The World Wide Web (internet) is made up of a system of internet servers that support specially formatted documents. These documents are formatted in a programming language called HTML, which is short for Hyper Text Mark-up Language. HTML is the authoring language used to create documents on the web and defines the structure of a web document by using a variety of tags and attributes.

When you type in a Uniform Resource Locator (URL), it uses a Hyper Text Transfer Protocol (HTTP), to define how messages are formatted and transmitted; as well as what actions web servers and browsers should take in response to the various commands that are issued. For example when you enter a URL into your browser, it sends a HTTP command to the web server directing it to fetch the corresponding HTML code and transmit it to your computer.

Lost yet? Don't worry! Quite honestly, you can be very successful on the internet, and not know HTML code from an orange. But, understanding basic HTML code can help make you more money, quicker. Let me explain why. Everything on the internet happens at lightening speed; a day, an hour, even a couple of minutes can make a big difference in your sales performance. Why wait for (and pay) a web designer to make small changes and updates to your webpage when you can quite easily do it yourself in only a few minutes. Sometimes it can take a few days or longer for your web designer to make the necessary changes and update your site. And what happens if they're off on vacation in the Bahamas for a couple weeks and you get a killer promotion that you want to put on your website, but can't, because you don't know how?

In this section we're going to concentrate on some basic raw HTML, even though simple web design programs allow you to make changes without any code knowledge. The reason is simple, a basic understanding of the code and how it works will make it much easier to understand exactly what you are doing and why.

Let me simplify HTML a little. HTML is the name of a simple programming language that web programmers use to create webpages. It essentially tells your web browser what goes where on the webpage. HTML is a universal programming language, which means that it can be viewed by anyone with an internet connection, no matter what kind of computer or web browser they are using. HTML uses a series of tags (or directions) that are integrated into a webpage, which silently tell the web browser what to do.

HTML tags are usually English words or abbreviations that are distinguished from the regular text because they are placed in angle brackets (< >). The job of tags it to dictate to the web browser how the webpage will be formatted, or how it looks. For example the simple tag <b> makes the text that follows it bold. In HTML language writing:

This text is <b> bold

Would look like this in your web browser:

This text is **bold**

The tag, <b> tells the web browser to make the text following the tag bold. One very important thing to note about tags is that they always travel in pairs. Every time you use a <b> tag, you need to close it off using the same tag with a back slash (/) in front of it. The "/" distinguishes the opening tag from the closing tag. The code from the above example should really read:

This text is <b> bold </b>

If you don't close the tag off, the web browser won't know when to stop making the text bold, so everything that follows the <b> tag would be bold.

Despite what you might have heard, you don't need any special software to create an HTML page; all you need is a word processor (Notepad, Microsoft Word etc.) and a working knowledge of simple HTML. And lucky for all of us, basic HTML is dead easy.

A basic HTML page begins with the tag <HTML> and ends with </HTML>. In between there are two sections called the header and the body. The header tag, (<head>) contains information about the webpage that won't appear on the page itself, such as the page title and meta tags. The title tag is quite simple, while the meta tags can get slightly more complicated.

Title Tag

<title>**Your Title Goes Here**</title>

Meta Tags

<META NAME="description" CONTENT="**Your Page Description Goes Here**">

<META NAME="keywords" CONTENT="**Your Keywords Go Here**">

As you can see, there are two main meta tags used – the description and keywords. The text contained in the meta tags is used by some search engines to help rank your webpage in their search results. You can learn more about this in Chapter 12.

The second section of a webpage uses the <body> tag. This is where the action is - everything that appears on a webpage is contained within the body tags.

Let's create a basic webpage. In this case we won't use a web software program; we'll do it from scratch. The easiest way is to create a new document, Notepad works well on a PC or SimpleText on a Mac. Open a new document and immediately save it as index.html (remember, it needs to be saved as a "text only" or a "plain text" file). The reason we're calling it index.html is simple, that is the file that browsers automatically open when going to a website. For example, if you type www.JustinMichie.com into your web browser it is really going to the file www.JustinMichie.com/index.html.

Your basic web document will look something like this:

```
<HTML>
<head>
<title>Your title goes here</title>
<META NAME="description" CONTENT="Your description goes here">
<META NAME="keywords" CONTENT="Your keywords go here">
</head>
<body>This is where the body of your webpage goes</body>
</HTML>
```

If you were to copy the above HTML code exactly as it is into Notepad and save it as index.html, you would have just programmed a basic webpage.

Design Software

When I created my first webpage back in 1994, I did it all by hand in raw HTML using Notepad. Lucky for you, few people hand-code their websites anymore. Thankfully, there are a variety of HTML editors available that are super simple to use. If you can write a document in Microsoft Word, you can make your own webpage. Microsoft Word even has an option that lets you save any document as a webpage if you wish, although I wouldn't recommend it, as it adds a lot of extra unnecessary HTML code which makes the file size larger and inefficient.

Though there are a variety of HTML editors available, the mainstream editors are Microsoft FrontPage which is quite simple to use, and Macromedia Dreamweaver, which is a little more advanced and used by more diehard web programmers.

Microsoft FrontPage is included with many new computers and Microsoft Office packages, so you might already have it installed on your computer. Dreamweaver is more expensive to purchase, but also performs many more complicated functions that FrontPage doesn't. Dreamweaver is used by about 80% of web developers mostly because of the control and more advanced features that it offers. I personally use FrontPage, only because I've been using it for a long time and haven't had a reason to learn how to use anything else.

If you're intimidated at all by technology, there's still an easier (and free) option, FrontPage Express, which is no harder to use than writing an email. Since it's no longer readily available, it can be downloaded from the members website (www.ssim.biz) for free. It doesn't really matter what you use, as long as you make an effort to try and learn something. It makes testing page variables much easier and allows you a little more control over your website.

A nice chart containing some of the more common HTML tags can be found on the members website. Of course you don't really need to know them when using a HTML editor, but it does make things easier. When using FrontPage I often find myself going into the raw HTML code to figure out why something might not be working the way I want, or even just to clear out unnecessary code.

II

Keywords

Keywords are words that are typed into search engines to find websites of a particular interest. If I wanted to find out more about hybrid cars, I would type the keyword phrase "hybrid cars" into my favorite search engine, which would return the results ranked in order of relevancy.

Most search engines use keywords in one way or another to rank your webpage in their listings, so it is very important that you select the proper keywords for the content of your site. Keywords can also useful for people that like to scan a webpage to see if they should bother to actually read it. Selecting keywords for your webpage isn't a difficult thing to do, so long as you know what you're doing. This chapter has some tips on choosing the right keywords and getting the maximum impact from them.

If you're just starting out on the internet, or haven't specifically selected any keywords for your website yet, a good place to start is to check out your competition and see what keywords are working for them. You can find out their meta keywords by viewing the source code for their site and looking under "meta keywords" in the header.

When you're selecting keywords for your site, you need to think as your customer would. Not everybody uses the same word to describe the same thing. You might call a couch a couch, while someone else may call it a sofa or chesterfield, so it's important to cover all the variations. When deciding on what keywords you might use, you can consult a thesaurus for any synonyms and consider using them as well. Some people also use common misspellings as keywords in case someone doesn't type in a search term correctly. I would very strongly recommend that you do not do this; as most people will view it as a spelling mistake on your part which is not good. Besides, most search engines have some type of spell checker which will automatically correct most mistakes, or will offer alternative suggestions if the keywords entered return low results.

Be specific, search engine users are. If you sell clothing, use keywords that describe what kind of clothing you sell. No one will go and search for "clothing" or "pants," that's far too general. They will search for "formal black evening dress" or "tommy hilfiger cargo pants" to find exactly what they want. If you were looking for a company or product like yours, what would you search for?

Yahoo! Search Marketing (formerly Overture) has a great search term suggestion tool that will tell you exactly how many times a certain keyword or phrase has been searched for in the last month. You simply type in your keyword or phrase into the search box and hit enter. Overture then looks through all its data and brings back the number of times the keyword or phrase was searched for in previous month, and also suggests other keywords that might be good alternatives with their respective frequencies. Go to http://inventory.overture.com and try it out, it's 100% free.

The only problem with the Overture search term suggestion tool is that it doesn't account for any other major search engines such as Google, MSN, AOL, Ask etc. This isn't really much of a problem though, the Overture family (Yahoo, AltaVista and Overture) make up about 25% of the market share, so multiply the number Overture gives you by four, and you'll have a more accurate net wide result.

Here are some search examples from Overture for June 2006.

Search Term	Number of Searches
"ebook"	146,703
"self help"	83,044
"auction"	502,192
"eBay"	14,209,935
"cookie recipe"	77,009
"sex"	7,482,002
"survey"	212,228
"free"	2,506,236
"discount vacation"	28,462
"internet marketing"	279,679
"seminar"	30,848

Google AdWords also provides a keyword suggestion tool that can be found at: https://adwords.google.com/select/tools.html. This tool functions a lot like Yahoo's, but does not provide the total number of searches for each keyword, it only provides a detailed listing of keyword suggestions.

If you owned a white water rafting company in Colorado, what would your customers search for when trying to find you? Go to www.inventory.overture.com and find out. By typing in "whitewater rafting" it brings back the following results:

Searches done in June 2006	
Count	Search Term
34603	whitewater rafting
1524	whitewater rafting california
1246	west virginia whitewater rafting
1141	whitewater rafting trip
834	colorado whitewater rafting

581	grand canyon whitewater rafting
550	american river whitewater rafting
500	whitewater rafting wv
432	whitewater rafting maine
405	whitewater rafting in California
383	whitewater rafting vacation

This is only the top ten keywords that apply to whitewater rafting and you probably don't need to go any further than this. Since your business is located in Colorado, any of the other state specific searches are not accurate keywords that describe your business. Using "whitewater rafting california" as a keyword is considered keyword spamming (more on this soon) and also doesn't make sense. If someone is searching for California, why would they want information for a place in Colorado? It's not like they're going to decide to drive all the way to Colorado because they came across your website.

Based on the results from Yahoo! some of your keywords would be:

- whitewater rafting
- whitewater rafting trip
- colorado whitewater rafting
- whitewater rafting vacation

People search in plurals. If you were looking for sport cars, you wouldn't type "sport car" in your favorite search engine, you would type "sports cars" or "sport cars." The nice thing about using plural forms of words is that the keyword phrase "sport car" is contained in the phrase "sports cars," and most search engines recognize this. You can also apply the same principal with longer forms of words as well, for example use "engineering" instead of "engineer."

You may have noticed that when I'm using names such as Colorado and Tommy Hilfiger, I neglect to capitalize the first letter as proper English would suggest. The reason is that most people search in lowercase and believe it or not there are still a few search engines that discriminate between upper and lowercase. Some search engines will automatically discount words that are written all in uppercase, so there's another reason to put all keywords into their lowercase form.

A recent study found that 65% of web searchers search for keyword phrases versus single keywords. It has also been found that there is a direct correlation between the number of words in a phrase and the likelihood the searcher is looking to make a purchase. So what's the moral of the story? Use keyword phrases instead of single keywords and you're likely to get more traffic to your site that is wanting to buy instead of browse. Phrases also often contain many single keywords, so both bases are covered anyways.

Prepare your keywords in advance and use them often. You'll find that you'll achieve a higher ranking in search engines as well as ultimately get more people to your site. Best of all - your sales will go up.

How Many Are Too Many?

So how many keywords should you use on each page of your site? If you don't use enough keywords on you page, some searchers may have a hard time finding you. If you use too many, search engines spiders may look at your page and say "well this page is about everything" and decrease your ranking. Everytime you add another keyword it dilutes the value of the others. Typically speaking one keyword per page is not enough and ten is too many. Aim to use two or three or four keywords per page; always use more than one, but never more than six or seven.

If your website has 5 separate pages, each page should be on a slightly different but related topic and have its own set of keywords. For example, if you're a real estate agent, one page of your site may list properties for sale, another may have tips on preparing a property for purchase, another on securing a mortgage and so on. Each one of these pages would have a different set of keywords that pertain to the specific topic of the page.

Where Do You Use Keywords?

So now that you know about keywords, what do you do with them? Where do you use them? The simple answer, everywhere you can. Keywords can be used in a variety of places including:

1. Webpage titles
2. Meta tag descriptions
3. Meta tag keywords
4. Header tags
5. Text on body of page
6. Alternate image tags (displayed instead of picture or graphic)
7. URLs and filenames
8. Search engine submissions

One of the best places to use keywords is in the actual title of the webpage that appears at the top of your web browser. Another good place is in the first few sentences of content. Some search engines will create your listing simply from using title of your webpage and the first couple sentences of text on the page. It is always important to make sure that the body (or text) on your webpage contains a healthy mix of keywords, while keeping the sentences user friendly.

When you're submitting your sites to search engines or directories, on the submission form they sometimes have a spot for you to add a title and description. This is very important and something that you should take much care in writing. The keywords contained in this title and description are often used by the search engine to match up with a users search. If the terms they are looking for aren't found there, then you'll be out of luck.

When incorporating keywords into the body of your webpage, is should not be obvious to the reader that this is what your doing. Use them frequently, but not too frequently. Don't overload your webpage with text. Keywords are most effective at the top of your webpage, so place them as close to the top of the page as you can. Just don't forget to include some at the bottom of the page and throughout the body. Always make sure that you have at least 100 words of text on your page, with the keywords mixed in – otherwise there may not be enough content for some search engines and your keywords won't achieve maximum results.

It's also a good idea to place keywords in headlines and sub headers. These are given some importance in some search engine's ranking systems and as well are useful to people who like to scan.

You can also place keywords in alt tags. An alt tag is a "text caption" which is displayed in a web browser if the user has the graphics turned off, or if the graphic file isn't found on the web server. If you hold your mouse over an image with an alt tag, it will display a little text description of the image. They are simply added to the HTML coding of your site. They are also visible and used by some search engines in the ranking of your site and are also used in some search engines with image/picture search capabilities. More can be found on search engines and keywords in Chapter 24.

In conclusion, use keywords wherever you can and as often as you can – just make sure you choose the right ones. They will do nothing but help you and when used properly and your foot traffic will skyrocket.

Keyword Spamming

Keyword spamming is the practice of repeating the same keyword too many times, or using inappropriate keywords that are unrelated to the content of your webpage for the purpose of gaining a higher ranking in search engines.

Most search engines have the ability to determine whether the use of keywords and their repetition on a page are appropriate. Needless to say keyword spamming can negatively affect your page ranking, or even get you banned from the search engine. Bans can last until the spamming is removed or fixed and the search engine updates itself, or it can be lifelong. It depends on the search engine – it's better to just play by the rules.

The following is a list of what search engines may consider keyword spamming:

1. **Simply writing a list of keywords on your webpage:** If your website was about boats and you had a list at the top of your webpages that said "boat, boats, fishing boats, jet boats, pleasure boats, fast boats, slow boats, row boats etc." the search engine may think that the list is there to fool them (and it probably is) which can lead to a decrease in your ranking.

2. **Using the same keyword an excessive amount of times:** In the above example of the boat website, the keyword boat is used eight times which could be considered keyword spamming. Many search engines have a maximum number of allowable repetitions of the same keyword and will penalize you if you use a keyword too many times. Read the rules and see what they say. Or if you're unsure keep keyword frequency to a maximum of four or five times.

3. **Using keywords on your webpage that are not relevant to page content:** An example would be using the keyword "Britney Spears" on an exotic car website to gain more visitors. I don't know why anyone would do this; someone that is searching for Britney Spears probably isn't interested in cars at that exact moment (if ever) and it certainly won't help your ranking.

Remember, search engines are there to serve their users (not us) and the more users they have, the more money they can make in advertising revenue. Keyword spamming degrades the relevancy of search engine listings, which results in a less than satisfactory user experience and therefore lost profit. That is why search engines dislike sites that spam them – it's like money coming out of their own pocket.

12

Meta Tags

The term "meta" comes from "metadata" which means "data about data." In the case of a webpage, the metadata, or meta tag primarily describes the contents and/or characteristics of a webpage. In the earlier days of the internet some meta tags were widely used by search engines to rank your webpage in the search results.

Meta tags are found in the header section of your website so they're accessible to search engine crawlers but aren't displayed in the web browser window. The header is the area of the webpage that contains all the key information about your site. It is readily available for you to see when looking at the source code of the webpage.

Meta tags are by no means a requirement for a functional site, but they are something that you will likely find in the source code of almost any website. It only takes a minute or two to add them to your source code and it could get you a handful (or more) of extra visitors to your site every week. A typical header with only the keyword and description meta tags looks like:

```
<HEAD>
<TITLE>This is where your title goes</TITLE>
<META name="keywords" content="Your keywords go here">
<META name="description" content="Your description goes here">
</HEAD>
```

There aren't really any rules that define the functions of meta tags (only their format is defined) so there are a number of different meta tags describing everything from a description of the webpage, to when the information on the webpage expires. Some search engines use meta tags as a component of their ranking algorithm and some don't. Meta tags, like keywords can increase your search engine ranking, as well as the traffic to your site if they are used properly.

There are many types of meta tags, only a couple of which directly relate to site promotion, which are the ones we'll focus on.

The Meta Description Tag

The meta description tag allows you to influence the description of your website in search engines that use crawlers that support the tag. Some of the major search engines actually use the description meta tag to display a short description of your page on the search results page of the search engine.

Take care in writing your description and put your most important information at the beginning. Most search engines cut off the display after about 150 – 200 characters. Be sure to use your most important three or four keywords in this description. A few search engines use the words in the description as keywords for their searches. This brief description of your site's content gives the searcher important information he or she needs to determine your site's value. If there's no meta description to display, most search engines pull the first few lines of text from the site's content and display it on the results page. It is definitely worthwhile to use the meta description tag for your pages because it gives you some degree of control with the search engines that use them and it only takes a couple minutes.

The Meta Keywords Tag

The meta keywords tag allows you to provide additional keywords or text for crawler based search engines to index along with your body copy. It is simply an extended list of your keywords, separated by a comma.

When writing your meta keywords tag, always write the most important keywords first, as they carry the most relevance for search engines that do use meta keyword tags. You should have a unique set of meta keyword tags for each unique page on your site. Any keywords that are listed more than four or five times may be considered keyword spamming and are not looked upon very nicely by the search engines that use them.

The meta keyword tag is also sometimes useful as a way to include keyword synonyms or unusual words that don't appear on the actual page itself. For that reason you can use slightly more meta keywords than actual keywords on the page itself, although there isn't really any reason to use more than ten or fifteen. Let's take the whitewater rafting example from the last chapter for instance; some people may search for "white water rafting" instead of "whitewater rafting." Since it is correctly spelled as one word and you don't want any mistakes on your webpage itself, it may help to use "white water rafting" in the keywords meta tag, which remember, is invisible on the webpage itself. Keyword meta tags are also very useful for internal site searches.

When meta tags first became popular, webmasters would load their pages with high ranking meta keyword tags that were unrelated to the content of the webpage on which they appeared. This is essentially identical to keyword spamming, except that it involves the meta tags. Because of the abuse of the keyword meta tag, major search engines no longer use those keywords as a significant factor in their rankings. So is it still worth it to use keyword meta tags? Yes, although don't obsess with them; spend a little time on them, but not too much. They will probably get you an increase in traffic, albeit a small difference. It's certainly not nearly as important as many of the other things you can do for your website to increase traffic and sales.

Other Common Meta Tags and Their Uses

Just because most of the search engines have largely abandoned the best known keyword and description meta tags, doesn't mean you should ignore them and the valuable functions they can perform. There are many other meta tags that exist beyond the description and keyword meta tags, in fact, there's a long list of established meta tags available for your use. Here is a list of some of the other, more common meta tags and their uses:

- **Abstract** - Provides a brief summary of the contents of your webpage.

- **Author** - Includes the author's name and any other information (email address, location etc).

- **Copyright** - The copyright date of the page.

- **Expiry** - Tells search engines when the page will be out of date. If you have a page for a seminar to be held in August 2006, you might want the page expiration date for September 2006.

- **Generator** - This indicates what HTML editor was used to generate the page and is usually inserted automatically by the HTML editor if you use one. I sometimes delete it as it is completely unnecessary.

- **Rating** - This meta tag allows you to rate your page much like movies are rated. As more parents use filtering software, many may block access to unrated sites. In the future, a rating meta tag may be necessary to increase your site's visibility.

- **Refresh** - Use this attribute to refresh the page and/or to redirect the user to another page or site after a certain period of time.

- **Revisit** - Indicates how often search engines should return to check for new content on the page. Some search engines use this, some do not.

- **Robots** (robots.txt) - Controls search engine spiders and crawlers, telling them what pages to index and which links to follow.

Meta tags can provide valuable information to search engines, site users and offer other features available for internal use such as a site search. It is something that can be beneficial if used properly, but can have an overall negative effect when used improperly. If you have any questions on how to use them, check with your web designer who should be able to help you - if they can't, get a new web designer.

13

What's in a Website

If you have a product or service to sell online as far as I'm concerned there are only three types of websites you should ever need:

1. Squeeze sites
2. Sales sites
3. Branding sites

And that's what we'll discuss in this chapter. Depending on the type of online business you have, or want to have, you could use one, two, or all three types of sites in your marketing strategy. I use all three, as I suspect most businesses would.

I should note that there are also other types of websites such as content sites which you might use to create an advertising revenue. They're not really used for marketing products and services, unless you want to place ads on them to drive traffic to your site or add an opt-in box to generate leads. Since this book is more on marketing your business, products or services, we're not going to get into other types of sites.

Squeeze Sites

A squeeze page (also known as a "shy yes" or "power squeeze" page) is basically a webpage designed to "squeeze" the name and email address out of the visitor. Here's how it works. You have a webpage where you give the visitor a free gift in return for them providing you with their name and email address. The free gift could be anything from a special report to an ebook to an audio or video download. Along with providing their email address, visitors opt-in to receive future emails from you. This system allows you to create an opt-in list or database of leads you can use to sell your products or services. On some squeeze pages, your only options are to opt-in or leave. On others, you are given a method to continue exploring the site without opting in.

You don't need to have an entire website or domain name for your squeeze page; it could just be www.YourDomain.com/freereport if you like. I usually use a separate domain name because it looks more professional and also makes tracking and promotion a little easier. For an example of a squeeze page that I use go to www.99InternetMarketingTips.com.

While there are many scripts which you can use to collect information about your visitors without them knowing even knowing about it, it is not ethical, not opt-in and in most countries illegal.

Creating a squeeze page is not hard. You just need some copy on a webpage that will entice the visitor to sign up and a signup form. Quite often the code for the signup form can be obtained from your autoresponder service. When the visitor enters their information, the autoresponder saves and stores the information then sends either a confirmation or a thank you for signing up email. The autoresponder service I use is integrated with my shopping cart system and can be found at, www.1StartCart.com.

The rationale behind using a squeeze page is that most internet marketers realize that the vast majority of visitors will not buy from a site on the first visit. If you can collect the email addresses of most of your visitors you can invite them back to your site again and again and have an opportunity to make a sale at a later date. If you don't collect their info, once they leave your site you may never see them again.

Driving traffic to a squeeze site is a little different than driving traffic to a sales page or branding site. Since there is no real content on the actual signup page search engine optimization is slim at best. That's why I primarily use paid traffic generation techniques like Google AdWords, Yahoo Search Marketing or some type of banner, online display or text ad.

Some squeeze pages experience "leakage" because some visitors may look at the HTML source code and locate the URL of the confirmation page. They can just enter that URL into their web browser to access what's behind the door. A good way to prevent this type of leakage (if you want to) is to encrypt the URL for that follow-up webpage, or to email a link to what was promised on the squeeze page. That way if the visitor supplies a bogus email address they don't get the free gift.

Another thing you can do with squeeze pages is personalize them. This takes the information that that visitor enters on the opt-in page and incorporates it into the copy of the confirmation page. It could be something as simple as:

"Thanks for subscribing [Visitor's Name]. An email has been sent to VisitorsName@TheirDomain.com with a download link for your free ebook."

Squeeze pages are popping up all over the internet simply because the technique works. Internet marketers are using squeeze pages on a regular basis to build massive opt-in lists for lead generation and sales. If lead generation is important to your business, you need to get your squeeze pages up and working for you as soon as possible, even if you don't have a product or service to sell yet. In fact, before you start selling anything you should use a squeeze page to develop a list of leads. That way when your product launches you may have 5-10 thousand qualified leads to offer your product to. With a $100 product and a conversion rate of only 4%, that is $20,000 - $40,000 in sales in only a few days.

While squeeze pages may irritate a small percentage of your visitors, they have been proven to increase your overall opt-in conversion rate by 100-600%. If you haven't already, seriously consider adding squeeze pages to your marketing arsenal.

Sales Sites

The purpose of a sales site is obviously to get your customer to purchase your product or service. Depending on the type of product or service you are selling and the target market you are selling to, a sales site can be anything from a site selling multiple products like an online store (www.Amazon.com) to a site dedicated to selling a single product.

Most information based products such as how-to courses, audio/video discs and ebooks have a sales page or website that's sole purpose is to sell a single product. These pages are just like a long sales letter used in direct mail (except with color, graphics and pictures) and can range from 5-30 pages or more. I'm sure you've probably come across the long sales letters that are used to sell these types of products if you've done a little surfing on the net. If you bought this book, there's a good chance that you came across the sales page at www.StreetSmartInternetMarketing.com.

When a visitor lands on a sales page you don't want them to leave before they buy, so don't have options (like links to other pages) that allow them to leave the site. If you want to, you can link to another part on the sales page (down the page) as long as they continue to read the copy. Most sales sites are simple one or two page websites, except maybe for a separate order and confirmation page.

Creating a Sales Page

A sales letter site generally consists of a headline that is usually proceeded by a pre-headline to setup the main headline, then followed by a post headline which clarifies the main headline. The three part headline is followed by an introduction that further draws the visitor into the copy and allows you to start the sales presentation by presenting the benefits of doing business with you. Next you need to build credibility through providing credentials, experience, testimonials, real-life examples and so on, so the reader knows that what you're saying isn't a crock of BS. Then describe the benefits and features (focusing on the benefits) of purchasing the product or service you have to offer, remembering WII-FM (What's In It For Me). Then you should build up the value of your offer in the mind of the visitor. A great way to quickly add a lot of value to your offer is to sweeten the pot by adding several bonuses with a high perceived value. After your offer, you need to clearly state a call to action that links to an order page.

If you're going the route of the online store, you can utilize any one of many design and copy layouts. The most important point here is to be sure that the products and navigation are easy to find and simple and easy to use. I used to own a retail store that also had an online component. We had about 4,000 products that were organized into ten main categories that each had between four-to-ten sub categories, which each had another four-to-ten sub categories and so on until the final product was reached. To give you an example of what I mean, consider the following category layout:

Sporting Goods
    Soccer
      Balls
        Official Balls
          Adidas MLS Official Matchball

If you have more than 100 products on your site, it is generally a good idea to have some kind of product search. If you're not sure how to do this Google (and some other major search engines) have a built in site search tool that you can install on your site. Just go to Google and type in "free Google site search" to get the details.

Branding Sites

The purpose of your branding site is to brand your company, products or services and/or you. Large corporations continually spend correspondingly large amounts of money establishing and supporting their brands. They do it because it works. Users of their goods and services do so for any number of reasons that all correlate to the establishment of the brand. Branding is the foundation for almost all successful marketing.

A brand is your identifying mark which is made up of a combined set of impressions and expectations that a customer has as a result of the interactions with you, or your company and its products and services over time. Everything you say and do establishes your brand. Branding does not only convey a message, it attaches an emotion to products and company names in the minds of customers. The ultimate goal of branding is to end up with the name of your product, service or business on your target markets mind. If you don't establish your brand yourself, your customers and competitors will define it for you – and that's probably not something you want.

Branding is not about selling a product, but selling a company or name. Just think of the war between Coke and Pepsi. They both spend an obscene amount of money every year trying to become the dominant brand. Most of their ads don't even try to sell their product; they simply sell the brand and try to create "brand awareness."

Branding sites should be fairly basic in nature and the number of options kept to a minimum. A very important element in branding any website is your choice of domain name. It needs to correlate to your site, your business and ultimately your brand. A branding site should convey information about you or your business focused on building your brand rather than selling your products. Use the branding site to highlight your strong points to customers and what they should expect from doing business with you.

For example this book will be listed on my branding/blogging site (www.JustinMichie.com), however only about 1% or less of my online book sales will come from my branding site. The reasons are simple. If I want to advertise for this book, I won't link to my branding site, I'll link to the specific sales site for the book. My branding site won't be search engine optimized for the book, or even optimized for the highest sales conversion rate like my sales site will. The goal of my specific branding site is to brand me and as such that will be the focus of the site, not making sales.

Doorway Pages

Although it's not a type of site, a doorway page is a type of webpage designed for a specific purpose. A doorway (also known as a bridge or gateway) page is webpage designed specifically to rank well in search engines for the particular topic of the webpage. These pages differ from search engine optimized pages because they are only made to please the search engines and do not have any real content. In fact they are never seen by web surfers. When you go to a doorway page, it automatically redirects you to the webpage the site owner wants you to see, and effectively skips over the doorway page.

Doorway pages have acquired something of a bad reputation due to their frequent use (and abuse) in spamming search engines. Some people have also used mass produced doorway pages with only a few small variations, to spam search engines. Doorways used in this manner add to the clutter that search engines and web searchers must contend with. For this reason many search engines ban websites that use these types of pages. In fact, just this past year (at the time of writing) a very major German car manufacturer had its site banned from Google because it used a doorway page.

Critics of doorway pages contend that the time and effort spent generating pages would be better spent optimizing pages that are integrated into the content of the website. A wide range of opinions exists concerning what constitutes a doorway page and when one is acceptable. One of the most common justifications is for sites that have database-driven content that would otherwise be invisible to the search engines.

Don't use a doorway page unless it is absolutely necessary and always be sure to check the search engine guidelines prior to submitting them. Submitting a doorway page to the wrong search engine could possibly get your site banned for life.

You can have as many sales sites or power squeeze sites as you want, but you should only have one branding site - unless you have different online businesses branded under different corporate names, where you could have a site for each business. I find it works best to have one of each (squeeze, sales and branding) all working together. The more unique power squeeze sites you have, the more traffic you can drive to your sales sites by way of direct email marketing. Depending on the type of products you are selling, you may want to have a sales site for each product (which is almost always better) vs. one sales site for all your products.

Websites are made up of many different pieces or elements that when arranged together can either make your site the ultimate online selling machine, or the ultimate dud. The next chapter will focus individually on each one of these elements.

14

Website Design

There are countless elements that go into the making of webpage, but if you make a bad design choice, it won't matter how great your content is, or how much advertising you do. If your site looks bad no one who visits will stay long, and if they don't stay long, you won't have much of an opportunity to sell them. To get as many sales as you can, you'll want to make it as easy as possible for people to buy from you. That involves making your website easy to navigate and friendly to use.

One of the hardest decisions website owners (or designers) face is how to balance artistic design with practicality and functionality. You must have a clear purpose for your site and every element on your site must contribute to that purpose. What we're going to discuss here are the elements that frame your content including your navigation menu, colors, graphics, gizmos and more.

Target Your Audience

It is imperative that you understand exactly who your target audience is, and that you tailor your site to fit their needs. For example, if your target market consists of adults between the age of 50 and 65, don't use a small font size on your site. Determine what you want your site to accomplish, and then set out to make sure that it does just that. Who your primary target audience is should affect everything from the layout, to the colours you use, to the personality of the copy.

Design and Layout

The layout is how things are arranged on your pages. There are many different ways to display your content and you need to choose the most functional design for your market, type of site and content. A great site will have a layout that is pleasing to the eye and all the parts will have a consistent look and feel. It should be well organized, logical and easy to navigate. A clean layout that uses a lot of white space enhance the way a site looks and is more pleasing to the eye. Create a template and keep it consistent throughout your site.

The name of your website, domain name, or business name should be prominently featured somewhere at or near the top of your pages either within your logo or near it.

The navigation should be prominently displayed and arranged on your page to fit with your design, name and logo. This should be your template. Most websites use a template for their pages as it keeps the layout consistent throughout your site, which helps build your brand and also makes it more user friendly and professional looking.

Use lots of white space and avoid clutter. Keep the focus on your content. Use fonts that will be available on all computers to prevent your site looking jarred. I prefer Arial, but Times New Roman and Verdana are popular as well and they don't require licensing.

It's important to understand that there are two types of readers: One will read absolutely everything, and the other will skim and scroll, looking for key points. Use sub headers and bullets for the skimmers. Appeal to both types of readers. Reading webpages on a computer is much harder than reading a letter in your hand. Design your site in such a way that it keeps the attention of the reader.

Unless you have a sales letter type site, don't make your pages too long. People don't like to read from a screen. Most web surfers don't read too far past the first screen of information, so make sure you put the most important information on the first visible screen.

Although many people have high resolution monitors, about half of my visitors still use a monitor with an 800 by 600 screen resolution. So you need to check to make sure your page will fit completely within this screen size. If you're using windows, simply change the screen resolution under the display properties settings tab to see what it looks like.

Another way to make sure your site will always fit on your visitors computer is to put the entire site inside a resizable table, that will automatically adjust itself to cover a certain percentage of the surfer's monitor. I don't recommend using resizable tables as they throw most of the other information on your site out of alignment, unless they are done properly with is both difficult and time consuming. You can also try using a fixed table width, centered, or left or right justified on your visitors screen such as Yahoo! currently does.

There are also any number of "crude design techniques" which include things like mouse trails, scrolling and blinking text and so on. These do not belong on professional business websites of any kind. Just because it is available does not mean you need to use it. There is not a situation I can think where it would be acceptable, unless you were a web design firm illustrating your capabilities, although those would not be big selling points to me.

Clutter

This is one of the most common mistakes of the internet newbie, and even some of the larger corporations. Clutter can mean any number of things, from having a navigation area with ten or more links to choose from, to a website where every little bit of space is crammed with information. It's even worse when the information that's packed together isn't even relevant to the site. Have you ever been to a real estate site that has the weather, news, sports scores and any other number of unrelated items on it? If that sounds like your website, you're killing the chances of someone staying, and buying from you.

Choosing Colors

A color scheme should be established, and the number of colors should be held to a minimum. Colors should compliment your website. The color scheme will help create a consistent look and feel, and the pages will flow more smoothly from one to another. Too many, or too bright of colors can be visually distracting from the content. As with graphics, color should only be used to help the effectiveness of the actual content.

Choose your colors carefully and keep in mind that your tastes may not be appealing to your target audience. Try a few different color schemes and get others opinions on them. As a general rule, don't use anything that is too outrageous, or too dull; a comfortable, happy but un-boring medium usually works best.

Colored text should also be used sparingly as black text is the commonly accepted standard, usually on a light or pale background. Keep the contrast with the background in mind. Since text is the content of most pages, it must be easy it read. Try to use colored text only to emphasize important information. For important points you can highlight the black text with yellow, which has a high contrast ratio, ultimately increasing the readability.

Backgrounds

Because a plain white background can be somewhat boring, most web designers make things a little more interesting by using a background consisting of either a solid color, a repeated image, or a single image. Backgrounds can really improve the appearance of a webpage, but you need to use some common sense. If the color of the text is too close to the color of the background it can make the text difficult to read, (like a light yellow text on a white page). Alternatively, bright colors on a dark background (neon green on black) is not any easier to read. Dark or oddly colored backgrounds will distract your visitors from your information and also can make reading more difficult.

Repeated or single images aren't used too often anymore, simply because they add to the clutter and make the pages take longer to load. It doesn't mean they can't be used, just make sure to use something that's actually going to enhance the content of your page, not take away from it.

Navigation

How many times have you left a website in frustration because you can't find what you're looking for? It's a silly way to lose visitors. Navigation links on your site play a big role in determining the stickiness of your site (how long your visitor stays and explores your site).

There should always be a consistent navigational method throughout the site that allows users to know exactly where they are and how they can get back to where they started. If you go to any major website, you'll quickly notice that each page has the same look and feel, and the navigations buttons are always in the same spot. There's a reason for this. Not only does it help to brand the look and feel of the site, but the visitors also always know where they are, and how to get back to where they came from. If you ever make it hard for your visitors to find their way around your site, they'll find their way to somebody else's site. Always use jargon-free labels for your navigation and make sure they are as clear and concise as possible.

Create a primary navigation system that will be available on every page of your site. Choose the top four-to-six or so main categories and place them in the navigation bar along with a "home" link and a "contact us" link. Supplying too many options can paralyze the decision making process, so six or eight works well and also happens to be how many you can comfortably fit across the top of a webpage. These days, visitors have an expectation that they'll find the "home link" on your webpages in the top left-hand corner, so if you put it anywhere else, you may be confusing your visitors and failing to meet their expectations. Navigation buttons are the same way, they're expected to be at the top of the page, and if they're not there, down the left hand side of the page. Navigation buttons down the side of your pages don't run into any length limitations due to the endless amount of vertical space on every page. Still, if you have any more than eight or so choices, it'll only make the decision making process more difficult and you'll wind up losing visitors.

Another essential navigation tool is a "search this site" option. It's one of the first things some visitors will look for when they get to your site, especially if you have a site with lots of content. Don't lose them - put your search link near the top where it's easy to find.

Many sites also include a second set of navigational links at the bottom of all its webpages, for the simple reason that when a visitor scrolls down past the first screen of information, most navigation buttons are lost.

Links

Links are what make the World Wide Web tick, and are the lifeblood in the navigation system of any website. It's very rare that a webpage doesn't have at least a few links on it - without them you can't go anywhere but away to another site. There are three different types of links, internal, external and bookmark links.

An internal link is a link to a page on your own site. Since you have complete control over these links, you have absolutely no excuse if they don't work.

An external link is a link to a page on a different website. Even though you have no control over these links, check them periodically to make sure they still work. A link that worked yesterday may no longer work today. Visitors to your page will find themselves very frustrated if your links do not work. In my opinion external links are at best a bad idea. If your goal is to make money from your website, how can you accomplish this by distracting your visitors with links to other sites? The only way this is considered acceptable, is if you are taking them to another money making site of yours.

A bookmark link is a link to a location on the same page. When the user clicks on a such a link, the browser scrolls the page to bring the bookmarked location into view. As with internal links, there is no excuse for non-working bookmark links.

Nothing shouts "unprofessional" like links that don't work. There is absolutely no excuse for this one. It's not hard to check to make sure your links work, heck there are even programs that can do this for you for free. Remember to regularly check external links to other websites to make sure that they still point to where they should.

Links are a key factor in the navigation process on any website, and knowing where you've been and where you are makes it easier to decide where to go next. If visited links don't change color naturally as they should, users exhibit navigational disorientation and may unintentionally revisit the same pages repeatedly, eventually getting frustrated, and leave. That's why you need to appropriately change the color of active and visited links. Always use the commonly accepted default colors – there's no need to deviate from the norm unless you want to confuse people. A regular link typically defaults to blue, while an active link is red, and an already visited link is purple.

Optimum Load Time

There is nothing more annoying than waiting minutes for a page to load. While many people are connecting to the internet faster than ever before, believe it or not, at the time of writing this book 90% of worldwide internet users still use dialup internet connections. I was recently on vacation and for three weeks had the pleasure of using a dialup internet connection for the first time in years. In case it's been awhile since you've used dialup, it is very, very, very slow; some webpages would literally take five-to-ten minutes to load. Call me silly, but I don't think that most people want to waste that much time waiting for a webpage to load. If you don't design your site for the lowest common denominator, you'll end up turning away the vast majority of users who still surf the web at modem speeds.

That means minimizing graphics and making sure that the ones you do use are the proper resolution and cropped appropriately. Optimize your HTML and make sure there's no unnecessary code. Flash and other scripts can also increase page load time, so if you don't need it, don't use it. Use Server Side Include (SSI) files wherever possible. SSI files help make your webpages more responsive and decrease page load time by cutting and pasting HTML. Ask your web developer if they can do this for you.

Webpages should almost always take less than 30 seconds to load, even for a dialup internet user. As I mentioned before, the average dialup speed is 4kb/s. To keep your page load time under 30s, that means a maximum total webpage size of 120kb (4kb/s x 30s) including all graphics, HTML and other scripts. The only exceptions would be when the user intentionally clicks a link to a page that they know in advance will take longer to load (due to a large number of graphics, video or other multimedia).

Graphics

Graphics, like anything else should be used only as needed. Be sure not to overdo it and to leave enough white (blank) space to keep the page balanced and uncluttered. Graphics should be used solely to improve the presentation of content and the functionality of your site. Do not use graphics to make a page prettier, if it will decrease the functionality of the page. Functionality breeds happy visitors, which breeds more sales, which ultimately means more money in your pocket.

If you have a lot of pictures or images that you need to display on a single page, thumbnails can help you out. A thumbnail is a smaller image (in physical size and file size) representation or snapshot of a larger image, usually intended to make it easier and faster to look at or manage a larger group of images. When you click on a thumbnail it links to the full size image. Thumbnails are useful because they help keep page load time to a minimum and help avoid clutter on your webpage.

As far as the technical aspect of graphics go, use .jpg formats for continuous color graphics (any real life picture or image) and .gif format for smaller vector images such as a logo or animation. Size does matter, so crop your images and cut out the extra space around what you want your visitor to see. When you're printing promotional material, your graphics should be at 300 dpi (dots per inch), but on the internet, you only need your graphics to be 72 dpi; sometimes 96 dpi at most. Computer monitors can only see this quality and by decreasing the quality you significantly decrease the file size of your graphics. Another helpful hint is to always include the image size (height and width usually in pixels) in the HTML code. Most HTML editors like FrontPage do this automatically for you. If you don't, the web browser and computer need to calculate where graphics fit in with the other content and the webpage will take longer to load.

Browser Bias

When designing a website, it is important to recognize that not everyone uses Internet Explorer to browse the internet and that your site needs to be cross browser compatible. While Microsoft still owns the majority of the browser market, it does not own it all. Depending on your site (and more importantly, the content of the site), there are other browsers that your visitors use including Firefox, Netscape Navigator, AOL and Opera just to name a few. To check compatibility of your site, check out www.anybrowser.com.

Sounds

It is fairly easy to play music or sound effects on your webpage and many people do so freely. In almost all cases I would advise against this. The chances that your visitor's choice in music would be the same as yours are quite unlikely and sound effects should be reserved for games. Other potential problems are that the user may already be listening to something else on the radio, or the baby may be asleep – who knows? There are a few exceptions, like if your site is about a specific musical artist or group, then background music could be justified.

If you must have music (only because it relates to your sites content), do not have it automatically start; let the visitor start it – and it is also a good idea to have several selections to choose from. You also need to beware of copyright infringement issues.

Something with sound that does work is a short audio introduction to your website. I usually have it start automatically, which I know goes against what I said above, but this is purely vocal and not intended to jar your visitors awake. It is especially helpful for getting people to sign up for your opt-in email list, take a variety of other shy calls to action and can greatly increase your conversion rate, so in this case only, it's acceptable.

Video

It is now easier than ever to add video to a webpage and it can be a very powerful promotion technique. If you want to add video to a page, it's better to either have the user manually start the video, or to have them click on a link to view it so it doesn't catch them off guard and pollute their environment for the same reasons as starting sounds. It also won't bog down page loading time. Always play the video in a universally accepted format, see the paragraph entitled "Non Universal Formatting" on the next page for more information.

Animations

Animations, scrolling text and other moving objects are somewhat popular, to the point where they have been grossly overused on some sites. Having some movement on your page can help call attention to certain elements of your page and liven things up a bit. But please keep this in mind: more is not always better. I'm sure we've all been to a website where it is impossible to decipher the content due to the mass of moving icons.

There's no reason for an animated "click here to email me" button when a static button will do just fine. Moving images sometimes have an overpowering effect on the human peripheral vision and distract visitors from the desired purpose of your site. Give your user some peace and quiet to actually read the text or see the product you are selling. I prefer not to use any moving stuff on most of my websites, as it takes away from the actual relevant content. If you really need to use anything that moves, do so sparingly. A good rule of thumb is that "the less movement they see, the better off you'll be." One of the only times when movement is good is when you're placing a graphical ad on someone else's site, as it helps your ad stick out from the rest of the page.

Flash

Macromedia flash must be another thing that was created more to annoy people than for its actual real-world usefulness. Websites went from splash pages to flash intros. Big corporations started it and everyone else followed. At least most flash intros let you skip over them, but only after you finish waiting for them to load. The ones you can't skip, well they're a lost cause.

The main reason flash has somewhat of a bad rap, is because it has been overused and because it is, well, "flashy." If you only have a few seconds to get someone's attention with the information on your website, why distract and waste the few precious moments you have with flash.

Don't get me wrong, flash can be useful in moderation and in the right situation. It is used over and over for banner ads. Though I don't recommend putting flash banner ads on your site because it's distracting; it's ok to use flash for your banner ads on other sites. Flash is also useful for adding audio intros to your website, or even playing short videos. If you've been to any of my sites with audio, I use a little flash script to play the audio since it's a universally supported format. If, and only if, adding flash can increase the value of your website then use it. But if you don't need it, don't use it just because you can.

Non Universal Formatting

This is another real problem people seem to forget in website design. Unless there is some very specific reason to use Acrobat Reader (.pdf) format for your webpage, avoid it. It's annoying and either requires the visitor to download Adobe Reader, or if they already have it, wait for it to load so they can view the page. Same goes for video and audio. If you absolutely need it on your website, play it in a format that most people don't need to download software to play. For example .ra files can only be played in the Real Audio Player, and .mov files can only be played in Apple's Quicktime. If your visitors need these programs to view the content, chances are they won't, and they'll leave your webpage and move onto the next.

Use what comes with most computers: Microsoft Windows. If you want to play a movie file that will work on most computers, play it in .mpeg format, or .wav for small audio files and .mp3 format for larger files. Windows Media Player, which comes with almost every non Mac computer, will play .mp3, .wav, .mpeg, .wma, .wmv files, and many others including .midi, .au, .avi and so on.

Frames

Frames divide webpages into two or more sections, with each section displaying a different document or webpage. For example, frames can have a table of contents in one frame and a main page in another. This way if you want to update your table of contents, you don't need to change every webpage. There are other ways to do this, but it's beyond my technological knowledge. That's why I have a web designer.

Like anything else, frames can be overused. Do not use frames just because they are available. In fact I don't recommend using them at all, unless you have a very good reason to do so and there's none I can think of.

Splitting a webpage into frames is very confusing for users since frames break the fundamental user model of the webpage. They also may prevent the visitor from using the bookmark feature. Thus, the visitor may not be able to remember your website address, URLs can stop working and printouts become difficult. If you must use frames, make sure they don't have a scrolling bar - besides looking ugly, they take up valuable page space. Another negative feature of frames is that they are not search engine friendly. What if the page the search engine references, doesn't have the navigation menu on it? How are your visitors going to navigate your website?

Scrolling From Left to Right

Have you ever been to a website where you found yourself having to scroll the screen left to right to read all the content? If you have, chances are that you didn't stay very long. While it is intuitive to read down a page, it's less so to scroll left to right. On some sites you need to scroll for the simple reason that the site developer forced an absolute size width on his or her webpage, instead of allowing it to fit on the users computer screen. The visual distraction of having content cut off on the right side is very disconcerting and having to scroll left to right is just not natural. Chances are, if you make your visitors scroll left to right, they'll likely click away to another website.

Advertisements

Ads are a seemingly unavoidable part of the web. If you have a website, you may want to advertise on other sites to help get visitors to your site. But should you place ads on your site? Maybe - it's completely up to you. But keep in mind, people do not visit your website to see the ads, they are there for the content. Ads should only be a secondary part of your page. They can be a great source of secondary income, but they should not be the focus of your page. In fact they should not really stick out too much at all. If you're going to place any ads on your site, they should fit in with the rest of the page.

Let's say that you have a website devoted to pets and you sell a variety of ebooks about various aspects of owning/caring for different types of animals. An ad or affiliate link for a specific pet food delivery website that you recommend would probably be a good fit. Instead of having an obnoxious animated banner ad on your site, you could seamlessly include it with your content like this: "If you own a wide variety of animals, and even if you don't, shopping for pet food can be quite a chore. To help me make my life a little easier, I get all my pet food delivered to my door each week. It's cheaper than the big box stores and takes no time at all. For more information, check out www.petfoodforless.com."

If you can go ad free, it's best, especially if you're selling a product, otherwise you'll simply take away from your sales and your conversion rate will suffer. However, if you must have ads, use them sparingly and take some time to consider their placement. Nothing is more annoying than having to scroll past a bunch of ads to get to the content. You can lose a lot of visitors very quickly this way.

This is the way I personally see it: if I have a website that's ultimate purpose is to sell some kind of product, I don't put ads on it. They are distracting to the user, unprofessional and don't add to the ultimate goal of the site – to sell products. The kind of site I might place ads on would be a content or information based site whose sole purpose is to generate revenue from ads, such as a Google AdSense site.

Opening New Windows – Popups

Have you ever been to a website where one popup opens, then another, and another, until it is snow-balling out of control and you can't keep up trying to close them? Most people see them as nothing but an annoying pain in the rear. However, the reason they're used so much is because they can be effective if used properly. Luckily, now there are a wide variety of popup blockers to choose from for those who don't like them.

If you are selling your own product or service, do not under any circumstances have someone else's pop up advertisements on your website. It won't produce favorable results, looks awful and creates an unenjoyable experience for your visitors.

Thanks to technology, some new, some old, there are four types of popups:

- **Original popup** – opens new browser window.
- **Pop-unders** – opens new window under browser.
- **DHTML pop-overs** – gives the appearance of popup without opening a new window.
- **Alert boxes** – grey dialogue alert box, usually reserved for error messages.

My testing has shown that DHTML pop-overs work best, followed by pop-unders, alert boxes then popups. Pop-overs are designed to look like a separate browser window is opened, without actually opening one – for this reason, pop-overs are immune to almost all popup blockers.

If you're going to use popups, here are the only two reasons why I think they should be used:

1. When visitors first enter your webpage, you can use a popup to give them an opportunity to sign up for your newsletter, or other opt-in list. You can also use a popup when the user exits to give them another opportunity to sign up for your newsletter (only if they haven't already done so).

2. The only other time you should ever use a popup is when it is user initiated; here are some examples:

    a) The visitor clicks an external link to another website (you of course don't want them to leave your site to go to another).

    b) They click on thumbnail of a graphic (when they click on thumbnail, it opens a new window with the large sized version).

    c) They click on a link to view a video, pdf document or other file type.

    d) They click on a link to go to an order form.

Other than those particular situations, don't use them popups. Quite frankly, they're as annoying as you know what, and will deter users from your site.

Under Construction

Would you move into a house that is under construction? Would you drive a car that wasn't finished? Then why would you put unfinished webpages that represent you or your company on the internet in a pubic domain? Never invite a customer to a section that has not been completed, it is a waste of the visitor's time which is both frustrating and disappointing. Either hide the section, or get enough content in that area to make it valuable to your visitors. Anything less is frustrating and disappointing to visitors - they came looking for something you advertised, so it should be there. Furthermore, if a visitor believes a section/page of your site is "always under construction," the chances that he'll mosey that way when you have completed it are slim to none.

Page Redirects

Many people are guilty of this internet feature. The only time a "page redirect" should be used is when you have changed domain names or site addresses, or if it is being used for ad tracking purposes. Some search engines don't like them and some cause page loading delays which surfers don't like either.

Bad Spelling and Grammar

To make this quick and simple, there are not, under any circumstances, any excuses for having spelling or grammatical mistakes on your website. If you do have mistakes, it looks like you're either extremely lazy, extremely stupid, or both.

Contact Info

You need to get a customer feeling like you are a real business, so always include your company profile and contact information. If it's possible, include your phone/fax numbers and actual physical mailing address in addition to an email address or contact form. It also doesn't hurt any to have an "about us" page on your site with additional information as well.

Scan Proofing

Scan proofing is when a webpage visitor scans the page to see if it is relevant to them. You can make it easier for them to do this by using bold to highlight certain points (such as benefits); also consider using bulleted lists for multiple benefits to make it more visually pleasing. This also helps add eye-pleasing white space.

Testimonials

Adding testimonials to your web page, (especially on the order form) can drastically help increase your conversion rates and adds instant credibility to your business.

Call to Action

You need to tell your visitors what action to take. I know it sounds silly, but you need to explicitly ask them for the sale. Place strong calls to action in different places on your webpage to test what works best.

Awards

If your business has won any awards or received official recognition, you could possibly display it on the "about us" page of your site. Awards are a way to gain recognition for you and your website. They bring prestige, more traffic to your site and they enhance your credibility.

Browser Hijacking (Mousetrapping)

Browser hijacking is one of the most extreme marketing tactics available on the net that is often reserved for sleazy porn sites. The ultimate goal is to extract maximum value from one-time visits, typically through the use of browser tricks in an effort to keep a visitor captive at a site. This includes things like bombarding visitors with a never-ending supply of popup ads, disabling the browsers "back" button and right click disabling among other things.

Right click disabling is perhaps one of the most annoying things I have seen. This is a feature quite often initiated to prevent people from copying pictures from your website. Not only are there at least two other ways that I know of to easily copy a picture from a website, but if you have an online business, you should want people to copy your pictures – the more they are circulated, the more free exposure you'll get. Besides attempting to make it slightly more difficult for someone to copy your pictures, it also disables some other options, including opening links in new windows, which is something I regularly do. Quite often it frustrates me so much I just leave the webpage – as I'm sure many other visitors probably do as well.

Another thing I've come across on some websites that would otherwise be impressive, is a script that prevents users from clicking the back button in their web browser. I don't really understand why some people think this works? If you can't go back to the page you came from, does that mean that you're going to spend more time on the page that's preventing you and actually buy something from them? Absolutely not! I can guarantee you that I'll never go back to a webpage that's hijacked my back button. So, never, ever disable the back button on the users browser to try and keep them on your site – it doesn't work, and if there was even a slight chance that they might buy from you, you've just ruined it.

Other hijacking techniques include webpages that automatically place their domain in your bookmarks folder or change your homepage to their website. Some sites automatically install toolbars into your browser without your permission, or download/install other programs such as dialer software with the hope that you'll actually use it. There are a bunch of other schemes out there, just make sure that you don't practice any of them.

Knowing the rules is good, but knowing when to break them is even better. If you (or your graphic designer) know the principals and rules that underline good design, you're a step ahead of the crowd, but if you know when to break the rules and principals you're leaps and bounds ahead of the crowd.

Hopefully by now you have a good idea about what goes into a webpage and how to implement it. By continually testing and tracking the design and layout, you can greatly improve the functionality of your site and consequently the money it makes for you. It's also important to note that web designers aren't marketers. It's up to you to make sure your site is marketable.

15

Accepting Payment on the Web

If you're doing business on the internet, accepting payment through your website is an absolute must. If you're not processing orders online, you're losing a great deal of money in lost sales. Furthermore, studies have shown, you can increase your online sales by up to 400% simply by accepting credit cards. Unless you're really bored and have nothing better to do, you probably don't want to spend the bulk of your time answering phone calls and processing orders by hand. That's where the most compelling benefit of the internet, the ability to automate almost everything, including accepting payment, comes into play.

Traditionally, when you make a purchase at a store the generally accepted methods of payment are:

1. Cash (everywhere)
2. Debit (most places)
3. Check (some places)
4. Money order (some places)
5. Bank/wire transfer (high end purchases – house, car etc.)
6. Credit card (most places)

Obviously, when you want the process to be as automated as possible, numbers one through five are not hands free, so they're out. To automate the payment process, you must be able to accept credit cards. In fact, if you want to do any type of business on the net, you absolutely need to accept credit cards. If you don't accept them, you'll lose massive amounts of business to people who do. Besides, accepting credit cards also gives you a measure of credibility - you will seem more like a real business than a faceless fly-by-night company.

The way people pay for products that they find online is broken down as follows:

- 80% through a secure server (credit cards)
- 7% by phone
- 6% by fax

- 5% through regular postal mail
- 2% through non-secured server (call with credit card number)

If that's not reason enough, I don't know what is. But here are some other reasons to accept credit cards: First is the unprecedented convenience they offer. Your customers pop a number into their computer and presto, the item is paid for and will shortly arrive in their inbox or at their door. That's it. That's all. Easy, simple and very little effort required. Credit cards also offer their holders some level of protection against fradulent purchases and allow users to spend money that they don't necessarily have.

A second reason is impulse. After reading your advertisements and hype on your site, buyers should be all fired up about your product, and as long as they can satisy their desire to purchase your product immediately, you've got that sale bagged. If you only allow payments by phone or snail mail (or even fax) by the time they get around to making payment (if they do), the may have lost interest or simply changed their mind.

Credit card payment is also a necessity if your customers are in a neighboring country or overseas. It automatically takes care of currency conversion, is instantaneous, doesn't have the same problems checks and money orders can have and it won't get lost in the mail.

Credit cards may offer convenience for your customers, but they also make your job a lot easier than accepting cash, checks and money orders because:

- They don't require any trips to the bank.
- They leave a clean paper trail.
- They can't bounce like a check.
- Orders are easy to trace and track for customer service.

This is how it works. When an order is placed on the secure internet server, the secure server calls the bank and authorizes the credit card while the customer waits for a few moments. While they are waiting a screen is displayed letting the customer know exactly what is happening. Once the order is approved, a screen comes up explaining that the order was approved (usually with a confirmation or order number) and where the product will be shipped. Remember to post your contact info on this screen in case they have any problems. It is also a good idea to tell them what name will show up on their credit card bill so there's no confusion that the charge is legitimate. For example, you could say something like this:

"$167.74 was charged to your credit card XXXX XXXX XXXX 1234. This charge will appear on your card as [Your Business Name]."

Some customers may feel uncomfortable giving their credit card number on the internet, but still want to place an order right away. To solve this problem, you can have a non secure order form (minus the credit card info) where they fill out all their details, including a phone number where you can call them to get their credit card number, or so they can call you to give their credit card number. You should also have a form available that they can print out and fax to you just in case they don't trust the internet with their credit card numbers, but trust a fax. You should also have a mailing address available where they can mail payment to you in the form of a check or money order. Some people won't give their credit card number out to anybody and some people don't have credit cards, so you need to make sure that they can pay another way.

Keep in mind that some people will want to call to place the order no matter what options you offer them online. This could be because they feel uncomfortable not talking to a live person, entering their credit card number online, or any number of other reasons. If possible always have a number that they can call to place an order. If you work out of your home, or even if you don't, there are companies that will take orders for you 24/7 for a nominal fee, usually about $5 - $10 per order. Just do a quick google for "fulfillment companies."

Checks by Phone

You've probably seen this pop up as a payment option from time to time, although not too many people know much about it. Receiving checks by phone or fax sounds like a great way to take a payment in theory, but in practice it's not such a wonderful idea. The way it works is you take bank account information from customers over the phone or by fax, enter it into a check producing program on your computer and print out a check. The check is supposed to be valid at your bank however this is not always the case. Banks don't like these types of checks, and unless you have a good relationship with your bank, they may not accept them. Some of the banks that do accept them may place as much as a 30 day hold on them. It is probably a good idea to check with your bank prior to considering this as a viable payment option. It's usually more trouble than it is worth - if you really want to accept checks, only accept real signed checks sent by mail.

Merchant Accounts

In order to accept credit cards on your website, you'll either need to get a merchant account, or sign up for a third party merchant account. A third party mechant is when someone else uses their merchant account to process transactions for you and you pay them for the service. In general third party accounts are usually cheaper and faster to set up, but have a higher rate per transaction. So, if you're just starting out, or do a low volume of sales (under $1,000/month), you're probably better off starting with a third party account, then getting your own account when business picks up. Also, if you'd like to set up a merchant account, keep in mind, you will also need a shopping cart system (next chapter) and access to a secure server.

The chart below lists some of the more distinguishing charactistics between a regular merchant account, and third party merchant accounts:

Your Own Account						
Setup Fees	Approval Time	Transaction Rate	Approval Rate	Deposit	Monthly Cost	Transaction Fee
$50 - $1,000	1 – 30 days	1.8% - 2.5%	90% +	$1K - $10K	$0 - 100	$0 - $0.30
Third Party Account						
Setup Fees	Approval Time	Transaction Rate	Approval Rate	Deposit	Monthly Cost	Transaction Fee
$0 - $100	1 – 15 days	2.5% - 14%	99% +	$0	$0 - $25	$0 - $10

As you can see, the initial costs of opening your own merchant account are higher than using a third party account, but if you do enough sales it is more than made up from the savings in the transaction fees and rate. Some third party accounts rip you off on the transaction fees with them pushing 14% per transaction. The big benefit to third party accounts is that almost anyone can sign up for one and they're quick to set up.

There are four ways to get a merchant account:

1. Go through your local bank

2. Go through a broker

3. Hire a fulfillment house and use their credit card accounts

4. Use a third party merchant account provider

Going Through Your Bank

The most direct route to gain a merchant account is through your local bank. Some banks will automatically send you details of their own particular service when you open a business account, or with others you may need to request it. Some banks require a security deposit before they will issue you an account, which can be anywhere from $500 to $10,000 or more. If they want a large security deposit don't worry, there lots of other places to get an account. Some banks also don't accept all four major credit cards, so check with yours to see if they do. The four major card types you want to accept are:

- Visa
- MasterCard
- American Express
- Discover

One of the problems with local banks is that they are set up to serve retail stores and not mail order or internet based businesses. So some charge a very high transaction rate or require a very large security deposit to compensate. Always check to make sure that your bank is set up for the net. The transaction rate is the percentage you pay on each transaction for the privilege of using their credit card services. In other words, if you have a transaction rate of 2.0 %, and you put through a $100 sale, you will only receive $98 of that sale because the other $2 goes to the bank.

The problem with many banks is that, as large powerful institutions many don't want to accept small businesses and startups. For example, twelve months or more of audited accounts may be required and business plans or evidence of considerable investment capital may also be required. Add to this the fact that many banks are still developing their e-commerce services, so going through your bank may or may not be a good option for your business. It depends on your bank and your credit.

Going Through a Broker or Intermediary

Going through a broker is my personal choice. It is usually much easier to get approved and most don't require security deposits. A broker will basically do the work for you and negotiate with various banks on your behalf for the best deal you can get.

Intermediate companies do exactly what it sounds - they form a defense between you and the bank. While this may at first sound like a disadvantage because there's another body to get authorized by, the matter is really quite the reverse. Intermediary companies understand the banks and what they look for in a new client. They can "pitch" your application right and many boast enviable acceptance rates.

Fulfillment Houses

A fulfillment house is a company that is designed to do all your "dirty work". They will take your orders for you, process the payments and ship your packages. They are there to make your business mostly hands free: all you need to do is periodically send them products to ship, pay them and of course market your product(s). These companies will use their own merchant accounts to process your payments for you. They usually charge you between 5% - 10% for processing the sale, and between $1 - $10 for packaging and handling depending on your needs.

If you are only processing a couple thousands dollars' worth of orders every month, this could be a good way for you to start. But if you are doing more business than that, it is more cost effective to get your own merchant account. Also, please note that most fulfillment houses will only allow you to charge orders to their credit card account when the orders come in through the 800 number (almost all will not let you use their credit card account for direct sales over the internet) which can lose you a lot of sales. Alternatively, you can process your own transactions and just have the fulfillment company package and ship your orders for you.

Third Party Merchant Accounts

Another method of accepting credit cards on your website is to use a third party service. In this case, your business is not granted its own merchant account, but rather you are utilizing the merchant account of another company. If this is the route you decide to go, you can be fully setup usually in a day or two. The obvious downside to using a third party account is that they charge a processing fee of 5-15%, instead of the customary 2-3% of a regular merchant account. Another downside is that your customer's credit card bill will show up the name of the third party processor you have used rather than that of your company.

Another item to take into consideration is that most merchant accounts deposit the money paid by your customers within 24-48 hours, while third party processors sometimes take between 14-28 days or more, depending upon the company. Some even pay you mid-month for the previous month's earnings - meaning you may have to wait up to 45 days for the settlement of funds. Most third party processors will also hold back a reserve fee to cover any charge-backs you may incur.

Setting up an account with a third party processor is tremendously easy - it's a case of filling in a simple form with your name, address, phone number and any other pertinent information and you're well on your way. Sometimes there's an activation, or an application fee and sometimes there's not. I'd regard using third party processors as a last resort, only if you've been unsuccessful at obtaining your own merchant account.

The following websites will process credit card orders for you among others:

www.ccnow.com
www.Clickbank.com
www.iBill.com

I have a third party account primarily for backup, in case there is some kind of problem with my merchant account. I've heard of cases where merchant accounts have been suspended because the account holder was processing too many transactions, or where long holds have been placed on the funds for the same reason. Merchant accounts, like anything else on the internet, can go down sometimes because of a connection problem, or simply because they are updating their site. Some people even have more than one merchant account for that same reason, although this isn't really necessary. I personally have never had a major problem and hope I never do, but it's nice to be prepared just in case.

PayPal

PayPal is another payment option, but should not be the only option. If you're only selling one or two low ticket items, or selling only on eBay, I suppose you could get by accepting PayPal as the only form of payment. But if you're serious about making money online, you need your own merchant account (or at the very least a third party account) to accept credit cards, along with PayPal as another option.

PayPal was started in 1998 as a way for people to pay easily over the internet. At present, there are well over 80 million PayPal users and it is accepted in 55 countries and still growing. PayPal doesn't charge a setup fee, there's no monthly fees, no monthly minimums and you can literally be set up and accepting payments in a matter of minutes. PayPal also offers free fraud protection, and there are no chargeback fees in the event you should ever incur a chargeback. The transaction rate charged by PayPal is slightly higher than most merchant accounts, and lower than a few. PayPal currently charges $0.30 for each transaction, plus 2.9% of the selling price. The percentage can drop as low as 1.9%, which depends upon your previous months volume of sales. It's nothing like the up to 15% charged by some third party processors.

Some people just prefer to pay by PayPal for their own reasons. Quite often when I'm on a site that I've don't know anything about, I often use PayPal because I know it is secure, it offers fraud protection, I don't need to give out my credit card information to a third party; it also allows me to pay directly from my bank account which I like.

By setting up a PayPal business account, PayPal allows you to accept credit cards, and people don't even need a PayPal account to pay you. There are tools that are designed to help you sell, like being able to create individual "buy" buttons for products. PayPal can also be hooked up with most shopping cart systems as a method of payment as well.

When someone pays you through PayPal, you get the money immediately in your PayPal account (unless they pay by eCheck where you need to wait for funds to clear) and you can transfer it to your bank account where it will show up within 48 hours.

By accepting PayPal on your website, you increase the number of orders you receive and have use of some handy tools. If you're just venturing out onto the internet, PayPal is a great way to start accepting payments immediately and get your business off the ground.

Minimizing Risk

Getting a merchant account for use on the internet isn't as easy as getting one if you have a retail store. When you're on the net, the credit card number is just typed in, there's no card to swipe or no signature to verify, so there's a greater risk of fraud. Some merchant account providers will also verify the credit card holders billing address along with the credit card information for added security and only allow you to ship to the card holders billing address as an additional security measure.

Most of the applicants that do get refused merchant accounts, or are required to pay a large security deposit, are refused on the grounds that they are high risk. Minimize the risk. Whenever possible, find ways to make your business appear a safe bet, and you will greatly increase your chances. If you're selling a $1,000 electronic information product you're higher risk than someone selling a $20 book.

The guarantees you offer on your products also influence the risk imposed on your merchant provider. The stronger and longer your guarantee, the lower your risk. You may even be asked about your finances including your monthly overhead, your anticipated or current sales or any number of other questions.

Getting a merchant account is much like getting car insurance. The cheaper, safer and more boring you and your car are, the cheaper your insurance will be. Merchant accounts are much the same, the lower the risk, the more likely you are to be approved and at a lower rate.

16

Selecting a Shopping Cart System

If you're planning to do any selling directly from your website, you need some kind of system to take and process orders for you. Choosing the right shopping cart system can have a huge impact on the success of your online business. Even if you have an amazing website with truckloads of traffic, you'll lose tons of customers if it isn't easy for them to buy from you. That's why it's so important to make the right choice early on.

In its most basic form, a shopping cart on the internet is a piece of software that allows your website visitors to shop on your website, much the same way they would shop in a real store. Here's how it works:

When the visitor sees something they would like to buy, they simply click on the "add to cart" or "buy now" button, and the item is added to their cart at which point they can checkout or continue shopping. At any time along the way, if they wanted, they could take an item out of their cart by clicking on the "view cart" link, then selecting the item they want removed and clicking on the "remove" button.

When they're all done shopping, they click on the "checkout" button or link (sometimes you need to click on the "view cart" link to get to the "checkout" link), enter their name, address, phone number and shipping info, along with their credit card and expiration date. Once they hit the final "submit" or "checkout" button, everything fits into place to send the money to your bank account.

Many people don't realize that the credit card processing is not done by the shopping cart. The shopping cart really only acts as the front-end and passes the credit card information (via a secure connection) to a merchant account provider who processes the transaction in real time. A few seconds later the merchant account provider sends back a confirmation or denial to the shopping cart software.

Choosing a Shopping Cart

The good news is that there are literally hundreds of shopping cart systems available. The bad news is also that there are hundreds of shopping cart systems available. Sometimes it's difficult to make a decision when all companies claim to be the best and there's no real way to tell who is unless you get a chance to try them out first. That's why a free or discounted trial offer is important, so you can try before you buy. This chapter is designed to give you some of the key tools you need in order to make a properly informed decision.

Free Shopping Carts?

I don't think so. Nothing is really ever free, and anything that is ever advertised as being free, will never be as good as something that you pay for. When it's the size of your wallet on the line, don't get free anything. Free shopping carts have all kinds of limits on them and if you go over the limit, you'll find out it's not free anymore. Besides, they're usually cluttered with advertisements and rarely have the features you need. If you're selling a $10 ebook part time, you'll probably get by with free software, but if you're serious about making money online, free is not the way to go.

There are essentially three ways to get a shopping cart system. You can get it custom designed for your website, buy a software license and install the software directly onto your internet server, or my favorite, use a remotely-hosted shopping cart account.

Custom Carts

Some webmasters may try to sell you a custom shopping cart system that could run anywhere from a few hundred to tens of thousands of dollars. The more custom or complicated the cart, the more money programming it will take, and they more money they will make from you. Even if you have a shopping cart system that's currently in the works, you might want to consider scrapping it. There are very few businesses that need a custom shopping cart and the time and money it takes to develop one is hardly ever worth it. One of the main problems with custom carts it that you will need to pay someone to make any changes for you, which can include adding/removing products, changing prices or shipping information and so on. I don't recommend this way, unless you have the time, the money and like more frustrations and stress than necessary. Trust me – it's very hands on experience.

Buying a Shopping Cart Software License

This in fact, can be a very viable solution, and quite often the software can also be custom programmed a little to integrate better with your sales and marketing system for a relatively small fee. This option is much better than getting a custom cart programmed; however, it still has its drawbacks: The first being the initial purchase price which can run from a few hundred dollars to thousands or more and the fact that it needs to be installed, configured and maintained on your server by a technically oriented individual. The software usually allows for configuration and maintenance through a control panel that is accessed directly through your web server. For the main part, you should be able to make changes from any computer with a web connection if you have the know how.

Remotely Hosted Carts

This is, by far the way I recommend you go. I can't really ever see a reason not to go this way, unless you have a ridiculously complicated online business that does hundreds of millions in sales annually. If that's you, then you might have a whole IT department to refer to and wouldn't be reading this book. For the rest of us, a remotely hosted account is the way to go.

Remotely hosted accounts are hosted by another company on their web server. Besides not having to worry about the technical aspect of installing and configuring the software, you can also save on bandwidth charges especially if a lot of your products are downloadable. Most remotely hosted accounts charge a monthly fee, some make you pay annually upfront and some charge setup fee. Many of the really good remotely hosted carts also offer many other features including, autoresponders, complete affiliate programs, ad tracking and much more. The costs to get a custom cart programmed to compete with some of the best remotely hosted systems would probably set you back $25,000 - $100,000. Most remotely hosted accounts have an online control panel, so you can access everything from any computer in the world with an internet connection.

PayPal

I know you're probably thinking, what does PayPal have to do with shopping carts? Well, PayPal is one of the best free ecommerce solutions around, which allows you to integrate some basic shopping cart features with their payment gateway and merchant account. Unlike some of the other integrated third party shopping cart and payment processors, PayPal doesn't charge you an arm and a leg to use their services. In fact they charge even less than some merchant accounts I've been quoted prices for.

You used to need to be a PayPal member to pay with PayPal, but they now have a new system where you can pay by credit card without even signing up for an account. Another nice thing I like about PayPal is that I can attach it to my bank account, so I can pay for something directly from my bank account, or transfer all or part of my PayPal account balance to my bank account whenever I wish. They also have a debit card that you can apply for, which you can use anywhere that accepts MasterCard, including ATM's. Just a quick note: You need to be a Premier, or Business account holder to receive funds… it's no big deal as it's free to sign up for.

PayPal makes it easy to set up subscriptions and recurring payments. When you set up your subscription, you can specify up to two trial periods. For example, the subscriber can be billed $0 for the first month, and $20 for every month after the trial period has ended. You can set your billing cycle to be days, weeks, months, or even years. You can also set up payment in installments; for example you can break a $100 item down into five installments of $20. PayPal can also generate unique username and password combinations if you want to give buyers access to "members-only" content, stored in a special folder of your website.

As mentioned before, PayPal also offers free fraud protection and there are no chargeback fees in the event you should ever incur a chargeback. They also offer web developers a wide variety of easy to use tools to assist with rapid implementation, so if you're unsure or only sell a few products, it's a great way to get started. Check out www.PayPal.com for more info.

What to Look For in a Shopping Cart

A really good shopping cart should not just be a shopping cart, it should be a cash generating system. If you're serious about making money online, it is important that you choose a good shopping cart system. And a good shopping cart system should include many of the features we'll discuss in the subsequent pages, which are essential to doing business online.

Good shopping systems will dramatically increase sales because they manage the entire shopping process including upselling the customer, making special offers, handling special sales and discounts, and completely managing your extremely valuable database of prospects and customers.

The list of what to look for in a shopping cart is quite extensive so bare with me here. It is quite unlikely that you'll find absolutely all the features I discuss in any one piece of software, so choose the ones that best suits your needs. Some features are important to some businesses and some aren't, so look for what you specifically need, not what might be nice to have, but will never be useful. Here's the list, in alphabetical order:

Ad Tracking

This is an extremely important feature and I wouldn't be privy to consider any shopping cart system without it. Ad tracking allows you to tell where each customer comes from and what action they take on your website. You may have an ad that is getting a tremendous amount of click-throughs, but it may only be generating a very small amount of sales. The better systems can follow and report to you each page the visitors visit, how long they stayed and which website or link they came from. It is imperative that you be able to track ads, otherwise it extremely difficult to test ads, and elements of your sales and order pages. Do not get a cart without this capability and if you already have one where it isn't included, make sure you get some kind of outside tracking software – you needed it yesterday!

Affiliate / Associate Programs

Does your shopping cart software have affiliate software built in? If not, you'll need a third party affiliate software that works coherently with your shopping cart. A shopping cart affiliate module can handle the signup process, provide statistics, streamline communications and keep track of payments to be made to affiliates. The convenience of having it built right in with your shopping cart is huge. It automatically and flawlessly keeps track of absolutely everything for you including tracking where the sales come from, and keeping track of and tallying up all your affiliate partners' commissions at the end of the month.

Autoresponders

If you keep in touch with your clients through regular email offers (as you should), you may want to consider shopping cart software that has integrated autoresponder capabilities. A simple autoresponder is a software program that sends out an automatic response to an email sent to a specific email address and a smart autoresponder can send out a sequential series of personalized messages at the time intervals you specify. There's more on this in Chapter 20. Only the most advanced carts will have this feature, as you typically need to contract out to another company if you want to use a sequential (or smart) autoresponder. Even some of the cart systems that come with autoresponders are quite basic and can only send one unpersonalized email per purchase whereas the more advanced autoresponders can personalize emails with any of the information that the customer filled out when ordering.

Backups

Does the shopping cart (if third party) backup its files? Does it have more than one connection to the internet in case one goes down? It should, or it could severely damage your business if there is a problem. A good shopping cart application should also have flexible exporting functions so you can make a backup of your own files. This can prove to be very valuable should you need to change cart systems at some point in the future, or if they haven't backed up their data appropriately.

Broadcast Capability

Many shopping carts require you to export your data to another system, where you have to massage the data in order to send emails back to the customer. Good shopping carts have integrated mailing capabilities that can allow customers to be sorted and broadcast to immediately. You should be able to email to all customers or only to ones that bought certain items. You should also be able to broadcast email to your affiliates right from the shopping cart system. Good shopping cart systems also integrate the database with an included mail merge program so that reaching your customers with personalized emails is simple and easy.

Compatibility with Your Payment Gateway

Unless you're starting an entirely new business you may already have a merchant account you can use to process credit card payments. Before you pay a dime for a shopping cart system, you need to make sure that it is compatible with your payment gateway. Does the shopping cart allow all the cards your merchant account accepts? Most carts are compatible with most gateways, but that doesn't mean yours will be. Also make sure your payment gateway is compatible with your merchant account. Always check to make sure they will work together before you commit to anything.

Control Panel

Does the shopping cart have a control panel which you can view/use in your web browser? Most do, but for some you need to submit a request to shopping cart hosting company if you want to make a change. If you have custom shopping cart software, you may need to contact your webmaster to make changes. If you have the ability to access your control panel via an internet connection, that means you can add/remove products, changes prices and any other information you like with any computer and an internet connection anywhere in the world. You want to be able to update and make changes yourself; if you need to wait for someone else to make the changes for you, it make take a day or two and you'll be light-years behind your competitors.

Conversion Ratio

This is something that goes hand in hand with ad tracking. Most shopping carts have the ability to track this and automatically calculate your conversion rate for you. They simply follow the click-throughs through to the completion of the sale by tracking the users IP address. Having this ability with your shopping cart will make your more money and save you time and frustration integrating other software to do the job.

Upsell / Cross-sell Modules

Some shopping cart systems will have the capability of suggesting related products that complement the customer's current selection. This is the "Do you want fries with that?" method of selling. If they're buying pants, why not suggest a belt? Cross-selling is a great way to fill shopping carts, but few programs offer this feature.

Upselling is something that is a common occurrence on the net, simply because it works even better than it does in the physical world. When you're booking an airline flight, on some sites right before you pay it'll say, "Upgrade to first class for only so much more!" When you're renting a car, it's only $5 more per day to upgrade to the next size. The reason they do this is that it works, it's simple and easy to do if you have the right software, and because it can make you a lot more money with very little effort.

Customer Support

Customer support for your shopping cart system is just as important as support for your web hosting. If there is some kind of problem and you can't process any sales, you can't make any money and that's a bit of a problem.

What kind of support do they offer, if any? Phone? Email? Live chat? As I mentioned before, live chat is better than email and phone is better than live chat, so don't just settle for email. Also is it 24/7/365? It should be.

If you're planning to purchase the software to install on your web server, tech support may be limited at best, unless you plan to pay for it. If you don't have the technical expertise to install and configure your shopping cart yourself, get quotes from the company or from a third party contractor.

Don't forget to test out the customer support by sending them an email prior to paying for anything and see how long it takes for them to respond noting the quality of the response.

Some shopping cart software companies also offer user forums or newsgroups as part of their service, where you can communicate with other users. This is an excellent bonus feature to have, as you can most often find a solution to any problem, no matter how technical it is. Sometimes the software company will even have its employees answer the more difficult questions.

Custom Order Pages

One of the biggest problems that internet marketers face is people going to the order page, changing their mind and exiting the page. According to a Forrester Research study the most abandoned webpage the internet is the order page. They estimate that 68% of people who go to the order page will not actually order. Something to keep in mind is that the order page information needs to be customized, depending on what is ordered. A good shopping cart lets you put customized text right on the order form page that recaps and reassures the customer why they should complete the sale. If you have the ability to add to the order page, but not fully customize it, you could restate your guarantee and add testimonials from people who have done business with you in the past, to reassure they buyer that they are making the right decision. This is an awesome feature to have and it will get more people to complete the sale, which means more money in your pocket.

Database Handling

What happens to all the data the customers fill in when they place an order? It should go into a database of some kind. The question is not where does it go, but can it be accessed and manipulated to your advantage? Good shopping carts allow you to reuse the information (usually in the form of an email broadcast) to contact past customers to send additional emails or offers. Customer data coming into a shopping cart system should never ever have to be retyped - what a waste of time and resources that would be. With a good system and only a few clicks of a mouse, you should be able to instantly email everyone who buys a particular product or products, with the ability to easily personalize the emails.

Discounts

Having the capability to use coupons and offer quantity discounts can tremendously boost your sales. Most shopping carts should allow you to offer and accept coupons. Here's how it works: The buyer simply enters a coupon code when checking out and the shopping cart automatically applies the discount to the purchase amount. Many of the decent quality shopping carts also allow for the calculation of discount rates based on the number of units a customer wishes to purchase.

Email List Management

If you have a newsletter or ezine, a better shopping cart system should be able to manage all the subscribers for you automatically. That means the cart can create a web-based form where people can subscribe to your list, provide unsubscribe instructions at the bottom of your emails, and allow broadcast email capability.

Multiple Website Capability

Some shopping cart systems will only work for one website. This is most always the case if you have custom-programmed software for your website. What happens then if you want to makes sales from another site of yours? If you purchase the software outright, sometimes you are required to buy a completely separate system license for each website on which you want to use the software. This can be enormously expensive, time consuming and make you want to pull your hair out. The solution: use a shopping cart system with multiple website capability. That way you can sell completely different products, on completely different websites with one system at one price. Be sure to check with the provider before you sign up with them.

Output to Your Accounting Software

This is a nice time saving feature that allows you to export your sales data directly from your shopping cart to your accounting software such as Quickbooks, Quicken and Peachtree. Not only will this save you time and money, but your bookkeeper and accountant will love you. While it's not necessary for integration of online sales, it certainly is a nice feature to have.

Receipt and Confirmation Emails

The ability to automatically send a receipt or confirmation email directly to the customer (via email) is another basic feature that your shopping cart should have. Not only does this reassure the customers by informing them that the purchase went through successfully, but it also serves as a receipt they can print out for their records.

Preferably, you should also be able to customize the look and feel of your receipt and dictate what information is contained on it. Although this is looks more professional, it is not necessary and should not be seen as a deciding factor in choosing one shopping cart system over another.

It can also helpful for you if the shopping cart allows you to print a receipt you can stick in the package with any products you ship. Another common feature is the ability to send an email order notification to a third party, such as a fulfillment or drop-ship company, so they can send out your orders for you without having to submit the information to them manually.

Recurring Billing

This is another important feature, especially if you plan to offer any kind of payment plan or a subscription service (such as a membership website that is billed monthly, or a paid weekly newsletter). Most systems with this feature allow you to automatically bill the buyer's credit card at whichever interval you want, such as every week, month or year.

Return to Shopping

Where you send your customers after they add an item to their shopping cart can make a big difference in the amount of money they spend with you. A good shopping cart will allow you to customize the "return to shopping" or "continue shopping button" so that you can send them to any webpage you like (like another sales or upsell/cross-sell page). This simple feature can dramatically influence whether the customer simply checks out, or continues shopping with you.

Sales Reports

When anyone orders a product off of a website, the shopping cart usually takes the buyers name, email, address and other information, then stores it in a database of some kind. The better carts don't only store the data, they also allow you to access it in the form of a sales report. The reason this is such an important feature is because it allows you to find out which products are selling the best and which aren't. That way you can try to improve the copy on the products that sell the poorest and leave things alone for the products that are doing well. It also lets you know what ad campaigns are working and which aren't so hot, as well as how much each affiliate is bringing in, among other things. Some of the best shopping carts even allow you to create custom sales reports with the exact information you want.

Some of the more common reports that are offered are:

Sales by product – This tells you how much of a particular product you sold, usually within a given time period.

Sales by date – This of course tells you what and how much you sold on a certain day, or during a certain period.

Sales by customer – This breaks down your sales by customer and tells you how much money each individual customer has spent and on what, during a specified time period.

Sales by ad campaign – This report tells you exactly how each one of your promotions performed in regards to sales made, which allows you to easily calculate your ROI.

Sales by affiliate – This report tells you how well each of your affiliates are doing, during a given time period.

Sales by payment type – This report breaks out the amount of money that come in from each of the different payments types you accept during a specified period.

If the shopping cart you are considering doesn't at least have these kinds of reports, I'd be very reluctant to use it. Otherwise it will be very hard to successfully grow your business without switching to something of a higher caliber or compiling information manually.

Shipping and Delivery

This is among the most basic of functions and is an absolute must. Many potential customers abandon the purchase simply because they weren't shown the shipping costs before they had to enter their credit card information. Make sure your cart has the ability to calculate and display shipping costs in advance. The simpler, clearer and shorter the process from cart to sale, the more money you'll ultimately make.

If you are only selling hard (or physical) goods that need shipping, choosing a shopping cart is a little easier as this is among the most standard of functions that all shopping carts should have. You should make sure that the shopping cart allows you to have several shipping options (with prices) available to your shoppers – some customers may want to get it fast, like next day.

If you are dealing in soft (or electronic) goods such as software or any other downloadable products, you'll want to make the product available online immediately after the customer has paid for it. Some shopping carts that are capable of delivering goods online redirect customers to a static download page after the transaction is processed. This isn't a good idea as the customer and his or her friends are able to return to the page to download again and again. A better equipped shopping cart will only provide customers with a temporary URL that will be unique to that customer and may only be available for a few hours after purchase before it is deleted. This is an absolute requirement if you plan to sell many downloadable goods.

Hard and Soft Goods (Physical and Electronic Goods)

As I just mentioned, hard goods are any physical products that are shipped to the customer whereas soft goods are products that are electronically delivered (downloaded), so no shipping is required. If you want to sell any type of downloadable product like an ebook, you want to make sure that your cart can differentiate between the two. There's two things to watch out for here: that the shopping cart can handle both types of products in the same transaction so your customer doesn't need to go through the ordering process twice; and that the shopping cart can automatically supply a download page that disappears automatically after a short time so that customer can't give the link to all their friends.

Taxes

Taxes are a part of life and a part of online business. Your shopping should be able to calculate different tax rates for different provinces, states and countries. It should also be able to distinguish between taxable and non-taxable goods in the same transaction. Most quality shopping carts allow you to select the taxes that are applicable to each individual item, as well as set state, provincial or country specific rates.

Tell a Friend

This is as simple as it sounds; it allows your visitors to tell their friends about your website. It traditionally means filling out a simple form on your website that will automatically send an email announcing your website to the addresses your visitor specifies. Some shopping cart systems have this capability, others don't – no sweat, there are tons of simple scripts that can do this automatically for you for free.

Upgrades

If you're purchasing the software outright, does that entitle you to receive upgraded future versions as part of the package, or are the upgrades only at an additional cost? If there's a problem or bug in the system, do you get the upgrade or patch at no cost?

What about if you need to increase the options or the database of the third party software you are using? Can you add more bells and whistles if you want? How much extra does it cost? It isn't uncommon for some companies to offer a basic shopping cart for next to nothing and then to charge an excessive amount for upgrades so you might want to check into it before you buy.

Hopefully this will help set you on the right track in regards to finding something that will work best for your needs. There are many options to evaluate, so just choose the shopping cart solution that is best for your business considering where it is and where you want it to be in the future.

My Recommendation

Quite often I'm asked what shopping cart systems are good, and which aren't so great, and what to avoid all together. You may have noticed I haven't recommended any particular shopping cart throughout this chapter; yet. There's a reason for that: the internet changes so much and a company that was around when I wrote this may not be by the time you read it. It's also irresponsible of me to recommend anyone I haven't personally used and continue to use. The company that I used when I started out on the net, amazingly enough, isn't around anymore.

However, that being said, there is now a system I can confidently recommend, which I have used for the last few years that has become something of a legend in the internet marketing shopping cart world. Out of everything I have looked at, used and considered, there is nothing that even comes close to competing with this system. It is one of the most powerful online marketing tools that I have seen since I started on the internet. It was designed and developed by 1ShoppingCart, although it has been branded under several different private label names. It consists of a sophisticated, feature rich ordering system as part of a complete integrated shopping cart suite, which also includes autoresponders, affiliate management and a host of statistical tracking and marketing tools.

The 1ShoppingCart system is a remotely hosted shopping cart system, which means there's no time and money wasted having it installed on your server. You'll never have any tech problems, or bugs to fix, and all upgrades are automatically included with your monthly hosting plan. One of the things I like about this system is that it is not run by a bunch of programmers who have no idea about online marketing and selling. The people at 1ShoppingCart are constantly looking for more ways to make their customers more money.

The best part of the system is that 1ShoppingCart takes several different modules you would usually need to purchase separately and seamlessly integrates them together into one very easy to use money making system. The shopping cart system is integrated with a full featured autoresponder, a complete affiliate management module and a bunch of other options including ad trackers, custom form generators, digital delivery, popup generators and more. Within only a few minutes of signing up, you can be up and running with no technical ability needed. They even have a video tutorial and an online manual to assist you in getting the most out of their system.

To try it out for free for 30 days simply go to www.1StartCart.com and click on the "free demo" link in the top right hand corner of the screen.

Why I Like This System

This is by far the most sophisticated and advanced shopping cart software on the planet and it comes to you at a very affordable price. If you do any business at all on the net, just the shopping cart software alone will pay for itself in less than a month. 1StartCart is multi website capable, which means you can sell marketing ebooks from one site and pottery clay from another site, and no one will ever know.

This system easily differentiates between soft and hard goods and can even create unique automatic download links for your downloadable products that expire after a predetermined amount of time. There's no need to worry about the download links getting passed around the internet and people ripping your stuff off. The best part is, downloadable products can be downloaded immediately, there's no waiting period. Even the download pages can be customized with your own look and feel.

Whether you want to offer coupons for percentage based or exact dollar discounts, or provide discounts based on the quantity of products purchased, no sweat, it takes care of all of that for you. It can even make the offer only available to the first 50 or 100 buyers.

One of the easiest ways to increase your sales is upsell your customers. That's "Basic Sales 101." While you can't be there 24/7 to upsell, your shopping cart can be there doing the selling for you.

Recurring billing is absolutely necessary if you want to offer any kind of subscription service, or even if you want to break a big ticket item down into easier to manage payments. With this system it is completely hands off, credit cards are automatically charged and the money is deposited directly into your bank account.

Sales reports come standard and can be organized by date range and grouped by clients, type of items sold, type and date, ad campaign, or by product sales by affiliates. This data can also be exported into standard formats including CSV, tab-delimited text, or HTML table formats.

1StartCart has many other areas you can customize that help you sell, including customizable order form sell-throughs, return to shopping buttons, sales confirmation and thank you pages just to name a few.

If the online manual, tutorials, tons of help files and videos can't answer your questions, live phone and/or email support is free and included in your membership cost. This is an awesome feature; hardly anywhere on the internet can you get a real person on the phone to help you with your problems.

Shipping and Taxes

I didn't even know there were so many different ways to calculate shipping until I started using this system. It allows you to calculate shipping in a number of ways including:

- **Flat rate** – single price charged for all sales.

- **Real time shipping** – calculated based on weight of products and the shipping address of customers, options of UPS, FedEx or USPS. At present this feature only works for shipping within the United States.

- **Order based** – shipping calculated based on the amount of the total order.

- **Quantity based** – shipping charges are based on the quantity of items ordered regardless of price or weight.

- **Weight based** – calculated based on the weight of each product, such as $1 per pound.

- **Product specific shipping** – shipping determined by a preset shipping charge on each individual product.

- **Free shipping** – you may set free shipping if the order total reaches a certain price level, such as free shipping on orders of $100 or more.

Calculating tax on the internet can be a bit of a challenge for some carts. With 1StartCart you can set up sales tax rates for any state or province you like which will be automatically determined by the customers shipping address. You can also decide whether to calculate the tax before or after adding shipping charges. Country specific taxes such as federal sales tax or GST can also be set based on the country of the shopper. When each product is entered into the database, it can be marked as to whether it is taxable or not.

Integrated Autoresponders

Integrated autoresponders are part of the package and there's no limit on how many you can have, or the number of timed messages you can send over as long as a two year period. The thing I find most useful is that it is fully integrated with your shopping cart. That means anytime someone orders a product, not only does that person get automatically added to your database, but you can send them a series of powerful sequential autoresponders, influencing them to buy again from you.

The autoresponders can even be specific to the product the customer purchased and used to sell them another product. When they purchase the next product, they are automatically removed from that autoresponder and started on the next. For example, upon purchase of a certain product the customer may receive five follow-up training autoresponder messages and then be transferred into another autoresponder influencing them to buy another product. Then, if and when they purchase the next product, they're removed from the first autoresponder cycle and started on another.

The autoresponders system works so well that I use it for all my autoresponder emails. As well with the broadcast email capability built in, I can send my whole list an email with a few clicks of the mouse. Email personalization (mail merging) is included and can be as general or as specific as you want, and you can easily add more custom mail merge fields than I know what to do with. Subscribes and unsubscribes are taken care of automatically and with a few clicks you can create a custom opt-in email list signup form. You can even check the potential of your email getting picked up by anti-spam software such as Spam Assassin with the click of a button. Lists can also be imported and exported with ease in a variety of the most popular formats including CSV, text tab-delimited and Excel spreadsheet (export only).

Affiliate / Associate Management

This is what sets this cart apart from all the rest. The integrated, two-tier affiliate module allows you to take on new affiliates, manage them, email them and give them access to your promotional tools including banner ads, text ads and a whole slew of other promo stuff. The signup, login, and affiliate backend can be customized to fit your site's current look and feel to provide your affiliates with a consistent interface.

You can also specify product specific, first and second tier affiliate commissions and exclude certain products from affiliate commissions if you like. Commissions can be paid per sale, per click, per lead, and/or per impression.

A minimum payout and monthly payment date can be set, so the program can easily calculate which affiliates need to be paid in a given month, along with the amount. With the integration of your affiliate module with your shopping cart, you can instantly track your affiliate sales.

Other Features

There are a whole bunch of other features integrated into 1StartCart that are there to make it as easy as possible for you to make as much money on the internet as humanly possible. It's these features that are not found in the traditional shopping cart solutions that makes this system so popular.

A solid ad tracking system lets you effortlessly track and test any online advertising campaigns using media such as text links and banners. It not only tracks click-throughs, but also sales amounts, and it can calculate various kinds of conversion rates. Whenever an ad is clicked on, the link code goes to 1StartCart where it is counted and a cookie placed on the users computer, then the browser redirects the user to the corresponding sales page on your website. Ad rotation is another feature that has proven itself again and again to be quite useful.

There is also a popup wizard, so in only a few seconds you can generate instant popup HTML coding for your website. Use this simple yet effective method to increase your opt-in mailing list signups. The input form code is automatically generated for you.

Pretty much all of the features on 1StartCart are available on the internet from other places. But here's the thing: Nowhere, are they fully integrated together, all in one place to create such a powerful internet marketing tool. Simply by using this amazing system for your complete sales process, you could quite possibly increase your sales by 100% - 500% or more.

Don't just take my word for it - try it before you buy it; I absolutely urge you to go to www.1StartCart.com and take a thirty day absolutely free, no strings attached, test drive and find out why the top internet marketers are the top internet marketers.

Section 3

Email Marketing Secrets

Effective Email Marketing – The Basics

Email marketing is the fastest and the easiest way to make money on the internet, period. Though email marketing on its own is often not enough to get the sale. If you try to sell to people directly through email, you'll find that you'll probably be most unsuccessful. The whole purpose of marketing by email is to get people to your website, where you can provide them with more information on your product or service and get them to purchase it.

Once its set up all you need to do is get people to your webpage, have them place an order and you're a money machine! Ok, maybe I'm getting a little excited and a bit ahead of myself; there's a bit more to it than that, which is exactly what we'll discuss in this chapter.

This is what the whole premise of email marketing pivots on: Create an email list which you constantly work on expanding. Use it to bring customers back to your website, where you convince them that your product or service and your value are outstanding. Then sell it to them. Never mention price or cost in the email, just get them to the website for more information where you can sell them.

According to DoubleClick, over 78% of online shoppers have made purchases because of a marketing email message and one third of email users have made a purchase directly by clicking on a link from an email they received. For us email marketers, that's good news.

In the past direct mail advertising was only done through the postal service, which can be very costly at up to a $1 or more for each piece. However, through the use of the internet you can send direct email marketing for almost no money at all. Take a second to understand exactly what this means.

If a direct mail piece costs $1 to send out (printing and design costs, postage and handling), it costs $10,000 to send it out to 10,000 people, and that's not including any costs occurred in getting and/or compiling the mailing list. Now, if you had an email list of 10,000 people, how much would it cost to send an email to everybody? If you subscribe to a broadcast email marketing service at a cost of $50 per month, with some simple math, $50 / 10,000 people is $0.005, or *only half a red cent per person*. If you sent out emails 5 times a month it would only cost 1/10th of a cent per person per mailing. What would it cost to send out emails to 100,000 or even 1,000,000 people? That's right, only $50 per month.

This is why email advertising can be so cost effective, but do not get email advertising confused with spam. With email advertising you need to be very careful and only use an "opt-in" email list, which users can easily unsubscribe from. How do you build a list? Keep reading, it's coming up in a later chapter.

As we can see, sending a piece of direct mail to customers can cost as much as a dollar per piece, with a response rate of typically less than 1%. Email campaigns, by contrast, cost much less than a penny… Clearly, there's no better choice in marketing for the business owner, no matter what the size of your company.

Text or HTML?

A dilemma many email marketers struggle with at one time or another is whether they should send a plain text email, or an HTML formatted email to their list. A text email is like any email that you may receive from a friend or colleague, it's all text. That means no pictures, no special formatting (bold, italics and so on), no nothing, just plain text much like this sentence. An HTML email is like receiving a webpage with graphics and colors in your email inbox.

It's been a long-time debate on whether text email or HTML email work better when sending out emails, whether it's a newsletter, or a simple announcement. You will even find many contradicting studies that have been published. One might say that HTML emails have a response rate of more than two times that of a plain text email, or that text emails offer a three times greater response than HTML emails. Then there are studies that say the response rate between text and HTML emails is equal.

Quite frankly, there are so many studies available you could probably find one to say whatever you want. From my experiences, I tend to believe that whether you send a plain text email, or an HTML formatted email, results are inconsequentially similar. Of course you'll do your own testing with your email list to see what works best for you, right? Here are a few things to consider when choosing your email format.

Plain Text

Plain text emails do have their benefits. Perhaps the most important is the fact that is more personal than a HTML formatted email. Receiving a text email is more like receiving a personal letter in the mail. Getting an HTML formatted email is like receiving a brochure in the mail, that has a sticker or label with your name on it. The reason text emails are more personal, is that they appear (with proper personalizing) as if you wrote it yourself especially for the intended recipient.

If you choose to go with the text version for your email messages, put a hard return (press the enter key on your keyboard) after every 65 characters or so to protect against distorted text, or the text being truncated prematurely by the recipients email program.

Some email readers (though there aren't many left, so it isn't really worth worrying about) can't display anything other than plain text or standard ASCII characters. ASCII characters are just the regular letters and symbols that are found on your computer keyword. Text emails are also more likely to get through spam filters than HTML emails.

HTML Formatting

The main benefit of HTML formatted email is that it looks more professional and is more likely to catch the reader's attention. One other thing to consider when exploring both options is that HTML emails are not only aesthetically pleasing and often easier to read, but you also have the ability to track your results with a tracking code embedded in the HTML links. That's something that's not available with text only emails, unless you display the crazy tracking code (www.YourDomain.com?Ad_12345&Vers_67890) in the email.

A downside is that HTML email may look wonderful on your computer, but the recipient's computer can change the layout, font type and size of the message the recipient sees. This means your carefully constructed HTML email masterpiece, may look nothing like it was intended to, making it hard to read. It may even show up as HTML coding if their email software doesn't support HTML, or if they have it turned off.

According to ClickZ 40% of emails received are broken. A broken email is an email that isn't received in the same format in which it is sent. For instance many email filters block graphics as an effort to combat spam; when an email is formatted using graphics and the graphics don't get through, the text and alignment can get out of whack.

HTML emails also take more time and energy to produce, and then you need to check each one of the links out to be sure it is functioning perfectly. If someone you send an email to ever clicks on a link that doesn't work, the next time they receive an email from you, they probably won't bother to read it because it might be a waste of their time.

If you have the time and resources, consider giving your customers the choice of receiving either HTML or text messages. By asking customers what kind of email they prefer to receive, you not only give customers the confidence that you care about them, but you will also increase the chance that your messages will be read and acted upon. When given the choice two-thirds of subscribers usually opt for the more attractive looking HTML version over plain text, but give them the choice if it's available.

In the battle between text and HTML email, a common ground that I often use is to format HTML email to look like text. That way it comes across as more personal and it still allows you to easily track click though results. It's also possible to set the font to fit their default chosen font, so that is comes across in the same font as their Aunt Martha's emails.

Some of the more sophisticated broadcast email senders provide another option, Multipurpose Internet Mail Extension, or MIME. MIME, in a nutshell, allows you to send both a text and HTML email at the same time. Then the email client that the recipient is using, chooses which format to display based on its configuration settings. However, if the email client is only text only, the email with just look like garbled HTML coding.

Regardless of whether you opt for text, HTML or MIME, let the words and/or graphics do the talking. Don't attempt to convey urgency or emphasis with excess capital letters, asterisks and exclamation points. By shouting in your email "***BUY ONE GET ONE FREE!!!***" you risk not only getting trapped by spam filters, but you also risk losing the respect of your customers. Use these tactics sparingly - if at all.

Personalization

Email marketing is about building a relationship over time. What better way to speed up the process than taking the same email and personalizing it? Study after study has shown the greater the number of personalization elements in an email, the higher the response rates. At a minimum, personalization can mean addressing a recipient by their first name. True personalization however, is when emails are tailored to the specific profile, preferences and interests of each recipient.

How often do you open or read postal mail that comes to you addressed "Current Resident"? If you're like me, it probably goes straight to the recycling bin. The power of personalization is huge. A study by GotMarketing.com reports that "personalizing an email marketing campaign can improve response rates by 45 percent." As far as I know there's no other single email variable that you can change that will consistently increase your response rate by almost 50%.

Personalizing emails gives the illusion to the receiver that you took the time to manually write the email just for the receiver, even though you didn't. Most people know that, but still seem to appreciate the effort.

This can be illustrated by the approach of a travel agency who regularly communicates by email with their customers who have opted in to receive email. The travel agency can create an email template that includes mail merge variables such as their name, their last travel destination, places they'd like to visit, how long they have been a customer and so on.

Hi [name],

We sincerely hope you enjoyed your vacation with us last [last travel month], at the [last resort name] in [last destination]. Since it's been [number of months] since you've traveled with us, we thought you might be in need another well deserved vacation. So, we'd like to offer you a special once in a lifetime experience in [place they would like to travel]. This five-star resort comes fully loaded with everything you could imagine to satisfy your every desire including:

[list resort amenities]

For more information, including the very exclusive one time price we have secured for you, please visit our website at www.TravelAgentsInc.com/[special ID], or call me at the number supplied below.

I look forward to hearing from you soon,

[travel agents info]

PS: Don't forget to visit our website right away; we're only able to secure this special price from our vendors until [time] [date].

After the mail merge this email would look like this:

Hi Charles,

We sincerely hope you enjoyed your vacation with us last May at the Paradise Island Resort and Spa in the Bahamas. Since it's been nine months since you've *traveled with us, we thought you might be in need of another well deserved vacation. So, we'd like to offer you a special once in a lifetime experience in Jamaica. This five-star resort comes fully loaded with everything you could imagine to satisfy your every desire including:*

- *9 International Restaurants*
- *12 Swimming Pools*
- *7 Dry Bars, 4 Swim Up Bars*
- *Full Indoor/Outdoor Spa*
- *Variety of Watersports*
- *And so on…*

For more information, including the very exclusive one time price we have secured for you, please visit our website at www.TravelAgentsInc.com/9745826, or call me at the number supplied below.

I look forward to hearing from you soon,

Gary Swane,

Travel Agents Inc.
123 Main St.
Maine, MN, 12345
USA
800-555-5555 x1234
gary@travelagentsinc.com

PS: Don't forget to visit our website right away, we're only able to secure this special price from our vendors until 12:01am January 17, 2007.

It may cost a little more to personalize the campaign (only for the software license or third party autoresponder access) but the response rate more than makes up the difference from taking the cheap, plain, generic route. If you don't already have (or use) a good autoresponder with mail merge capabilities, check out the one provided by www.1StartCart.com.

When is the Best Time to Send Email?

The day, time of day, and even the time of year can affect the overall response rate you receive from your email marketing campaign. This detail may not be as important as the target market you select, or the subject line you choose, but it still is a factor that should be considered. I always work to achieve the largest response rate possible and every little thing I can do to help tip the scales in my favor, I will.

Many a time on the net, things are time sensitive and the sooner you can get the email out, the more money you stand to make. This section is for those emails that aren't super time sensitive, such as a special deal on a new product you are offering. Sure, if you send out the email a day or two earlier you start making money sooner… but your overall total sales may not be as high. It's your job as a marketer to find the balance between the sales lost or made by waiting or not waiting. As a general rule, if an email is time sensitive I send it out right away and if not I'll wait for a higher response rate time.

It is important to note that not all target audiences respond the same to the suggestions I've given below. The days and times are to be used as a good starting point and may need to be refined and tested to suit your exact target market. The suggestions in this bit assume a general target audience of middle class people who work Monday thru Friday. It's good to have an idea of the general behavior of your audience before sending a message at an inappropriate time.

So, when's the best time for you to send your email? There are many studies that have been done in an attempt to determine what day and at what time is best to launch your email campaign and although no conclusive result has been drawn, they pretty much all agree on one thing: Monday morning is the worst possible time.

Time of Year

The time of year does indeed have an impact on the response rate. Your offer and time of year need to mesh together. For instance, don't offer a tropical vacation on the hottest day of the summer, instead offer it in the dead cold of winter.

Also avoid sending emails on holidays, or the day after a major holiday. Even sending an offer in the middle of the holiday season should be avoided if at all possible. You don't want to catch someone just after a vacation when they have 200 waiting messages and are looking for stuff they can delete quickly. Most people vacation during the summer months, especially July and August when the kids are out of school and the weather is nicer.

Time of Week

Since many people use their business or work email as their primary email address, and the majority of people work Monday to Friday, Saturday and Sunday are by default not a good day to send out an email solicitation, since your audience is generally out of the office then.

Mondays are no good for a number for reasons, the most obvious being is that it is the beginning of the week and most people are not yet in business mode. Most people tend to have a morning ritual of "cleaning" their relatively full inbox of any spam that arrived overnight, or over the weekend. You don't want them to see your message when they are in a deleting frenzy, trying to find anything they can "clean up" quickly. Also, on Mondays people usually have a number of things to do and are not quite interested in offers or solicitations.

On Fridays, most people are interested in wrapping things up and getting home for the weekend. If you start something new on a Friday, it may be forgotten over the weekend and then ignored in place of new things the following Monday. Needless to say, Fridays aren't a great time either to send email solicitations.

Wednesday for many is hump day and most people just want to make it through the day and past the mid week point, so they are not as receptive to offers.

It has been my experience that the best time to send emails is Tuesday, and if Tuesday doesn't work out, Thursday is a close second. The reason Thursday isn't quite as good is simple, it's the day before Friday and the end of the week for many. Some people even take Fridays (or ever second Friday) off, so Thursday becomes their Friday. If you must do Thursday, aim for the mid morning so it doesn't go unread till Friday and then passed over to Monday where it may be deleted.

Time of Day

How much does time of day really matter? You probably want your message to reach your audience at a time when they are going to be most receptive to it and have the greatest likelihood to respond to it.

In a perfect world you want your message to pop up while your audience is sitting at their computer. The ping people hear when they receive an email, elicits a response for them to check their inbox and see what has arrived. At this time they are much more receptive to a solicitation. They want to see who's trying to contact them and are more likely to read the email and then act on it.

The best times of the day are around 10:30am and 1:30 pm. That is when you are most likely to catch your audience at their computer. It also gives them ample time to sort through and respond to their inbox in the morning and after the lunch hour, so that it is organized and uncluttered by the time your email comes along.

I urge you not to place too much emphasis on this area. It's often very difficult to ensure the precise time your message goes out. And even if the message is launched at precisely 10 a.m. in one time zone, there are other time zones to consider.

Don't wait for the perfect time or you will never launch your email campaign. As you've probably experienced there are times during the week, month or year when you are extremely busy and not as receptive to offers or messages. Do your best to pick a time when your clients will be most likely to act, but don't obsess about the launch time.

Email Tracking

Did you know 26% of email marketers fly blind? That is, they don't use any sort of email tracking. If you don't track, you can't test, and if you don't test, how can you know what works and improve your performance and sales? One of the greatest things about email marketing, besides all the money it can make you, is the ability to test with very little effort and incur amazing results.

Without some sort of tracking, it's difficult to tell how many visitors are responding in some way to your mailings. When you send out an email at the very least you need to how many sales you made from it. You also should want to know how many people took some kind of action. How many people clicked on a link in the email? Which link did they click on? How many people went to the sales page? How many of those went to the order page? How many actually bought something? Do you see what I'm getting at here? If you don't know what kind of results you're getting, it's hard to improve and you're missing out on business you should have gotten.

For instance, if I sent out 1,000 emails to my targeted opt-in list, I might get 400 people to click though to my sales page, have 200 of those people go to the order page and 50 of those people order.

What if I wanted to see if I could get a better than 5% response rate? I could try testing different variables, but in order for the testing to be effective, I need to track my results. Suppose my email list had 10,000 people on it, and I wanted to test four different variables. I could take part of my list, let's say 4,000 people, and send the original email to 1,000 people, then change the subject and send it to another 1,000 people, change the headline and send that to another 1,000 people, and so on. If you are tracking the results, you'll know how many click-throughs each email generated. You could take the winner and test it with another 10% of your list, or you may choose to send out the email at this point. Another thing that you can test is the sales and order pages. You can send one part of your list to one sales page, then another part to a different sales page and so on.

Other Things to Know

Here are a few other things you might want to know about sending email: Don't include attachments with your emails. Not only does this bog down the email server, but many free email accounts do not accept attachments over a certain size and many virus scanners don't allow the email to get through for the fear that the attachment could be a virus. If you need to send something, include a link to your webpage where the recipient can download any files that they need. That way if they don't want it, they don't get it and it also eliminates any fear that the email may not be from you.

"You had me at hello." - *Dorothy in Jerry Maguire.* This is so simple that many marketers forget to say hello in their emails. First impressions mean a lot. Say "hello" and personalize it.

Always create a sense of urgency in your emails. It's not just enough to say "Hurry, this is a limited time offer." Tell why it's a limited time offer. "I only have 17 seats available." If you want to use an expiration date, be specific and firm: "This offer will expire at 12:01am on October 12th, no exceptions."

Stay in frequent contact with your subscribers. How frequent? Well that's up to you, but keep this is mind. There's a fine line between maintaining your visibility and overwhelming your customers with too many messages. Email too infrequently and they'll forget about you. Email too often and they won't have time to read the emails, or worse, they'll unsubscribe. Once every one-to-four weeks is best. Any more than that and they won't have time to read your emails and any less, contact is not frequent enough to build a binding relationship.

And lastly, if I didn't mention this, it's funny how many people might forget to include a link to their website. The whole purpose of sending email to your list is usually to get them to visit your website. Always include a crystal clear link to your site, no matter the purpose of the email. Instead of having a plain old link, you can make it a little more interesting, and have a line that says something like "check out my newest internet marketing articles at www.JustinMichie.com."

Spam – No Viagra Please!

Did you know that the average online consumer receives over 300 emails a week, 62% of which is spam? This means for every piece of valid mail, the internet has to transfer a 1.24 pieces piece of junk mail. This costs internet service providers (ISPs) a ton of extra money. Instead of having 100 mail servers, they need to have 224. So instead of investing in more servers and bandwidth, ISPs are investing in spam filtering technology. If they can block an email before it enters their system, that's less mail that they have to manage, serve and support. Needless to say, spam filters save ISPs a ton of money.

The problem is, spam filters are not perfect. Although many of them do a good job ensuring legitimate emails get through, they sometimes classify legitimate email as spam that doesn't get through. As a permission based opt-in email marketer, the relatively small percentage of emails that don't get through can have a huge impact to the total number of sales you do. If 10% of your emails don't get through (which is common) on $10,000 in sales, you'd lose $1,000.

The simple definition of spam, as it applies to email is: unsolicited bulk email. Unsolicited email (first contacts, inquiries etc.) on its own is normal, as is bulk email (newsletters, customer communications etc.) - it's only when you put the two together it is considered spam. Email marketing is quite often confused with spam, but believe me they are not the same thing.

Sending spam is illegal in most places, not to mention the fact that it is also very bad for the reputation of your business. If convicted, the consequences of sending illegal email can be quite severe, including fines and potential jail time. Be sure to check the laws where you live and make sure that you are well within the guidelines.

Spam Filters

For those of us who are prone to receiving a lot of junk mail, spam filters may be the best thing since sliced bread. But when you switch yourself over to the side of the email marketer, spam filters can pose a serious obstacle between you and your email subscribers.

Even though you may be sending a perfectly legitimate email to an opt-in email list, unless your email is properly written and formatted, it doesn't stand a chance. Many spam filters may not see the email as it was to be intended, and may automatically assign it to the spam folder, or even worse send it directly to the trash bin.

As a monogamous permission based email marketer, we need to slip past the spam filters, and to do that we should understand a little about how they work.

Types of Spam Filters

Password Filters

This type of filter is fairly airtight and spam proof. It only accepts emails that contain a preset password in the subject line. Unless you know the password, there's no way to get past this type of filter. Don't worry though, because they're very uncommon, and the people who use them generally won't use that email address when signing up for an opt-in email list.

Content/Rule Based Filters

Content or rule based filters block spam by analyzing the whole email including the subject, headers and content. Then, based on how it conforms to the pre-determined rules, the filter catches spam by finding tell-tale signs, like odd punctuation and keyword triggers.

Over the years, spammers have been aware that their messages were being terminated by these content filters and have resorted to ever more desperate tricks to try to fool the content filters. This would explain why you get so much mail for "Vi@gra," and "Mort.gages."

Some of the better spam filters can now see through much of this word obscuration which makes a lot of spam messages virtually illegible in their attempt to fool these filters.

It's quite simple to get past this type of filter, just make sure that your email doesn't look like or appear to be spam. The easiest way to do this is to test it against the filter's rules. If you use the 1StartCart shopping cart system, it has a built in feature in its broadcast mailer that will analyze your emails (against Spam Assassin) and let you know how likely it is that it may be considered spam.

Alternatively, if you don't use this system or another one with a similar ability, you can go to www.lyris.com/contentchecker to check your emails for spam content. Simply paste the email you want to check into the text box along with other relevant information and it will automatically email you a report within a few minutes.

Bayesian Based Filters

Reverend Thomas Bayes developed a formula which allowed him to determine the probability of an event occurring based on the probabilities of two or more independent evidentiary events. So, Bayesian filters "learn" from studying known legitimate and spam messages. Each message is split into single "word bytes" or "tokens," which are placed into a database along with how often they are found in each kind of message.

When analyzing a new message, the message is split into word bytes and each byte is given a value according to the following criteria:

- The frequency of the token in spam messages that the filter has been trained on.
- The frequency of the token in legitimate messages that the filter has been trained on.
- The number of spam messages the filter has been trained on.
- The number of non-spam (or legitimate) email messages the filter has been trained on.

From applying Bayes' formula to these results, a value is extracted that gives the probability of the message being spam or not. This value is often called the "spamicity" rating. Bayesian filters typically are capable of achieving very good accuracy rates (>97%) and require very little ongoing maintenance because of their complexity.

Since each person that uses these filters has his or her own set of spamability rules, there's no set formula to get past these filters. The best you can do is make sure your emails don't look like spam by checking in one the spam checkers mentioned on the previous page and analyzing them yourself.

Whitelist/Blacklist Filters

These are very basic types of filters which nowadays are rarely used on their own, but are still used as part of an integrated filtering system comprising some of the other methods discussed in this chapter.

A blacklist is a collection of email addresses, domain names, IP addresses and email servers that are known to send out a lot of spam. Blacklists are mostly compiled by volunteers who send in emails that they believe are spam, which are then examined to determine if the sender should be added to the blacklist. Spam filters automatically block emails from any email addresses, domain names and/or email servers that are found on a blacklist. It is a good idea to do an internet search to make sure that your broadcast email service provider (if using third party provider) has a good relationship with ISP's and doesn't show up on any blacklists. If you somehow end up on a blacklist is it almost impossible to get off, so try hard not to end up on one and if you somehow do, you'll need to make some changes to your domain, IP and ISP.

Blacklists are usually stored and administered on a web server system and are referenced in real time via the internet. Blacklists available on the internet (which can be referenced in real time) are referred to as Realtime Black Lists or RBLs.

A whitelist is the opposite of a blacklist. It is nothing more than a list of approved email addresses from which you will accept email. If the sender is not on your whitelist, the email may bounce back. While this may seem like a good idea, it doesn't allow legitimate non-approved senders to reach you via email. Some filters use a whitelist along with the other variables it considers. That way if an email address is on a whitelist, it will get through for sure, and if it's not on the list, then it needs to go through some other type of spam filter.

Many filters have the ability to check your email message information against a blacklist, along with the other filtration techniques they employ. While being quite effective, they do tend to suffer from "false positives" where good messages are incorrectly identified as spam.

The only way to avoid this is to make sure that your domain name, email address, IP address or ISP don't appear on any blacklists. Go to www.dmoz.org/Computers/Internet/Abuse/Spam/Blacklists/ or your favorite search engine to search the readily available blacklists to make sure you're not on one.

Challenge/Response Filters

Challenge/Response filters are characterized by their ability to automatically send a response to a previously unknown sender asking them to provide a return confirmation of your email address before your email will be delivered. This usually means the sender needs to click on a verification link, or enter a hidden graphical code into a web based form. Once the email is initially verified, all future email from the same address will automatically get through.

This is often used when all other methods fail to appropriately block spam and let in legitimate email. If you want to get past this kind of filter, you need to be able to access the bounced emails and manually follow the instructions to verify your email address.

Community Filters

These types of filters work on the principal of "communal knowledge." When a user receives a spam message, they simply mark it as spam in their filter. This information is sent to a central server where a copy of the message is stored. After enough people in the community have marked this message as spam, the filter will stop it from reaching all other people in the community.

This type of filtering can prove to be quite effective, although it stands to reason that it can never be 100% effective as a few people have to receive the spam for it to be "flagged" in the first place. This system can also suffer from false positives though it's fairly unlikely. AOL is by far the largest advocate of community based email filtering. Send the wrong email to a few AOL customers and none of your future emails will get through. AOL has very tough anti-spam policies, so be sure to take extra care when you're sending an email to an AOL based email account.

In theory, as long as you don't send spam, you shouldn't be blocked by a community filter. There's nothing you can really do to prevent from being chosen as a false positive, except making sure your emails don't look like spam.

Filter Placement

One final distinguishing factor to consider between spam filters is their placement. There are four main schemes for filter placement:

Email Client Based Filters – All the major email clients such as Microsoft Outlook have anti-spam capability in the form of "message rules" that can be used to reduce spam. Spam messages are usually simply moved to a "Junk Mail" folder where they can be reviewed and/or deleted. You can also usually set certain email address or domain names that will always get through and can also select emails that got labeled as spam and mark them as legitimate so that it doesn't happen again.

Stand Alone Filters - These are filters that act as a "proxy" between the mail server and your email client. These filters reside on your computer run in the background to filter spam on your email as you receive it. This type of filter blocks spam before it makes it to your mail client and also represents another layer of security between the internet and your e-mail client. They usually will not run any applications or scripts found in email messages that could be a virus. Stand-alone filters are by far the most popular because they offer the best spam removal rates without requiring you to switch email clients.

Server (ISP) Based Filters - These filter spam at the ISP's location before it is delivered to you. Since they are a "one size fits all" filter without access to most of your email activity, they are not very effective. Many ISPs have this service available. The downside is that you don't have any control over which messages get blocked and usually aren't able to view the blocked messages. False positives may be lost to you forever. Since these types of filters are often employed, it's very important to make sure that your emails don't have any characteristics identifying them as spam.

Integrated Filter/Clients - Integrated filter/clients can eliminate spam by requiring every new sender to verify their address. The email is usually sent through a third party site for verification. You can usually tweak the filters so that it only requires messages that slightly appear be spam to verify their email addresses. This way, most regular email will get through without having to hassle the senders. In case some people don't bother to verify their email addresses, you can usually check the list of messages that went unverified. When sending out your broadcasts you need to make sure that you are able to check and manually verify the bounced emails.

Most filters use a point or flag system to decide which emails to block. Instead of using single criteria to block spam, they set rules for the formatting and content of an email. Each time an email breaks a rule, it adds a point. Depending on the sensitivity of the filter, if a certain number of points are reached - the email gets blocked. So, the more you can do to avoid getting points attached your email, the better.

Words and phrases that are commonly found in spam receive a higher point value and thus the higher the combined point value of the email, the higher the risk that the email is spam. In order to slip past most spam filters you need to know what the keywords and phrases to avoid in the subject and body of your emails.

Some of the more common keywords and phrases associated with spam are listed below. This is by no means an exhaustive list:

Free	Cialis	Profit
Seminar	Won	Click here
Remove	Diet	Winner
Offer	Insurance	Information
Limited	Credit	Opportunity
Weight	Loan	Health
Cheap	Save	Buy
$	Deal	Guarantee
Price	Enlarge	Subscribe
Loan	Act now	Blogger
Viagra	Debt	Gift
Sex	Win	Discount
Money	Nigeria	You've been selected

Most spam laws dictate that bulk email must have your full contact information including your physical address (no PO boxes) and include simple unsubscribe functions. Contact information also allows a potential customer to contact you should they have a question. Email must be sent from your actual email account and all "from" and "reply to" email addresses must be accurate email accounts that are checked regularly. Here's a couple of sample emails to consider:

Subject: FREE TELESEMINAR TOMORROW!!!

Hey There,

I'm hosting a free teleseminar tomorrow and want you to be on the call. I'll be interviewing the king of internet marketing, Mr. Larry Smith.

Mr. Smith has been on the internet since 1993 and does 10's of millions of dollars a year in online business. He makes more money then the next 5 top online marketers combined. Get on the call and find out why!

Go to http://www.JustinMichie.com/teleseminar to get the details!!!

Also, just a reminder, you can still get my new 8 CD Street Smart Internet Marketing audio course at www.JustinMichie.com. Get it for half price if you're one of the first 23 people to order it. That's only $148.50. Get yours today!

PS: Act Now!!! - You don't want to miss out on the opportunity of a lifetime!

This email is not spam, and is in compliance with the Can-Spam act!
--- Please click here to be removed or unsubscribe from the list ---

Detailed Results	
Our SpamAssassin scored this message at a **1.8**. Most SpamAssassin servers confidently mark spam at **5**.	
Explanation	**Score**
Subject starts with "Free"	0
Subject is all capitals	0.4
BODY: Claims to not be spam	0.7
BODY: Millions of something.	0.3
Subject has lots of exclamation marks	0.4

-- If you stick the word Viagra in the subject the score jumps to 5.1 --

Now, take a look at this next example. Same information, different wording:

Subject: Important Teleseminar Tomorrow!

Hey There,

I'm hosting a free teleseminar tomorrow and want you to be on the call. I'll be interviewing the king of internet marketing, Mr. Larry Smith.

Mr. Smith has been on the internet since 1993 and makes more online sales than the next top 5 online marketers combined. Get on the call and find out why!

Go to http://www.JustinMichie.com/teleseminar to get the details!!!

Also, just a reminder, you can still get my new 8 CD Street Smart Internet Marketing audio course at www.JustinMichie.com. Get it for half price if you're one of the first 23 people to order it. That's only $148.50. Get yours today!

PS: Act Now!!! - You don't want to miss out on the opportunity of a lifetime!

If you believe you received this email in error, please click here to unsubscribe

Detailed Results
Our SpamAssassin scored this message at a **0**. Most SpamAssassin servers confidently mark spam at **5**.
Summary
This email does not appear to be spam.

See how just a few words can make a difference. Even though the first email only had a score of 1.8, chances are that it won't get though to as many inboxes as the second email. If there's a difference of only 5% deliverability, and you're doing a mailing to 10,000 people, with a conversion rate of 2.5% for a $100 product, that's $1,250 in lost sales (10,000 x 5% x 2.5% x $100).

Other Factors to Consider

Another thing ISP's spam filters look for are email messages that are sent to a high degree of invalid email addresses. A common spam approach is to blast a domain name with a randomly selected list of possible email addresses. If you take a closer look at some of the spam that you have received, you might see addresses such as george@domain.com, george1@domain.com, george2@domain.com, or info@domain.com, support@domain.com, service@domain.com etc. Therefore if a message is sent to a large list of recipients and a lot of them are invalid email addresses, the message gets coined as spam and doesn't get through. So make sure you remove invalid addresses or bounces without delay and ensure that list members that have opted-out are removed promptly. A clean list is more likely to get delivered than a dirty one.

If you have an email list of a few thousand or more, it can also help to break it down into separate groups that all have a characteristic in common. Then email a slightly different message, at different times, to each category referencing the characteristic they have in common. That way when an ISP receives your messages, they're not all the same and they're not all coming through at once. This can help reduce the likelihood that it may be perceived as spam.

If you're sending a HTML message, check and recheck your HTML coding. Keep it simple and error free. Excessive use of different colors, fonts, sizes, images and so forth will result in a higher spam filtering rate. Broken images, missing tags, and non web safe colors are also some of the other things filters look for. Also don't forget to run your email through a spam checker. Either use the Spam Assassin email checker available at www.1StartCart.com or the email content checker found at www.lyris.com/contentchecker.

Never just send a giant graphic – that's what spammers do. If you choose to send an HTML email it needs to be a healthy balance of graphics and text. Graphics overall should be kept to a minimum, for optimum load time. Also many email filters won't let graphics through for fear that they may be spam or even a virus, so if you don't need graphics, don't send them.

Always make sure it is easy to opt-out. One sure-fire way of getting your emails reported by recipients as spam, is if you don't provide, or don't make it easy to opt-out. Always make is as simple as possible and give instructions on how to do so in each email you send. If people do opt-out, make sure that they are actually removed from the list immediately. Don't use the word "remove" in your email. It is commonly found in spam and will add points to your score. Something else that can prevent you messages from being classified as spam is to use a signature, including your name and mailing address.

The subject line is another one of the easiest way to get your email filtered as spam. Try to avoid using punctuation such as exclamation points, asterisks, dollar signs, question marks, quotations and others. It can trigger some spam filters. Also do not use misleading, untruthful or unbelievable subject lines. Not only will the user not open the email, but they may also forward it to a blacklist because it looks like spam.

It can also be worth your while to sign up for as many free email accounts as you can. Hotmail, Yahoo! mail, and GMail are among some of the most popular. Before you send an email to your list, send it to your test accounts first. If the newsletter ends up in the junk folder, then you've got some work to do. Remember, only change one variable at a time so you can accurately determine what the problem is.

If you can personalize the email, besides getting a better conversion rate, it will also slip past more spam filters. Most spam doesn't address the recipient by name, and if you do, it's more likely that your email is legitimate.

Don't use an anonymous email address to send bulk mail. Send your emails from a reputable domain name, or even better yet your own domain. Avoid free email addresses, such as harry_mo123@hotmail.com. In addition to looking unprofessional, it's easy to get a false positive with spam filters this way. Some spam filters will also check to make sure that an email claiming to be originating from a domain name actually did originate from that domain name. This is called "authentication" and it's slowly becoming more and more common. Emails that aren't "authenticated" are either classified as junk or flagged as suspicious.

Don't type all in caps. This is both rude, unprofessional, and looks a lot like a Nigerian Bank scam. It can also get you blacklisted, or blocked by the spam filter quicker than you could say tiggity boo. Make sure that you also use proper punctuation, spelling and grammar, as well as proper sentence structure. Also avoid sending email too frequently. Some sophisticated spam filters track frequency and it can play a part in the decision to block your email. Not only do the filters not like it, but most people don't want to receive the same or similar messages from the same people over and over.

Get yourself on a whitelist. Being registered on an ISPs whitelist will practically ensure that your email always gets delivered, or at least delivered to your recipient's email client. It takes some time and a little work to get on a whitelist, which usually involves an authenticating process to ensure that only reputable addresses are considered. It's definitely worth the time if you have a larger list. To start the process, contact your ISP and the ISPs of your major recipients and ask for information about their particular process for whitelist registration.

It's also always a good idea to keep opt-in records. Some spam monitors might contact you with a spam alert and give you an opportunity to prove that the recipient actually did opt-in. To successfully prove your case you must maintain a record of opt-in data, usually including the date, time and IP address of the opt-in message. It's also a good idea to put the customer's opt-in data in the email, such as the name and email they used when registering for your opt-in list. That way if people forget what email address they signed up with, it will serve as a reminder.

If you implement some of the things I've discussed in this chapter, you should notice an improvement in your email deliverability rates. When you are sending bulk email to substantial lists, a failure rate of only a few percent can mean a lot to the amount of cash that it brings to your bank account.

Building an Opt-in Email Database

The most important tool of any email marketer is their email database. Your email database needs to consist of targeted prospects, which have opted in to receive email from you. A good, highly targeted and focused email list can be worth millions, yes millions, in the right hands. It costs six times more money to acquire a new customer, than it does to sell to an existing customer. An easy way to sell to existing customers – email them. The problem is: How do we get an email list? Well, lucky for you, that's exactly what this chapter is about.

I'll never forget when the power of an internet database was demonstrated to me for the first time. I sat in my chair at a seminar, and the speaker sent an email to a list of 1,500 people. Within 15 minutes, they had made almost $3,000. Within 24hrs it was up to just under $10,000; all in about 5 minutes of work. Now they did send out an awesome deal to a highly targeted list, but it doesn't mean you can't do the same. You simply need an email list that you know how to use and have something to sell to.

At one time or another most of us have probably seen an ad, or come across a website offering to sell us an email list, ranging from a few hundred addresses to hundreds of millions. Truth be told, an email list that has the kind of highly targeted audience that we want should cost $0.10 - $0.50 per name. So how can someone offer what they claim to be a 30,000,000 name, opt-in email database for $29.95? Easy, the list is not targeted, not opt-in, not legal and most of the addresses on it probably don't work.

Buying or Renting Email Lists

What happens if you don't have an email database? You can buy one, rent one, use someone else's or build your own. I don't really recommend buying mailing lists – no matter how cheap they are. Most of the addresses on them are by no means "opt in" (think spam) and you can be sure they'll include a very small percentage of your primary target audience.

Though, if you don't have your own list, you can rent (not buy) one from a reputable company or broker, just be prepared to pay for it. The price varies greatly, depending on the quality of the list, and how targeted it is. All reputable companies will send the email for you, so they don't give up the identity of the email addresses you could use for future mailings. I have not yet come across a reputable company that sells actual lists, everybody rents. If they offer to sell, walk away.

Some of the people on these lists may be agreeing to receive emails in return for receiving coupons, discounts, or free prizes. So, the chances that they are really interested in reading your emails are very questionable at best. Even if the company you rent from has true opt-in lists, there's another big problem: they have probably rented these same email addresses out over and over again. You could easily be person number 358 trying to reach an already desensitized audience.

But if you still want to go this route, be sure to research the company thoroughly before giving them a dime. The chances that someone has opted to receive email from you - someone they don't know - is highly unlikely and highly risky. Always ask the seller how they opted in. What specifically did they opt in to receive? How long ago did they opt-in? When renting email addresses, there are far too many variables to consider, not to mention all the things that could go wrong and negatively impact the reputation of your business. So if you're going to do it, be careful.

There are also programs that can automatically harvest email addresses from the internet at about a rate of 10,000 addresses per second. These programs basically search through HTML code for email addresses (much the same way a search engine spider works), then adds them to a list. They offer a very minute targeting; you can select the country, sometimes even the state or province that you want to search, along with a few keywords. In addition to being unethical, and the resulting problems it causes, this procedure just doesn't work. Harvested email lists normally generate click-through rates of less than 0.001%. Do not, under any circumstances, use one of these programs; it is spamming, it is illegal, and it is bad for business.

There are methods that are considered ethical and responsible for collecting email addresses, and others that aren't. Be ethical, and use permission marketing techniques. Your customers will appreciate it and you'll see much better response rates and fewer angry emails and spam warnings.

Creating and developing your own opt-in list is an absolute must. Opt-in lists provide you with the ability to create a targeted list of potential customers to whom you can advertise to on a continual basis. No matter what strategies you're currently using, if you're not collecting the email addresses of your potential customers, you're literally guaranteeing your failure.

So, what's an opt-in email list? The uncontested core definition of opt-in email is: any email that is actively requested by the recipient. Usually opting-in involves entering your email address and name into a form on a website, then submitting it to the list owner. If a customer asks for a specific piece of information, you only have the permission to send them that information and nothing more.

Double Opt-in

A double opt-in is when subscribers actively confirm their subscriptions. This is typically done by replying to an automatically generated email, thus confirming your subscription, or by clicking on a special link contained in the confirmation email. For instance, if Harry signs up for a special newsletter with a double opt-in system he would receive an automatic email that he would either need to reply to, or follow a link contained in the email to confirm his subscription.

One of the major benefits of using a double opt-in system is that you are much less likely to get accused of sending spam.

If Harry's friend Bill was peeved with him, and signed Harry up for a whole bunch of newsletters, when Harry started receiving them he would most likely consider them to be spam. He may or may not take action. With a double opt-in, Harry would receive an email confirming his subscription, and if he didn't sign up for the newsletter, no further action would be required on his part.

One of the problems with double opt-ins is that you can lose a lot of the people that originally sign up for your newsletter; either because they just never got around to confirming their subscription, or because they've changed their mind. Some studies have shown that by using a double opt-in system you can lose up to 60% of your subscribers, and that's a big deal.

Another branch of double opt-in, is to send out a confirmation email and unless the recipient takes explicit action to remove themselves from the list, their subscription would be confirmed. This is not really a true double opt-in as all emails need to have an unsubscribe feature anyways as required by law. The only benefit to doing it this way is that you are likely to have less people take the effort to remove themselves from your list. But keep this in mind: Someone who doesn't want to be on your list isn't going to buy from you and will more likely than not cause you problems down the road.

In conclusion, a site visitor is a terrible thing to waste! If you're not collecting email addresses on your website at every opportunity, you are missing out on opportunities to turn one-time visitors into some of your best customers. If you're not providing a way for visitors to communicate with you in the future and come back to visit your site, your promotions are nothing more than a one shot deal. Never miss an opportunity to ask people to join your mailing list.

Building an Opt-in List

The whole principal behind email marketing is to drive people to your website, and sell your products or services to them. If you want to get them to your website through an email campaign, you need to have an email address to send the messages to. Increasing your opt-in list of targeted email clients is the most important email marketing strategy you can use. So, how do you get someone to "opt-in?"

People don't like to give out their email address just so they can "be on a mailing list." You need to offer them something in return (remember the phrase "what's in it for me?") to get them to give you their email address. Offering subscriptions, whether to a newsletter or ezine is the number one legitimate method of increasing your email list. But, with the splurge of newsletters and ezines taking over the net, often the valuable content contained in a newsletter or ezine is not enough to convince someone to sign up. They want more before they'll part with their email address.

One of the easiest ways to get them to give you their name and email is by giving them an ethical bribe or a gift in exchange for their email address. An ethical bribe can be anything that has a high perceived value to the visitor like an ebook, audio download, mini email course, special report and so on.

In exchange for the ethical bribe, the prospect agrees to opt-in to your email list. You probably want the ethical bribe to be something the subscriber can download using an autoresponder. Imagine if you had to mail out 100 CDs each day to all your new subscribers. The money and time it requires would be a complete and unnecessary waste of resources. Autoresponders are coming up in the next chapter, but in a nutshell, it would automatically send out an email to the subscriber at the address they supplied. The email sent out by the autoresponder could have a link embedded in it, that the subscriber could click on to download their bribe (or should I say gift?). Another advantage to using an autoresponder to email the ethical bribe is that if the email address they supply is fake, or does not work, they don't get the free gift – simple as that.

Of course, you can also set it up so that after clicking on the submit button, it automatically goes to a page where they can download their free gift. The downside to doing this is that they could give any name and email address they want. Though if you think about it, if the only reason they want to join the mailing list is to get the free gift, their email address may not be of much use to you anyway, and they'd probably just unsubscribe as soon as they get what they want.

When giving away your ethical bribe you can also use what is known as a negative qualifier. A negative qualifier is when you get people to pay a small sum for the ethical bribe (like $1.95 for s/h). The only reason you would want to do this is that it helps weed out the worthless (for lack of a better word) people who join your list. It also helps justify why you are giving them a fantastic gift for nothing. I don't recommend that you use this often, if at all, unless what you are sending to them has a very significant value in the eye of the prospect.

If you use this technique (the free gift, not the negative qualifier), you should see response rates to your subscription requests go up tremendously. Don't have time to write an ebook or special report? No problem, go to www.elance.com and hire someone to write one for you, or simply buy one with master resale rights that allows you to give it away.

Opt-in Form - Make it Easy

If you want people to sign up for your newsletter, you need to make it as easy for them as possible. People don't like hard, they like easy. Making it more complicated than in needs to be often breaches the fine line between whether they sign up or not.

It's amazing the number of online businesses that have their subscription forms tucked away deep in their site – so that even when you're looking for it, it's hard to find. Your subscription form is one of the most important aspects of your website. People rarely ever buy on their first visit, and once they leave your site, if you don't capture their email address, you may have lost them forever. That's why email marketing is so important; it gives them a reminder and a reason to come back.

Take a minute and go to www.JustinMichie.com. Notice how prevalent the subscription form is. It's impossible to miss. You don't need to click on a link and go to another page. You don't need to scroll down the page. You don't need to look for it. It's right there, popping out, asking, begging for you to opt-in.

Make sure you place the subscription box in a prominent area. People naturally read from left to right, so the left side of the page usually has the highest signup rate. Of course, you should test different places, until you find one than consistently pulls the largest conversion rate for your site.

Be sure to have at least a link (but preferably an actual signup form) on each and every webpage on your website, offering visitors the chance to subscribe. Otherwise, people will go to your site, look around, and forget that they meant to sign up for your newsletter. Your visitors may also enter your website from many pages other than your main page. They may never even visit your main page, so it is best if your subscription box is visible on every page of your website. Here's what I do: Build the subscription box into the design template or navigational bar of every page. That way it's always there, in the same spot frequently reminding the visitor to subscribe.

You can't rely on the customer to take the initiative to look for the sign up form, or to send you an email asking to subscribe. It simply won't happen.

Alternatively, you could create a pop under that appears when they leave, asking if they would like to subscribe (if they haven't already). You can also have a popup when they first arrive at your site asking them if they'd like to subscribe. Don't let them leave your site without offering them as many chances as possible to sign up and give you their email address.

How Much Is Too Much?

Some sites ask you for your life history just so you can sign up for their newsletter. That's absolutely ridiculous, you're not getting married - heck you're not even dating. It doesn't matter when they're born, or what their income is. You primary and _only_ objective is to get them to sign up. That's it, nothing else. All you need to ask, and all you ever should ask for, is for their primary email address, and first name. Any other information you can get from them at a later date, like when they order from you.

I used to own a retail brick and mortar store that also had an online component. At one point we were running a particular contest for a trip for two to the Caribbean, which we promoted both online and offline. The primary purpose was to generate an opt-in list of email addresses we could mail to in the future. We tested two different online entry forms and the results were staggering.

The first entry form we tested had nine different fields including the entrants name, email address, contact info, income, date of birth and so on. The second entry form we tested, asked only three things, their name, email address and phone number so we could contact them in case they won.

Before I tell you the results, I should let you know that the contest was advertised on some major websites, newsletters and ezines that would bring people directly to the entry page. We also had in-store flyers advertising the contest, along with newspaper ads, and of course a large ad for it on our website.

To get to the signup page, the user had to click on a link, either from the main page of our website, or from any of the other sites that we advertised on to get to the contest page. People who clicked on the link had already partially qualified themselves because they had some intention of signing up before they got to the signup page. Therefore, the conversion rate was significantly higher than you would expect to receive for a newsletter signup form on the main page of your website. Also, remember this was also back in 2003 where opt-in forms weren't overused as much as they are today.

Anyways, here are the results: In the first entry form with 9 fields we had a 28% signup rate. In the second entry form with only 3 fields, we had an 87% signup rate. That's more than a 300% increase.

Here's why. First, some people don't like to give out quasi-personal information like their date of birth and income. Second, most people, by definition, are lazy and don't want fill in a long entry form. Since my goal was to get their email addresses, I don't need their addresses, birth date, income, or any other information. All I needed was their name (so we know who entered), email address and phone number (so we could call them if they won). That's it.

Your subscription box is not meant to be marketing research and shouldn't be used this way. At this point, you are creating an initial contact with potential clients. Simply ask for their name and primary email address. Don't even think about asking them for their last name, you don't need it. You don't address your emails, "Dear John Smith," you address them "Dear John." The less information you ask for, the less intimidating it seems to the prospect and the more likely they are to give you their information. Always use lower case when asking for the customers name and email, it is less formal and appears to be less threatening. Also don't ask them to repeat their email address; if they want what you have badly enough, they will make sure it is right.

Down the road, when they know you better, you can always send out surveys to find out more about them. At that point, you can let them know you're trying to improve your customer service and their experience when visiting your site. Then they'll know who you are and will feel more comfortable giving you information. And when they order, you'll get their mailing address and other info anyways.

Easy Opt-out

It really boosts your credibility to have an easy-to-use opt-out process. If people feel they can stop your email at anytime, they are more likely to join in the first place. Be sure to include instructions on how to opt-out in every correspondence sent to your mailing list. In the old days email marketers would have something as simple as replying to the email with the words "remove" in the subject. While this is still used occasionally today, more often than not the email recipient clicks on a link in the email and is automatically opted out, or removed from the list by the autoresponder, or broadcast mailing program.

Make it easy, make it simple, and above all when someone opts out, make sure it is immediate. None of this "Your email address will be removed from out list within 7-10 business days." That's BS; there is no reason it can't be removed immediately and automatically.

Privacy Policy

It's never been a bad idea to have a privacy policy available for your "soon to be opt-in" subscribers to view. While you can have a link to a long winded privacy policy, it is unnecessary and causes the visitor to leave the signup form, thus denying the impulse to signup. You need to guarantee the prospect that you will keep their information private and confidential. Here's an example of the disclaimer that I often use:

We hate spam as much as you do! We will not sell, rent or share your email address with any unauthorized third parties.

Notice, how I say any unauthorized third parties. This still enables you to use your email list for joint venture email marketing. You also want to be sure that your prospects understand that they are under no obligation to buy anything from you in the future and that they can remove their name from your list any time they like.

You can also have a link to a more in-depth privacy policy at the bottom you webpage, but it's not necessary for the opt-in signup form.

Ways to Grow Your List

Although there are a whole truckload of ways to grow your list, if you expect someone to enter their name into an online or offline form, you need to give them a good reason. Newsletters work, but as discussed above they are most often not enough, so don't forget to give an ethical bribe, gift, content etc. that has value in the eye of the visitor. That being said, here are some of the best ways to grow your list.

Joint Ventures

One of the easiest ways to quickly build a list would be to joint venture with another similar but non-competing business and use their email list in return for paying them a percentage of the profits or sales that you do. (We will discuss joint venture marketing more in depth in Chapter 36.) The person or business that you are joint venturing with will not actually give you their email database. They will almost always send out an email on your behalf (written by you – edited by them), and if you're lucky, they'll endorse you and whatever you are offering.

Their customers already know who they are, but most likely they'll have no idea who you are, so if they are willing to endorse you, all the more power to you. Then you sell your product to their list and split the profits or sales with them 50/50 or any other agreed-upon percentage. Remember you're trying to build an email database, not strike it rich, so you might need to sell your product at a ridiculously low, never before seen, unheard of price. Even if you don't make a ton of money right away, you'll have a huge list that you can market other products to on the back-end.

Tell-a-friend Forms

Something as simple as having a tell-a-friend about this site form (or an article or information found on it), can be a great way to cost effectively grow your list. You simply have a form on your site that allows your visitors to easily send an email to their friends letting them know about your site. Just ask them to enter their friends email address and have a pre-written, editable message to go along with it that might look something like this:

To: [Your Friend's Name]
From: [Your Email Address]

Subject: [Friends Name], check out this great website I just found.

Hey [Friends Name],

I just found this great website on chicken feeding that I thought you might be interested to know about. Simply <u>click here</u> to go to the website, or copy the following link into your browser:

<u>http://www.YourDomain.com</u>

talk to you later,

[Your Name]

This is a one time message sent by [Your Name] at [Your Email Address].

Keep in mind that you can't add the email addresses from the tell-a-friend form to your email list. These people have not opted-in to receive email from you and unless they sign up for some kind of opt-in list you cannot mail them again. You can also ask your past customers to refer a friend, or give them some kind of free gift for referring people to your site. It doesn't cost you anything to do, except a few moments of your time.

There are tons of free scripts that you can find on the internet which you simply need to cut and paste into your HTML code, and change the email copy. Just do a google for "tell a friend script (or code)," or ask your web developer and they should be able to easily program it for you.

Contests

You can also arrange a contest or sweepstakes. If you have your own products take one of the more expensive ones and give it away as a grand prize. It shouldn't cost you much to produce and in order to enter contestants need to supply a valid email address. To get the best possible results, declare that the winner will be contacted by email and needs to claim the prize within a certain time period. This will enable you to eliminate the problem of people giving out bogus email addresses, or ones they don't check frequently or use for junk email for fear that they might lose out if they actually win.

Members Only Sites

Members only sites can be another effective way to grow your list. Still, continue to allow everyone to access most of the content on your site, but also simply add a "members only" area that contains special information like articles, ebooks, audio etc. In return for the special information, visitors must register and by doing so give you their email address.

By going this route, you could also at some time in the future make the membership area a paid feature of your site, thereby collecting a small fee for the information offered. Of course you then need to have a good amount of high quality content to justify the charge.

11 +1 Other Ways to Build Your List

1. Direct traffic to a power squeeze webpage via PPC ads.

2. Have a "subscribe to our newsletter, and get a free gift" in the signature line of your and your employee's emails.
3. Hand out signup forms (or a variation thereof) at speaking engagements, seminars, tradeshows and other events.
4. Add email opt-in features to warranty or product registration cards.
5. Promote your newsletter or email list in the tag line of any articles that you write.
6. Include opt-in message boxes on shopping cart checkout pages.
7. Ask for opt-in email address on any direct mail order forms.
8. Ask customers if they would like to join your list on any customer service or support calls.
9. Setup co-registration/partnerships - allow customers to opt in via partner's website or thank you page.
10. Include links on your customer surveys, invoices and promo material.
11. Try and match your customer list (names and address) with an email appending service. Email appending services look through huge databases of email addresses and physical addresses trying to match your customers physical address with their email address. Then you get their emails, and can send a one time email to them asking if they would like to opt-in to your list.
12. Even through it's not a way to actually build your list; it's a way to keep it strong. Have a change of email address link in your mailings; 31% of email addresses are changed each year.

I Have a List – Now What?

What do I do with the email address once I get them? Follow up, follow up, follow up. That does not mean sending out an email saying "Well, you got my free gift, now buy my $900 audio CD set."

It does mean you can start to introduce your list to your products, affiliate programs or joint ventures. Not everyone will buy right away. When I'm sending email offers, I'll eventually offer something that is so enticing, so valuable, so interesting, so rare that you too, would want to be one of the few who can take advantage of the special offer.

Remember don't over-send offers (not emails), anything more than once or twice a month is too much. If you over-send email offers to your list, they will ignore your messages and your sales will plummet.

Although there are countless ways to build and market to an email list, this should give you a good place to start. There are many real world examples of online marketers that can easily do a million in sales year after year, with an email list of only 10,000 people. Of course it must be extremely targeted and extremely high quality. If that's not something that gets you excited about building your list I don't know what is.

If you master only a handful of the strategies and techniques outlined in this chapter, you should be in a position to make a very comfortable living doing whatever it is you do online. A properly developed, opt-in mailing list is, metaphorically speaking, worth its weight in gold.

Autoresponders

Perhaps the biggest benefit in the internet marketing business is the complete and total automation of the process. In order to automate the marketing and sales process you need the correct tools for the job. Keeping in close contact with your customers and responding to their inquiries in a timely manner is essential to the success of any online business. The vast majority of online businesses that have failed have learned this the hard way. This is where correct employment of an autoresponder plays an important role in the ultimate success of your business. It takes care of the most tedious aspects of online marketing, automatically.

The purpose of this chapter is to give you a balanced and objective review of the issues involved in choosing and using an autoresponder. Autoresponders have been around almost as long as email and in their simplest form are "old technology." Needless to say autoresponder technology has evolved and become a very successful email marketing tool, which is a vital part of many online businesses.

An autoresponder can de defined as a software program that sends out an automatic response to an email sent to a specific email address. The very first autoresponders were created when mail clients could not deliver email to a given email address. They created simple messages such as "Your email was not delivered because…" I should also note that autoresponders are sometimes referred to as "automatic responders" (which is where the got their name) – they are exactly the same thing and the terms can be used interchangeably.

Simple Autoresponders

There are two main types of autoresponders: Simple (or auto reply) autoresponders, and smart (or sequential) autoresponders. Simple autoresponders respond directly to an incoming email message the instant it is received. Many of us have either received an autoresponder message of this type or used one at some point. The most familiar simple autoresponder is the "Sorry, I am away on vacation until next Monday, and will respond to your email when I return." Simple autoresponders can also be used for sending information that has been requested or for something as simple as letting a customer know that you have received their email and will respond as soon as possible.

Most web hosts offer this type of single reply autoresponder free in the email accounts that come with their hosting package. Though, quite often the autoresponders services which come with your web hosting account are insufficient for business use. The problem with this type of autoresponder is that it is designed to send out only one basic message reply to an email that it receives. This is often not enough to maintain the continued contact, or to deliver the content you want to offer your visitors. It also lacks some important features needed to do proper follow-ups; for example, it cannot add prospects to a subscriber list and then send them a series of personalized, follow-up messages, or remove them from the list if they so desire.

This brings us to what is known as the smart or sequential autoresponder. Smart autoresponders are just that, smart. They can send out prewritten emails whenever you want based on the schedule you specify.

Sequential Autoresponders

A sequential or smart autoresponder is a program that is designed to capture email addresses and then send out a sequence of prewritten follow up messages at a schedule you specify. For example, suppose you had a decorating website, and had a mini email course available on "decorating on a budget." If you had to send out the emails by hand to everyone that signed up, imagine how long it would take to send out email to 100 people? 1,000 people? 10,000 people? It would consume an absolutely ridiculous amount of your time.

That's where a sequential autoresponder works its magic. If your mini course had five parts, the sequential autoresponder would send the first part instantly when the prospect signed up for the course. It could send the second part two days later, then the third part two days after that, and so on. Once you get it set up, it is 100% automated and consumes zero time on your part. Just remember that autoresponders must get through the spam filters as any other email, so keep that in mind when creating your pre-written messages.

Every marketer knows that repetition creates familiarity, which creates trust, and trust leads to sales. So the odds of getting a sale after sending multiple messages are much higher than getting a sale from a single email or webpage pitch. It is also a fairly well known fact that it takes on average of seven contacts to close a sale.

Another big benefit of autoresponders is that they tend to decrease return rates, especially on big ticket products. By following up with a simple automated series of email messages you can reassure customers that they made the right decision in purchasing your product and that you are there for them if they need you.

Sequential autoresponders are also known as smart autoresponders, not only because they can be sent out on a predetermined schedule, but also because they give the sender the ability to insert personalization characteristics into the emails. Simple autoresponders can sometimes insert the email address, subject line or some other very basic information into the email reply it is sending. However, sequential or smart autoresponders can insert an endless amount of information into the emails they send out. The information is usually stored in a database of some kind and can be pulled out by the autoresponder software and inserted into the email that you are sending. This way it appears to the recipient that the email was personally sent from you to them. Marketing principals dictate that the more an email is personalized, the more likely the recipient to take your desired call to action.

When used correctly, a sequential autoresponder can also make your site more sticky by reminding your visitors to come back and visit again. Since it's sequential autoresponders that are most useful to us as an online marketer, I'll be using the term "autoresponder" to refer to sequential autoresponders from now on.

Choosing an Autoresponder

There are three ways that autoresponders can be set or hosted which is vital to how they work, and consequently to what type of autoresponder you choose to use. First, there is the remotely hosted autoresponder, which is hosted by an outside company and is accessed through your web browser. Second, if you have a dedicated server (and sometimes even if you don't), you can buy autoresponder software outright and install it on your server. And lastly, you can buy software that you can run on your office or home computer.

Remotely hosted autoresponders operate on the provider's infrastructure and are usually configurable via a web-based control panel. You pay a monthly subscription fee for as long as you use the service. This is much easier to implement then installing software on a server (or even your computer), which requires some technical ability or the help of someone with technical ability. It is also much more expensive to buy the software outright, which is why I recommend using a remotely hosted autoresponder.

One thing I should note is about IP (internet protocol) addresses. When you use a remotely hosted autoresponder, the server usually uses the same IP address for all the emails it sends out. What that means for you, is if someone uses the server to send spam and the IP address gets blacklisted, your legitimate email may be getting blocked since is originates from the same IP address. If you have your own server, chances are you have your own IP address (check with your hosting company) and that way your IP address won't be blacklisted because of someone else's poor email habits. Before you sign up for a remotely hosted autoresponder, it's always a good idea to ask them what their IP address is and do a search on it to see if it appears on any blacklists. Some remotely hosted autoresponders use many different IP addresses for sending emails and have very strict spam policies. That way if an IP address gets blacklisted, not only is the spam sender banned from the system, but the company will discontinue use of the blacklisted IP so it doesn't hurt other's mailings.

Price

Price is by far not the most important thing to consider and it usually never is. The difference between how much money a good autoresponder and a great autoresponder can make you, more than makes up for the price difference. Compare the other features, benefits and qualities of the autoresponder first, then if a couple offer the same features, benefits and support, you can go with the cheaper one if you want. Though, I would usually choose the more expensive autoresponder because it is likely (though not always) to be higher quality and have better customer support since it costs more.

The price for a remotely hosted autoresponder is usually determined by the number of autoresponders you need, as well as the number of subscribers you expect to have in the autoresponder database. Most services have several hosting plans available depending upon your needs. Always make sure they allow you to upgrade the size of your database if need be, and check how much they charge for it first. Some autoresponders might start out super cheap, but once you get more than 10,000 subscribers the price jumps exorbitantly.

Most remotely hosted autoresponders will either provide a free, or heavily discounted limited time trial period. The trial period usually lets you try all the features the paid version offers, but usually limits the number of autoresponders, and/or subscribers you can have. Some free trial offers have even been known to place a small advertisement at the bottom or each email message, so watch out for that. Other issues to consider in the purchase price are the quality of technical support and some of the other options as outlined below.

If you plan on buying the rights to use the autoresponder software on your computer, or your internet server, the price can range from several hundred to several thousand dollars or more. Depending on your preferences and your budget it may or may not be a viable option for you. Just remember it requires a lot more money upfront and some technical expertise. If you do however decide to buy the software, make sure you have the ability to try it out first to see if it fits what you're after.

Personalization

A common feature of almost all autoresponders is the ability to personalize messages. This allows you to insert fields into your messages which will be automatically substituted with recipient's information that you may have captured from an online web form, database, an email they sent to you or any other source. This is something that is an absolute must have. Personalizing emails dramatically increases the response rates and makes you look better and more professional at the same time.

Does your autoresponder allow you to customize web forms to enable greater personalization of data? If so how many customizable fields can you have? Customizable fields are for non-standard data, such as favorite website or color.

Import / Export

The ability to import a subscriber database that you may already have into your autoresponder system is another must have feature for me. Some systems don't allow you to so this, and make you enter additional subscribers by hand. Any decent autoresponder will allow you to directly import a database from a file that you may have on your computer as long as it is in the correct format. Basically any spreadsheet should be able to be formatted and imported within five-to-ten minutes.

The ability to export a list to a spreadsheet or a comma separated text only file is also very useful must have feature. Suppose you wanted to mail a sales letter directly to your database; it would save tons of time if you could export names and addresses directly to your sales letter template, automatically insert them, then press the print button on your computer. I always also export a backup copy of my list to my own computer in the unlikely event that there is some kind of problem with the autoresponder's servers. An email list is one of an online marketers most important assets, so it's worth protecting.

Backups

Any worthy autoresponder should periodically make a backup of the information that you have on their servers, just in case something goes woo woo. As I mentioned in the previous paragraph, it's also a good idea for you to keep a backup as well. After learning the hard way several times I always backup all my important information and store a copy at my house and another one in a safety deposit box.

Bounced Emails

No matter how good of an email database you have, it's a fact of life that there will always be some unreachable emails. Returned emails can be a huge problem for a mailing server, especially if you have a large mailing list. Some autoresponders can automatically remove or archive (for your review) bounced or returned email addresses from their list which ensures your list stays clean. Some spam programs add email servers to a spam list if the repeatedly send emails address to an incorrect address, so it is important that your autoresponder has some way to deal with this and/or remove the addresses.

Click-through Link Tracking

Another must is the ability to be able to do click-through link tracking. This allows you to track the number of click-throughs for a particular link in your email messages. It also usually allows you to track how many of the click-throughs went to the order page, and how many people that went to the order page actually bought something. If you want to do any type of split email or sales page testing (and you should) this is something that is an absolute requirement. Without it, it would be almost impossible to track stats such as your conversion rate and so on.

Statistics

Good autoresponders should provide you with statistics such as the number of signups, number of unsubscribers, bounced or rejected emails, click-throughs and more. These statistics can sometimes be automatically sent to you by emails each month, or are available through the control panel, or both.

Blacklists

Something else that can prove to be useful is the ability to run a blacklist. This allows you to not send out emails to your competitors, or unwelcome visitors if you choose. You just enter or import a database of people or domains names you don't want to send emails to (even if they sign up on your site) and anytime you do a mailing, it automatically excludes them. To me this isn't a deciding factor, but I can see why it would be useful to have.

Duplicate Emails

Another important autoresponder tool is the ability to remove duplicate emails. While this may seem like it should be a standard feature, it isn't always. This small feature prevents you from looking unprofessional by sending out more than one email to the same subscriber, who may have registered more than once or be on more than one autoresponder sequence. Some spam filters also block multiple emails to the same recipient when the emails are exactly the same so it can be useful there as well.

Control Panel / Interface

The interface is similar to the control panel of your web hosting account. This is where you control the scheduling of when emails are sent, have access to your database to add, remove or modify subscriber details as necessary and have the ability to setup and store autoresponder sequences. The control panel should also provide access to detailed stats as we discussed a couple paragraphs ago as well as a whole bunch of other features.

All remotely hosted autoresponders must have a control panel, which is viewable and usable though your web browser. If you install software on your own server, most programs do have an easily accessible and usable control panel, but some are more complicated and may require technical ability or training to use.

Attachments

Can you send attachments with your emails? This isn't something you would usually want to do, but it might possibly be useful to have if you wanted to send a small file to a select group of people such as an inner circle. Usually it is best just to supply a download link for any files that need to be sent. Just don't let it be a deciding feature in your choice.

Text / HTML / MIME

Do you have the ability to send messages in text, HTML or MIME email formats? If you can send HTML messages, is there a built in HTML editor? If there is it can save you a lot of time going back and forth between programs. And if there is an HTML editor does it allow you to preview messages before you send them?

Is there an email message editor for text and MIME emails? Does it have a spell checker? A link checker or verifier? While none of these options are absolutely necessary to have, they make life a little easier.

Spam Checker

Does the autoresponder have a spamability checker? This will check how likely it is that your email may be perceived as spam by various spam filters such as Spam Assassin. It will usually give your email a score or percentage of how likely it is that it may be perceived as spam; and some of the better ones will even tell you why.

Some of the other features to look for that may or may not be important to you are:

- Do you have the option to select different "from" email addresses?
- Is the autoresponder double opt-in compatible?
- Can you customize double opt-in, subscribe and unsubscribe messages?
- Can you time-synchronize your emails? In other words, can you tell the autoresponder exactly when you want it to send your email?

What I Recommend

Given the importance of an autoresponder to your online business, it may be worth your while to do some research to find the best autoresponder that meets all of your major requirements. This will save you a lot of time, money and frustration in the long run.

The autoresponder software I recommend is part of the 1ShoppingCart network and can be found at www.1StartCart.com. It is one of the best autoresponder programs on the market and the program that I personally use. Chances are you received an email from me after you bought this book: guess where it came from?

If you're signed up with 1StartCart for your shopping cart software, the autoresponder software is part of the package and won't cost you anything extra. If you use someone else for your shopping cart system, the autoresponder system can be purchased separately for a relatively low monthly fee. Since this is a remotely hosted autoresponder, you can access it via a web interface from any computer anywhere in the world, so long as you have an internet connection. This system has very strict anti-spam policies which keeps its IP addresses off the blacklists, so that's not something you need to worry about.

The big benefit to using the same system for both your autoresponders and shopping cart is that they automatically mesh together. Anytime a sale is made, the contact information automatically gets added to the autoresponder which can send follow up to them as necessary.

Another popular autoresponder is available from www.aweber.com. It has most of the same features as 1StartCart, but it is a standalone system that doesn't come with any of the other shopping cart features, although it can be integrated with your shopping cart software. There are some other decent systems, but those are the by far the best I have come across.

Through the utilization of autoresponders you can put a good part of your business on autopilot, which will ultimately save you time and make you more money. Staying in contact with your customers builds a quality relationship, trust and credibility, all of which will make them that much more ready next time you ask them to purchase something from you.

Writing Killer Emails

Writing great copy for your email marketing campaign is very important if you want your campaign to succeed. If what you say, and how you say it, isn't carefully crafted, you may as well not waste your time marketing by email. Writing promotional emails is not the same as writing copy for any other medium. In a print ad you have graphics to enhance your message and you don't solely rely on text. Most emails are text-based (even if it's HTML format) and therefore need to be short, concise, informative and to the point; or no one is going to read it. You need to focus on your objective, find out what makes your audience tick, then talk to them in their own language and you could have the makings of a beautiful friendship.

If you don't believe you have the skills to write good copy yourself, then outsource – find someone who does; it will be well worth the money. On a quick side note, one of the most important lessons I have learned in business is to do yourself what you are an expert in and hire experts to do what you're not an expert in. This does not mean to hire employees - if you've ever had employees you know what a pain they can be; simply because they need to be trained, managed, guided and babysat. www.elance.com is a great place to find quality work at a good price.

One of the most prominent reasons electronic marketing is the best business to be in, is that you don't need employees. Instead of hiring employees you can contract out to an individual or business who is an expert or specializes in the services you require. For instance, my graphic designer lives 2,000 miles away from me. I have never personally met him and I have no reason to. What matters is what kind of finished product he presents to me and that he doesn't charge an arm and a leg for it. Why would I want to waste time meeting with someone, when I can communicate with them from the freedom of my own computer, at a time that is most convenient for me?

The sole purpose of sending email to your list should be to get them to your website where you can sell them. Peak their interest and leave them wanting more, or give them a free gift to get them to your site. Do whatever you need to do.

Subject Lines

When we send out emails to potential customers, we want to avoid having them hit the "delete" button. The goal is to get our emails opened, read, and acted on. Recent statistics show that the average click-through rates for email advertising are declining, in spite of the fact that the amount of money spent on email advertising is increasing each year.

What is the first thing that you look at when sorting through your emails? For me, it's the person whom it's from, or the subject line. If I don't instantly recognize the sender, then I quickly move on to the subject. If the subject doesn't catch my attention, it only takes a fraction of a second to hit the delete button. No big surprise, studies show that most email users do the same thing. No matter how well the email is written, if the subject isn't something that is going to grab the attention of the receiver and ultimately get them to open the email, nothing else really matters.

Six words in three seconds. That's what you have to work with when writing the subject of an email. Most users email users decide in three seconds or less whether they want to open your email, based solely upon who it is from and the subject line. Most subject lines are truncated at around forty characters or approximately six words, so that's all you've got to make an impression. Choose your words very carefully and always put the most important words first, just in case the subject is cut short. Also, in some email clients like Outlook Express, people can vary the width of the subject lines to whatever size they want and sometimes only the first few words will be seen. Just remember to always place the most crucial parts of your message at the beginning of the subject line and chances are greater that people will actually open your email.

The subject line of an email is similar to the headline of an article or ad in a print publication. It should be used as the opener, or introduction to your email. When crafting a subject for your emails, you need to grab the attention of the recipient, without sounding gimmicky, or like you are trying to sell something. It is also very important that the subject sounds believable. If you promise the world, no one is going to believe you. Even, if your subject is true (Make $10,000 a Month on the Internet), very few people will believe it if it sounds unrealistic or fake, and will hit the delete button in the blink of an eye. Instead, try something more believable and usable like, "Replace Your Income Selling Information Online."

That last subject line brings up a good point; don't over-generalize your subject lines. Instead of saying, "Do you want to succeed online?" Try something like "Ten Expert Tips for Writing Killer Emails!" This headline will grab the attention of anyone interested in email marketing much better than a generalization.

A recent survey by Forrester Research showed that 65% of emails people receive are some form of advertising. This is why the art of writing excellent subject lines is so important and takes time and practice. But don't feel that it's impossible; by following some of the tips here, yours will be better than your competition's from the start and your response rates will be higher than average.

You could create the most powerful marketing message on earth, create a killer subject line and your email will be instantly deleted if the reader isn't interested in the topic it addresses. If it's wintertime in Canada, you're probably not going to sell too many beach towels. The subject should make it clear what the email is all about, while being short, concise and informative and to the point. What few words, or phrase might entice your target audience?

Personalize Your Subject Lines

I have found, as have many other direct email marketers, that personalized subject lines generate higher response rates than unpersonalized ones. Just adding the person's name to the subject line can greatly increase the chance that the email will get opened. Something like "Chad, Double Your Email Response Rate" will have a higher response rate than simply writing, "Double Your Email Response Rate."

Another highly successful method of personalization that is often overlooked is addressing the readers by their job title. "Tips Human Resource Managers Need to Know." This subject line just got the attention of every human resource manager on your list, since they aren't used to getting emails addressed to them and they feel slightly flattered that you singled them out. You may also personalize email addresses by using other customer information that is familiar to them, such as the city they live in, or referencing the last purchase they made from you.

Honesty

Don't create emails with dishonest subject lines ("Jon, about the conversation we had the other day…", or "You've Just Received a Payment From…" or even blank subject lines). These are cheap tricks and don't bode well for a happy customer. If you trick them with your subject line, how trustworthy can your business be? Also always use your actual, working email address. Don't hide it or use fraudulent ones. It's perfectly ok to have a special email address like news@YourDomain.com set up for replies, just don't make one up or leave it blank.

Finally, never promise something in the subject line that you don't deliver. If you promise information on living a happier life, make sure it's in the email. If you ask a question in the subject line, answer it in the body of your email. If you don't follow these simple rules, people won't see any difference between you and a spammer.

If your subject lines are honest and reflect what your email is really about, you will create a positive impression in customer's minds and they will be more interested in doing business with you. Dishonesty and concern about scams are some of the biggest attributes that block a customer's willingness to do business online. Don't ruin your chances, before you even get a chance. Be honest, clear, never send email to someone who hasn't opted-in to receive it and your customers will look forward to doing business with you.

Don't Look Like Spam

Spam is among the most disliked parts of any internet experience. Don't let your email get unfairly lumped into the "spam" box. Instead, try your utmost to avoid spam trigger words in your subject lines and be sure to only mail to a targeted, opt-in list. Also, emails or subject lines that look like spam are almost guaranteed to receive the grace of an instant deletion, if they get through to an inbox. By creating targeted subject lines that address the concerns of your audience, you'll avoid creating a headline that sounds like spam, and increase the chances that your email will be opened.

Test Your Results

As with any form of marketing, testing subject lines against one another is key. I once had a subject line that pulled twenty-two times better than another; exact same email, different subject line. You'll often find, simply changing a subject line can improve results dramatically, but you won't know until you test them. Other crucial things to test are the lead or opening of the email and the offer or call to action. Researching what works, and what doesn't, can help you greatly increase the effectiveness of your marketing efforts and save you a lot of wasted time and money.

Body of the Email

The body of an email has one important job - and one only: to get the reader to visit your website. With that being said, the first few lines are very crucial. They let the reader know what the email is all about so they can decide if the email is for them.

Not only does the subject need to be short and to the point, but so does the rest of the email. Donald Trump is well known to spend a lot of time on the phone. But his phone calls are not thirty minutes long; they're only a minute or two each. He's very busy and doesn't waste time with small talk or meaningless chatter. You should pay the same respect to your email subscribers. Do not waste their time, life is short, and so should be your emails. When I receive an email that peaks my interest, I quickly skim through it. If I can't do this in five-to-ten seconds and get a general idea of whether or not I should actually read the email, forget it, the email is trashed.

Studies have shown that most other people do they same thing. Generally two-to-five short paragraphs consisting of no more than two-to-four sentences each is a good length. Use choppy copy, meaning mix up the length of sentences and paragraphs. Keep emails short, for the mot part, three-fourths of a page works best. Any longer and your subscribers may not bother to read it; and if it is any shorter, you may not be able to provide enough information to get them interested. Make sure the email flows nicely and is easy to read and follow. Use bulleted lists to condense information, and leave some white space for visual relief. Let the recipient get further information via your webpage. Remember, your email is competing with others for the time of the readers, so don't give them an unnecessary reason to trash you.

Since emails shouldn't be very long, it can be hard to try and fit absolutely everything that you want to say into an email, so don't. Give the reader just enough information to entice them to go to your website. The sole purpose of the email is to peak their interest and then get them to your website, not to get them to buy right then and there. They won't. The email is a quick synopsis, like what you would find on the back of a novel. Direct the subscriber to your website or sales page for more information either by peaking their interest or bribing them with a free gift.

Another reason for directing users to your website, is that you can track your response rate. A good stat/ad tracker program (list at www.TopAdTrackers.com) can provide you with a special link that will count the click-throughs, then redirect the visitors to your website without them even knowing. Another option is to get a free counter (www.digits.com) and place it on a special webpage and let it count your visitors for you. If you're using a counter make sure it is set up to count unique visitors, otherwise every time someone goes back to that page with the counter, or reloads it, it will count them again and again. Many web hosting companies also have an invisible counter that can count your visitors as well. If you're planning on using a counter, make sure the only way the user can get to your webpage is through your email. Do not link to it from your website, or post it in the search engines, as you just want to track the effectiveness of that particular email campaign.

Emails should be written in a conversational, informal tone. Email inboxes are very personal spaces that give you the unique opportunity to talk to your subscribers as friends, rather than as a faceless sales or marketing department. The best way to check your email is to read it out loud to yourself. If it sounds clumsy to the ear, it probably won't work too well. It needs to flow smoothly, like a conversation with a close friend.

We all like being addressed by name and it's no different with emails. You may send your email to hundreds or thousands of different people, but it needs to seem as if it is written one-to-one. It is worth the little extra time and money and with proper software it can be a breeze.

Even though emails are written in an informal tone, that does not mean that there can be spelling and grammatical errors. There is absolutely no excuse for a spelling mistake, or a grammatical error with today's spell checkers and other software. As well, your emails should not be sloppy or disorganized; they need to be carefully written, specific and easy to follow.

Over the years, I've reviewed hundreds of resumes, and I guarantee you that any resume with a spelling mistake, grammatical error or that didn't make complete sense, no matter how good the qualifications were, immediately got tossed into the shredder. If someone who is trying to get a job does not care, or try hard enough to submit an error-free resume, I do not under any circumstances want them working for me.

Emails are no different. It's one thing if you're writing to a friend where a small mistake may be acceptable once in awhile, but when you're trying to sell something (as the end result) to someone, it is completely unacceptable. If they see errors when you are trying to get their business, what is going to happen if you actually do business with them? Will your product have errors or mistakes as well? Will it work properly?

Not only do bad spelling and grammar look very unprofessional, but they also divert attention away from your message and consequently your sales. When you send emails, your customers will judge you by what you say and how you say it. Don't give them a reason to choose a competitor instead of you.

Since email is paperless people don't feel bad trashing it as they might if they receive a flyer in the mail. Most people certainly won't rip an ad out of a newspaper or magazine if it doesn't interest them. But they'll trash any emails they don't want in a heartbeat.

Testing is the only sure-fire way to tell what works and what doesn't. Studying and researching will help point you in the right direction and will enable you to make a very educated guess; but it is just that, a guess. In theory it may work, but in reality there might be something that prevents everything from working the way it should. Something may have been overlooked, or things might not pan out the way they should due to some unforeseen circumstance or obstacle. As I mentioned in Chapter 6, write a few variations of your message and send it out to a small sample of your list first. If you have a list of 10,000 addresses, you could send out four variations to 1,000 people each. Track the results to find out what version works best. At this point, you can either try tweaking the email that yielded the highest results, then test it again, or you can send it out the way it is to the rest of your list.

5 Simple Steps to Write an Email:

The Headline

Your headline is the first thing customers will see when they open your email. The headline will determine if a person is interested and reads further, or if they close the email. Putting headlines in quotes has been successfully proven to increase readership by 28%.

The Lead

Begin the communication in an interesting way. Your lead must be interesting, catching and cultivate the reader personally. Personalization is a definite must. The lead can also make or break your email as the subject can; if you can't motivate the reader to read on, they probably won't. Know your audience and write for them. Use a warm, friendly, conversational tone as if you are speaking directly to them.

The Body

Before you start writing, jot down the main purpose of the email and what you hope it will achieve. Decide what is most important and state that in the first paragraph. Don't leave any important information for a later paragraph, as some readers may not scroll past the first screen so it won't get read. You must know your target audience and to whom you are writing. Your emails should address the problem your customers face and offer a solution, your solution.

Sit down, and ask yourself: "Why do customers buy my product or service?" and "What problems am I solving for them?" Then write your message as a one-to-one communication. Pretend you're sitting down to talk to a friend. Focus on the reader, not yourself: try to use the words "you," "your" and "yours" frequently. Use the word "you" more than "we" or "I". People don't really care that much about how great you are; they care about how well you will meet their needs. By addressing them in the second person, you are unconsciously letting them know that they are the important ones, and in selling, that's vital psychology.

What are the benefits the reader would get from visiting your website or buying your product? Make them clear and relate them to the reader as specifically as you can. Explain the purpose of the email clearly to the subscriber. If you're trying to sell them something, let them know. If you are giving away free information, tell them. Explain the benefits. Use bullets if you need to.

If you went out of your way to get a special deal for the client, you need to make that offer unique or exclusive to the subscriber base that will be receiving it. Let them know how exclusive it is, then give them a strong reason to act immediately. Let them know that this special offer is only being made available to them and that it will only be available for a limited time.

The Call to Action

The last part of your message should spur readers to action. People don't know what action they should take unless you tell them. Create a strong call to action. A call to action can be as simple as a link they click on to find out more information. Make this link as enticing as possible. You could say, "click here to visit our website," but that doesn't really draw the reader in. Why not try, "Click here to preview 3 chapters of my new book." Giving them an incentive or reason to visit your website will definitely help get them there.

Always have a "P.S." After the headline, the P.S. is the second most frequently read part in the body of an email. Since it's more likely that it will get read, you should place you incentives there, along with a strong call to action.

Creating an irresistible email takes research, effort and some hard work, but pays off substantially when done.

Signatures and SIG Files

A signature is essentially a short block of text that can be automatically added to the end of an email message. The purpose of a signature is to identify the sender and provide some additional information about him or her. A SIG file is basically the same as a signature, except that it is a file that can automatically be attached to an email, with a .sig extension. The term SIG file is also used to identify blocks or groupings of text used for similar purposes through different forums such as discussion or newsgroup messages. For the purpose of simplicity, I'll be using the terms signature and SIG file interchangeably.

Your signature is really an extension of your identity and should be displayed proudly anytime you send an email, or post a message to newsgroups, message boards, or forums. Some moderated forums discourage and disallow any form of self-promotional signature so fully read the terms and conditions to get a feel for what is acceptable before posting.

You may be wondering to yourself, "What's the big deal with signatures?" The big deal is that they allow you to passively advertise wherever you go on the internet with very little effort. Signatures quietly and effectively tell everyone that you email, and anyone who reads a message you post (which can have a life span of a few years or more) who you are, what you do, and why you might be of benefit to them. A signature is a great way to identify yourself and promote your business passively for free at the same time.

An email signature is best limited to six lines or less. It needs to create curiosity, clearly state what you are offering and invite readers to click on a link to learn more - all in a nano-second - because that is about how much time you have to get the attention of the readers of your email. Keep the lines of your signature short and concise and easy to read quickly. Include only enough information to create curiosity to encourage the reader to click on the link to your website.

If you want the readers of your messages to click on the link to your website in your signatures, be sure your email is professional and attractive to the target group. I personally use several different signatures, depending on whom I'm replying to, or where I'm posting a message.

Most email programs have a feature that allows you to create and save multiple signatures and include them automatically in your emails. If you're not sure how to do this with the program you use, go to the help section, and type in "email signature" – it should provide detailed instructions. Some message boards allow you to save a signature that is automatically attached to any messages that you post. If it's not automatically attached, you can save your various signatures into a notepad document on your computer. Keep it open and when you are posting to a message board, just copy and paste the desired signature into your message. It's quick, easy and effective.

So what does an email signature look like? Quite often when a signature is used for a personal email it contains the person's name, maybe a famous quote, humorous saying, a funny message or some other such thing. With some email programs it's possible to rotate, or change the quote or saying at the bottom, so frequent recipients do not see the same message every time. Here's an example of a simple personal signature:

> *Cheers,*
>
> *Jon Halloway*
> *www.jonhalloway.blogger.com*
>
> *"It's been said that if you're going to quote someone, quote someone funny. But if you really want to be funny, misquote someone serious!"*
> *- origin unknown*

A business signature is a little different. It serves as a subtle statement that you're in business and is a legitimate way to have an ad on every email you send, or message you post. Your signature can include any of the following – your name, job title, company name, phone/fax number, email address, website, tag line, current offers and/or a brief benefit of your website, products or services. Always keep your signature short, concise and to the point. Remember, time is of the essence. Don't use visuals or graphics because they look too much like an ad and graphics may not show up in some text-only email programs. Here's an example of a signature that I might use to promote this book:

> Justin Michie
> Internet Marketing Specialist
> San Diego, California
>
> **WARNING!** *Don't waste another <u>PENNY</u> marketing online before you read this book:* **Street Smart Internet Marketing**
> Download 3 free chapters @ www.StreetSmartInternetMarketing.com

With a signature, you only have one chance to capture your reader's attention – make sure it's a good one.

This probably seems obvious, but when you're all done writing, don't forget to check the spelling, grammar and punctuation of your entire email. Take the time to edit your message for errors and for goodness sake, run the spellchecker. Even still, proofread for punctuation, spelling and proper grammar. It also helps to read it out loud: This will not only to make sure that your email is easy to read, but is also helpful in testing the tone to make sure it sounds friendly and informal. If possible, have some other people read over your email and get their feedback. Also don't forget to make sure all of your links work before you hit the send button.

22

Newsletters and Ezines

Publishing an email newsletter or ezine is the most direct and cost-effective methods to reach your target audience on a regular basis and build a quality lasting relationship with them. They also happen to be one of the most effective forms of marketing for your online business.

Reasons for publishing a newsletter (or ezine):

1. Sell advertising – this is one of the most common goals in ezine publishing, although it isn't recommended in certain situations.

2. Generate website traffic – newsletters and ezines are great at subtly reminding your subscribers to go back to your website and buy from you. Even if this isn't one of your explicit goals, your newsletter will probably do this anyway with a simple link back to your site.

3. Build trust and loyalty with your list of clients and prospective clients.

4. Establish yourself as an expert – an ezine is great at establishing yourself as an expert or authority in your area of expertise.

5. Promote your own products – if you have something to sell, a newsletter or ezine can be a great way to generate new business.

6. Network or make contacts – this involves publishing an ezine to meet others interested in the same topics, usually for business reasons.

7. Add value to something else – if you have a fancy "how to" course, having a specific newsletter published exclusively for people that bought that course can increase the perceived purchase price of the course.

The Distinction

Quite often the terms ezine and newsletter are used synonymously, which isn't entirely incorrect. Depending on who you ask, you'll probably get a variety of different definitions for the two terms. Although a newsletter and ezine share similar characteristics, they are not always the same thing.

A newsletter traditionally provides news or information to a specific interest group or target market. An example would be a real estate agent sending out a weekly newsletter on all the latest real estate market trends, properties for sale and so on. Newsletters are always emailed to the recipient and can be in text only, or HTML format. Newsletters are generally put together by a business to mail to their past customers or clients to keep in touch and usually do not contain any outside advertising from other businesses. Newsletters are generally shorter than an ezine and are usually sent more frequently.

An ezine is more like an electronic version of a print magazine. The "e" part of ezine, of course, stands for electronic. Most people assume the "zine" part is short for magazine. Many internet purists, though, believe it stands for fanzine; a word that usually refers to a low-budget print publication which covers a defined topic put out by a hardcore fan or enthusiast.

Ezines are almost always emailed in HTML format and sometimes recipient's are just emailed a link where they can view the ezine online. Publishers put out ezines to share information about a common topic of interest for anyone who wants to sign up; but usually the real goal behind publishing an ezine is to generate a source of advertising revenue. A large percentage of ezines are entertainment related covering topics such as sports, travel, theater, nightlife and so on.

For the sake of simplicity, I'm going to use the terms ezine and newsletter interchangeably for the rest of this book.

Newsletters (or Ezines)

A regularly published newsletter can be a very powerful promotional tool when used correctly. And it is something you should definitely use. It allows you to stay in touch with clients, past customers or prospects while constantly reminding them about your products and/or services and it helps you build credibility (which in turn builds trust) with everyone on your list.

Having a newsletter will allow you to keep in regular contact with your clients, for next to no money, and in a very small amount of time will establish you as an expert in your field. Your main goal should be to build a binding relationship between you and your list.

If you do decide to have a newsletter, it must be well done. A poorly written newsletter can actually do your business more harm than good. If your newsletter does not offer valuable information that is desirable to your list, it won't get read, and if it doesn't get read, it won't make you any money. Those that do subscribe will unsubscribe in the blink of an eye, and you'll lose any chance you ever had at doing any future business with them.

You don't write a newsletter so that people will buy from you right away, because most of them won't. But, it is extremely important for you to stay in touch with those prospects, until they are ready to make their decision. Your newsletter will help you build that bond until your subscribers do make their decision to buy from you.

Repetition is in the heart of marketing and the more someone hears about your products or services, the more likely they are to purchase it. With a newsletter you can continually and subtly present your products and services to your customers while offering them valuable information at the same time. That way they're happy, and you're happy because you make more sales.

Consistency

If you plan on sending a regular newsletter or ezine it's a good idea to use a template to keep things consistent. That way all your newsletters look and feel the same. It will also enable your readers to distinguish your newsletter instantly so as to not accidentally hit the delete button or report it as spam. It will also add a touch of professionalism and branding to your business.

Being consistent with your timing of the newsletter also helps. For example, if you send a newsletter every two weeks, aim to send it out on the same day, at the same time every two weeks.

For an example of what a properly formatted newsletter should look you can always visit www.JustinMichie.com and sign up for my newsletter.

Mailing Frequency

How often should you mail your newsletter or ezine? Well that's completely up to you, but keep this is mind what I said back in Chapter 17. Any less than once a month is too infrequent to build a quality relationship with your database. If you mail more than once a week and bombard your subscribers with email - you may lose some subscribers; and those you don't lose may not have the time to read it. If you're just starting out, until you become comfortable as a publisher, twice a month is fine. Then you can bump it up to weekly if you want, but it's up to you. In general, anything between once a week and once a month is considered kosher.

It's much better to send a short newsletter every week than to send one long one every month. People are busy and tend to put off reading long newsletters till later. I know I do.

Newsletter Content

Content

For your email newsletter to be effective, it has to be read. That means you'll have to work to make your newsletter issues so tantalizing that your subscribers will make opening your messages a priority. To do that you need you must offer useful content that informs, teaches, or enriches your audience. By doing so, your company's name and the products or services you offer are brought to the subscriber's attention each time he or she receives your newsletter. It's a great way to stay in touch with your customers and keep them coming back.

Most newsletters offer information in the form of:

- How to articles
- Tips, tricks or tactics
- Answers to common questions or concerns
- Discussions of newsworthy events or other related topics

Many newsletter owners don't want to write their own articles because they either don't have the time, or don't have the writing skills. Thankfully there are many alternatives to writing yourself. You can easily hire someone to do it for you for a small fee per article, or newsletter, or even give them a percentage of the advertising revenue it brings in. There are many writers, waiting for their big break that will be glad to write for you at a reasonable rate. Some of these writers can be found on websites like www.elance.com. There is also a huge supply of articles you can use on the internet for free. The only catch is you need to give the author credit for their work, which is usually included in the form of a byline or resource box at the bottom of the article, with a link back to their website. Just do a quick search for "article directories."

Always make sure you read and abide by the rules and stipulations that go along with using an article for free. Most articles can't be altered at all and some can't be used for paid newsletter subscriptions, so be sure to check first. Also, some newsletters have links in them to the author's website, or to an affiliate account of theirs. Some authors will allow you to replace the affiliate links with your own, and some won't. Read the rules, if you can replace the affiliate links, it's probably worth doing.

If you're going to write your own content, write as though you are speaking to a friend and keep the tone conversational. Some people actually record a conversation with a friend, get it transcribed and turn it into an article. This is especially useful if you're just starting out and are a little unsure, or if you're a particularly bad or slow typist. Also, don't write in tech jargon. Not only will this confuse some readers, it also might bore them to death.

The easiest way to decide what to write about in your newsletters is to ask your list. You could have something at the bottom of the newsletter that might say "Have a question or an idea for an article? Simply reply to this email with your thoughts." I usually get a fair number of questions from my websites each week and they give me a good idea of what people want to know about. Alternatively, you could look at the topics in newsgroups and forums to see what's hot.

Other things you could have in your newsletter are lists of how to tips, book reviews, freebies (such as a free ebook or special report), product reviews (with your affiliate link), information about you, your website or business and more.

You can also inform your readers of other websites that would might help them out, in your subject area. Write a short review to go along with the link including why this site might help your readers. If the site sells something, sign up for an affiliate link, and use that to link to the site. The same goes for product reviews. Whenever you link to another site, always include an affiliate link if you can. It's a subtle way to make money from a newsletter and it sure beats blatant ads.

Make sure there are no careless mistakes in your newsletter such as spelling or grammar. A newsletter can be loaded with good content, but if it looks like it was put together by a child, it doesn't say much for your business.

Length

Keep your newsletter relatively short. If you want to include several articles, use a table of contents at the top of the newsletter. Here's an example:

1. *Effective Email Marketing Part 1*
2. *Good Adwords – What You Didn't Know*
3. *Certified Email – Messages of Tomorrow*

Many newsletters email only the headlines and the first few sentences or so of the actual articles. That way, if it's something the recipient is interested in they can follow a link to a website where they can read the rest of the article. That way people aren't scrolling through articles they don't want to read and the actual email isn't more than a page or so long.

Ezine Advertising

Depending on the type of newsletter or ezine you offer and the number of subscribers you have, you may want to consider placing ads throughout. Think about this for a second. For every 1,000 subscribers you have, you can charge about $25 for an ad. Let's say that you have 5 ads per issue, and 52 issues (weekly circulation) per year. With some simple math ($25 x 5 x 52) you could make $6,500 a year in advertising revenue for every 1,000 subscribers you have. Let's look at what this means:

Subscribers	Ad cost per 1,000	Ads per issue	Issues per year	Total sales per year
1,000	$25	5	52	$6,500
1,000	$25	10	52	$13,000
10,000	$25	5	52	$65,000
10,000	$25	10	52	$130,000
100,000	$25	5	52	$650,000
100,000	$25	10	52	$1,300,000

In advertising alone, how much is one subscriber worth to you? With the above example, take your yearly sales ($6,500) and divide it by the number of subscribers (1,000) and you'll see that each subscriber is worth $6.50 a year. If that's not incentive enough to build your list, I don't know what is. Remember, before you can start selling ad space, you need a minimum of at least 1,000 subscribers, but the more the merrier.

Once you get enough subscribers, advertisers may start to come to you and then again, they may not. It's always a good idea to have a little text ad at the bottom of your newsletter letting subscribers know that ad space is available. You should also have a link to your website where you can post the rates, number of subscribers you have, specifications and your contact info.

Mailing a Newsletter

If you have more than a few handfuls of subscribers you'll need email broadcast software to send out the emails for you. If you're a 1StartCart user (www.1StartCart.com), they have an excellent broadcast email capability built right into their system. If you don't need a shopping cart system, simply sign up for their autoresponder service to get the same capabilities. Alternatively, you can purchase a program like Infacta's Groupmail available at www.infacta.com, that allows you to send broadcast email right from your computer.

Effective Newsletter Promotion

When you own an online business, your opt-in mailing list is your lifeline to your potential customers. Building this list and developing loyal readers is very important. To do this effectively, there are numerous ways of promoting your newsletter. Some of these promotion strategies are more involved than others, but they are all effective if you partake in them consistently.

Before a visitor leaves your site, it is important to get them onto your list, otherwise you might never see them again. In order to get the most subscribers, place a prominent signup form on each page of your website. As I mentioned before, be sure to do your own tests to see which placement works best for your signup form, don't forget to offer an ethical bribe.

Promote your newsletter or ezine just as you would your website. Some simple ways to promote your newsletter include:

- Ad swaps with other related newsletter publishers
- Listing your newsletter in specialty newsletter directories
- Using PPC or paid search engine ads
- Having an opt-in button on product order forms
- Email joint ventures
- Banner or graphical ads
- Text ads
- And much, much more

Section 4

Search Engine Optimization

23

How Search Engines Work

At any given time approximately 25% of all people searching on the internet are searching for sex-related material. The good news is that the other 75% are searching for something else. A good portion of the something else includes "how to" tips or information, entertainment-related fields, world affairs, politics and news. You just need to make sure you tap into one of these main fields.

If you go to your favorite search engine and type in anything, nearly instantly the search engine will sort through millions of webpages and present you with ones that match your topic. The matches will even be ranked, so that the most relevant ones come first. Of course, the search engines don't always get it right, but by and large they do a fantastic job.

According to a study by IMT Strategies Research, 46% of websites are found the first time through the use of a search engine. Just that fact alone makes search engines a very important part of the internet and of your total marketing plan.

Most people don't look past the first few pages of search results, so if your listing doesn't show up there, then you're out of luck. The higher your website is ranked, the more people will visit your webpage – for free. Although there is no set formula to achieve a high ranking, the goal of this section is to give you as much information as possible to get your site as close to the top as possible.

Search engines are a great way to get new prospects to your website and since they are mostly free, it is very important that you utilize them to the fullest. Search engine optimization (SEO) is a very confusing and technically challenging subject.

Search engine optimization means ensuring that your webpages are accessible to search engines and are focused in ways that help improve the chances they will be found, and ranked favorably as related to your site's content.

Basic site optimization may involve nothing more than ensuring that your website actually shows up in the major search engines. Advanced SEO can include significant research into every element of page design, site structure and off-the-page criteria to get you listed in the top results.

A large part of optimizing webpages is finding relevant keywords, determining their popularity, assessing the amount of competition and deciding which keywords can be best supported with quality content.

Getting your website listed in the search engines is actually quite simple, but getting it ranked high enough to make a significant difference, is a much more difficult and complicated task. In fact, there are books, companies and individuals that devote their entire business life to getting you to the top.

An important thing to know and recognize about search engines is that they're not working for you; the reason they exist is for people who are searching for things. Search engines primarily make their money by being able to sell ad space based on the number of people who use their site. The better their content and listings are, the more people will use their site and the more money they can justifiably charge.

Many websites appear poorly in search engine rankings, or don't appear at all, simply because they fail to consider how search engines work.

This next section provides information, techniques and a good grounding in the basics of search engine optimization. By using this information where appropriate, you may tap into potential customers who may have previously missed your site.

Please note: This section is not a guide on ways to trick or spam the search engines. Realistically, there aren't any big secrets that will guarantee a top listing. However there are a number of small changes you can make to your website that can potentially produce huge results.

How They Work

The term search engine is actually used quite loosely; all "search engines" aren't really search engines. There are actually two categories of what are commonly known as search engines. There are the actual search engines like Google, Lycos etc. and then there are human-powered directories, of which Yahoo! is the most well known. It is important to distinguish that these two types of search engines gather their listings in radically different ways.

Search Engines

A search engine is a collection of links and descriptions that are gathered and organized into a huge database. Search engines find information for their database one of two ways: by accepting submission forms from people who want their website to gain exposure, or by getting the information from what is commonly referred to as a "web crawler," "spider," or "robot," which are just different names for the same thing.

A web crawler is a computer program that works by visiting webpages that are in its database, then following the links on these pages to other webpages. As it goes along, everything the crawler finds, it sends back to the search engine to be indexed or cataloged. This is what it means when someone refers to a site being "spidered" or "crawled." The index, (also sometimes called the catalog or database), is like a giant book containing a copy of every webpage that the spider comes across.

If you have a something on a site that you do not want indexed by a crawler (such as a paid membership site), you can let them know using a robots.txt file. A robots.txt file is located in the root directory of your site (www.YourDomain.com/robots.txt) and instructs crawlers what you want indexed and what you don't want available in the search engine's results. For a free robots.txt file generator, go to www.seochat.com/seo-tools/robots-generator.

Web crawlers will periodically return to your site to look for changes. So if one of your webpages change, crawler-based search engines will eventually find these changes and update their databases. Also, if you make changes you think will increase your page ranking, you can go directly to the search engine site and click on the "add site" or "submit your site" link, then follow the instructions to add you site to the list to be crawled.

As a general rule, if a webpage is ranked fairly high, don't change or resubmit it, as your ranking may drop. If a page isn't doing too well, you can try making some changes then resubmit it every few weeks until the ranking becomes more favorable. Be patient, sometimes it can take awhile for new pages or changes that the spider finds to be added to the index. A webpage may have been "crawled" but not yet "indexed."

When you perform a search in your favorite search engine, the search engine software (different software from the spider) sifts through the millions of pages recorded in its index to find matches to your search, which it then ranks in the order of what it believes to be most relevant.

Directories

A directory is a listing of websites (usually in alphabetical order) organized by category. The only way to get your website listed in a directory is to submit your site directly to the directory. When a website is submitted, prior to acceptance and it being indexed, it is reviewed by a real person.

Directories require websites to adhere to rigid guidelines in order to be included in their indexes. Directory reviewers are very busy, and if they don't agree with the category you chose, they're not likely to correct it for you. As a result, directories' indexes are very thorough, accurate and contain a comparatively small number of high-quality links.

Perhaps the most important thing to know about directories is that changing your webpage has no effect on your listing, but it does have an affect on being listed in the first place. Things that are useful for improving a listing with a search engine (meta tags, title, keywords) have nothing to do with improving a listing in a directory. Therefore, no search engine optimization is necessary for directory-only listings. What's important here are the title and description that you use when submitting your site to the directory and the keywords contained in them.

Always read all the directions and rules for submission. Some directories (and search engines) will give you some really valuable tips about how to get the most out of your listing. Others will only list the terms and conditions for being listed.

To register with a directory an online form must be completed and submitted for review. This is rather time consuming, as a different form should be submitted for each webpage you submit, to each directory. You can either do this yourself or have someone do it for you. I always do this part myself, for the very reason, that once the form is submitted and your site is accepted, you usually can't make any changes to the way your site is listed in the directory – so take the time to do it right the first time. A mistake or error could have a huge impact in your online search engine presence.

Many directories allow you to enter in the description and keywords for your site exactly as you would like them to appear after selecting the category you want it cited under. Directories will not list your site and will never become aware of it until you register it with them.

It takes time for your site and the thousands of others submitted daily, to be reviewed and approved, so getting listed in a directory can take a few months or more. Be patient. Most directories usually don't confirm placements so keep checking back to see if your site has been indexed. Some of the most popular directories are:

www.yahoo.com
www.dmoz.org
www.directory.google.com

Hybrid Search Engines

In the earlier days of the internet, a search engine was a search engine and a directory was a directory. Hybrid search engines combine a directory with a search engine to give their visitors the most relevant and complete results. Today the top ten search sites are hybrids. For example, Yahoo! started out as a directory, but around 2002 it supplemented its manually compiled listings with search results from Google. Then in February 2004, Yahoo! announced it would start displaying its own crawler based results. On the other hand, Google uses Open Directory Project's (dmoz.org) directory to enrich its automatically generated listings. Hybrid search engines usually favor one type of listing over another; for example, Yahoo! favors its directory listings.

Submitting Your Site

Most submission forms ask you for a brief title of your site, as well as a short description and your email address. The title and description are very important and something you should prepare ahead of time. You need to give as much care (rewriting, proofreading, spell checking etc. to the title and description as you would give to your most important copy. Each search engine allows a different number of characters, or words for your title and description, so write a description with 20 words, 25 words and 50 words and so on. The title and description should be filled with as many keywords as possible, while keeping the description in logical, well written sentences. The title you give to your page will usually be the title displayed in the listing, so make sure it is good as it's what most users scan through first when deciding which listing they will click on.

When filling out the application, be sure to fill in all the information even if it is optional. Your application could be rejected simply because you failed to provide enough information about your site. Always be truthful – most of the time websites are visited by a spider or a person before they are listed and any falsified information could get your application quashed.

Some people are under the impression that the more you submit your site to a search engine the higher in rankings it will be. This is the rule I use: If your webpage is doing well in the rankings - and continues to do well, leave it alone. If your webpage is not doing so well, you can try to resubmitting it to search engines every few weeks (changing it a little each time) until you obtain a more favorable ranking.

When submitting a site to a search engine you have several choices (ranked in order from best to worst):

1. You can do it manually and painstakingly submit each site by hand. This is by far the best way and the effort and time it requires will pay off many times

over in only a short time. Go the homepage of the search engine and click on the link that says "add your site," "suggest a site" or "register URL." In some directories like Yahoo, you need to go to the actual category where you want to list your site. Click on the "add your site" link and follow the instructions. Always remember to take the time and do things right, some search engines and directories don't allow updates or revisions.

2. You can hire a company to do it for you. If you've spent much time on the internet you've probably seen the ads "Top 10 Search Engine Placement – Guaranteed!" While nobody can 100% guarantee that they can get you into the top ten listings, they can certainly try. If you decide to go this route, make sure you hire a reputable company with a strong money back guarantee. The fees charged by these companies are usually quite large, as they spend a lot of time researching and analyzing competitor's sites and various search engine ranking systems. It's also important to note that these companies usually do much more than submit your site; they optimize each webpage specifically for the search engines they are submitting it to. Find out more about this in upcoming chapters.

3. Buy a software program to do it for you. The only real benefit of doing it this way is that you can easily and quickly submit your site to many of the smaller, insignificant search engines, which may save a lot of time on your part. Many search engines are reported to place automated submissions in a lower priority. Some, like AltaVista, require a registration code (which is text hidden in a graphic that a computer can't read) to submit a site, thereby cutting out automatic computer generated registrations.

4. Auto-submit your site using a free web service. There many websites that claim to register your site with as many as 10,000 search engines for free (as far as actual money is concerned). In return, some require you to add your name to the mailing list. You'll generally have you fill in an information form, and their computer program automatically submits your site for you. This is similar to purchasing a software program to do it for you – only the website runs the program and it doesn't cost you any money. I don't recommend you go this route – the quality of submissions are low, it doesn't work with sites that use registration codes and it is unlikely to make a noticeable difference in your web traffic. In fact submitting using a free service can do more harm than good, by devaluing the ranking of any previously submitted sites.

How Long Does it Take to Get Listed?

Some search engines will search for a site immediately, verify that it exists and add it to its database right away. Others will take two to four to six weeks or more. The Open Directory Project had been rumored to take up to a year or more because of backlogs. Some search engines and/or directories also allow you to pay a set fee to get your site listed much more quickly. Yahoo! is one of these and currently charges $299 to get your site reviewed and if accepted, listed within seven days, whereas it might otherwise take a couple months or so.

24

Playing the Game:
How Search Engines Rank Webpages

Different Engines, Different Rankings

One thing all website owners want is for their website to rank well in the major search engines. To do this you need to, at the very least, show up in the first page of results, which usually means in the top ten. No search engine strategy will immediately propel your site to the top of the rankings. Sometimes you may need to wait weeks or months before the spiders visit and index your site. After the first visit, they may not return for a long time, so be sure your site is ready before you submit it to search engines.

Every search engine uses its own unique formula, called an algorithm, to index and score websites. Search engines' algorithms give a different weight to various elements of your site, such as the title of the webpage, meta tags, keywords, page design and layout to rank pages in their search results. By constantly refining and improving their algorithms, search engines strive to give their visitors the most relevant results. Search engines keep their algorithms secret for competitive reasons and to prevent people from making pages that spam them.

Even though some search engines rely on very similar factors in composing their rankings, they may still rank the same site quite differently. For example, imagine two search engines that only use meta tags and keyword density to rank webpages. One search engine may weigh both meta tags and keyword density equally at 50% each, while the other may weigh keywords at 80% of the site's value and meta tags at the other 20%; which would make their results completely different.

Understanding Ranking Factors

Before we can understand how each search engine score websites, we need to understand the various factors they consider. These factors can be divided into two categories: Inside factors, also sometimes referred to as on-the-page factors. This is anything that has something to do with the design/content/coding of your webpage. Some examples of inside factors are: meta tags, keywords, site layout, design and title. The second category is outside, or off-the-page factors. This is everything that happens outside the actual HTML of your site, some which you have very little control of. This includes things such as the number of incoming links to your site or the number of click-throughs your listing gets in the search engine.

Inside Factors

Using Your HTML Title Effectively

An HTML title describes the contents of your webpage in one sentence. The title is tricky, as it needs to appeal to both search engines and your visitors. It is also likely to appear in search engine listings and in will appear in people's bookmarks. Every webpage should have a unique title that gives a short, one sentence description of what the page is about, while containing two-to-three content related keywords.

It's also important to note that your title is the first thing a search engine's spider sees on your page, and as far as most search engines are concerned, the title is one of the most important elements of your webpage. Your title should appear in your HTML code, directly under the <head> tag. If you're using a software program such as FrontPage, or Dreamweaver you may want to quickly check and make sure it is placed correctly. Having it placed below its usual hangout could severely decrease its power and cost you rankings.

Also be careful not to repeat a keyword more than two times in a title, otherwise some search engines may see this as spamming and ban, block, or decrease your sites ranking.

The title of your webpage is also the title that shows up in most search engines results, as the title that a searcher sees along with the description of your site, so it also needs to be searcher appealing.

Longer titles are better than shorter titles simply because they contain more keywords and allow you more of a description to convince searchers to visit your site.

Keyword Frequency, Density, Prominence and Proximity

There are many issues to consider when placing keywords into the text of your pages. Most search engines index the full text of each page, so it's vital to place keywords throughout your text. However, each search engine uses different ranking algorithms. Difficult though it may be, you need to keep all of them in mind. Make sure your main page is full of keywords.

Some engines rank a page high if it has at least 100 words, so make that your minimum content. Some directories rank pages based on the quality of their content, so make sure your pages aren't simply lists of keywords.

Many search engines also value keywords contained in H1 and H2 HTML tags (header tags) for headlines and subheadings, and sometimes bullets are even deemed more relevant than the general text found in the body of the webpage. The assumption is that header tags (and bullets) are used to highlight the most important items or themes that appear on a page which makes them important.

Keyword Prominence

The best place to place keywords in the text of your webpage is right at the top of the main page. Most web crawlers assume that any page relevant to the topic will mention these words right at the beginning. This concept is known as "keyword prominence." You'll frequently see it used to describe search engines' algorithms. Some engines also say the bottom of the page is another important place for keywords.

Beware! Search engines view pages differently than people do. Here's a quick example:

Home	About Us	Contact Us

*At **Widgets** International, our business is selling **widgets**.*

You may think you did pretty well by placing the keyword "widgets" at the top of your page. A search engine, however, sees your page this way:

"Home About Us Contact Us At **Widgets** International, our business is selling **widgets**."

Try to place keyword-rich text at the *very* top of your page. If your navigation system currently uses text links and is at the top of your page, make it graphical so the first text the search engine sees can be relevant.

Keyword Proximity

Some search engines, such as Google, use the concept of keyword proximity as part of their ranking formulas. As suggested by the name, "keyword proximity" means the how close keywords are to each other. By putting your keywords as close together as possible and making sure your sentences are clear, concise, and make perfect sense you're likely to rank better. Here's an example:

1. *Smith Brothers has been selling **puppy food** for more than fifty years.*
2. *Smith Brothers has been selling **food** for your **puppy** more than fifty years.*

The two keywords are obviously "puppy" and "food." If a user searches for "puppy food," the first sentence will rank higher because its keywords are closer to each other.

Keyword Density

Keyword density measures the relationship of your keywords as compared to other text on the webpage. The higher the percentage of keywords in relationship to other text, the higher the keyword density is.

Here's an example of how it's measured. Let's assume the keyword phrase is "*beach volleyball.*"

***Beach volleyball** is my favorite outdoor sport.*

Since the keywords "beach volleyball" show up two times out of six, the keyword density is 33%, which is excellent. However, keep in mind that the text on your page needs to make sense and interest the reader, not only the search engines. The sentence above isn't worded as smoothly as it could be, but to word it better, we give up keyword density. Your job is to find a happy medium between both.

Realistically, keyword density is never as high as 33%. The recommended keyword density is 3-7%, per keyword or keyword phrase. This means you should repeat all your keywords three-to-seven times for every 100 words of content on your webpage. Imagine trying to do this if you have ten or fifteen keywords. Not only is this very impractical, but it is also virtually impossible. Remember your copy needs to make coherent sense to reader. Instead, pick at least two, but no more than five keywords per page and repeat them throughout the copy.

Keyword Frequency

Keyword frequency is a measure of the number of times keywords occur within a page's text. It's tied to the concept of keyword density. Search engines want to see more than one repetition of a keyword in your text to make sure it's not an isolated case. The recommended keyword repetition is three-to-seven times per page, any more than that and it might be considered spamming. Also, always include at least 100 words on a page: remember searches are looking for valuable content, and that's what search engines hope to give them. Any less than 100 words and the page's content is deemed to be indemnifiable.

Also avoid search engine spamming. Don't be tempted to use tiny or invisible text to put keywords at the beginning of your pages. Search engines define this behavior as spam and can reject your site for it. Also sites that list keywords and/or repeat them over and over can also be rejected for keyword spamming.

Proper Use of Meta Tags

The meta description and keyword tags describe your site's content, giving search engines' spiders an accurate summary filled with multiple keywords. Meta tags are hidden in a document's source code; the search engines can see them, but they visitors can't (unless of course they view your source code). Some search engines, however, use it as a site's summary on their results pages. If they do, the reader may actually see this hidden tag, so make sure its contents are somewhat enticing to the reader.

Meta tags are incredibly important to some search engines and others couldn't care less about them. There are a handful of search engines that use only meta tags to rank webpages, although the weight of meta tags in general is dropping across the board. Search engines don't penalize sites that use meta tags properly, so it's recommended that you always include them.

Here's an example of what a meta description tag looks like in the HTML coding:

```
<HTML>
<head>
<meta name="description" content="Your sites description goes here.">
</head>
</HTML>
```

The meta description tag should contain multiple keywords organized in a logical sentence. Place the keywords at the beginning of your description and close to each other to achieve the best possible rankings. Search engines vary in their preferred size for meta tags. Anywhere between 150-200 characters is the standard accepted size.

Meta keyword tags are much the same, except that they are a short list of keywords. For more on meta tags, refer back to Chapter 12.

Also, avoid repeating keywords more than three-to-seven times in your meta description - some search engines also consider that to be spam.

Using ALT Tags

Search engines don't see images and they won't index any text that is presented or embedded in an image format. To help fix this problem, there are ALT tags. An ALT tag provides an alternative text when non-textual page elements (images or graphics) cannot be displayed. If someone is using a text-only web browser (handheld device such as a cell phone), or on a slow dialup connection has their images turned off, or if an image is no longer available, an ALT tag would take the images place on the user's screen. Also, if you hold your mouse over an image with an ALT tag, the tag will be displayed in a little box in the surfer's browser.

ALT tags are not commonly used on most webpages, whether it's the smallest personal page or a million dollar corporate website. However, if properly used, ALT tags can be quite useful in helping achieve higher search engine rankings, among their other benefits. Search engines also don't penalize for using ALT tags or even for packing them with keywords, so there's no reason not to use them. Still, to be safe you should adhere to the generally accepted rule of not repeating keywords more than three-to-seven times.

An ALT tag embedded in an image link HTML looks like this:

```
<img src="http://www.YourDomain.com/YourImage.gif" alt="alt tag goes here">
```

Always add ALT tags to your images to make sure search engines recognize all the content on your site. ALT tags filled with keywords can also be used to boost your keyword frequency and will help you achieve better rankings.

Note: ALT tags also make your site more accessible to visually impaired people using text readers. That's because text readers can't read images, but they can detect text in ALT tags.

Comment Tags

Comment tags provide a way for webmasters to make notes right on their pages. They're hidden in the HTML code and so are not visible to the site's ordinary users, but some search engines can index them. That means comment tags are another great way to add keywords to your site, thus increasing keyword frequency. Always abide by the keyword frequency rule, don't use keywords more than three-to-seven times. This is what a comment tag looks like in the HTML coding of your site:

```
<!--please keep your comments to yourself-->
```

Frames Can Kill

Some of the major search engines cannot follow frame links, or will not index them properly. Most search engines will index each page within a frame window as a separate page. That means that if the matching search query is in one of the panes, the visitor will only be brought to that page, not the full frames page as it was designed. Avoid them if at all possible, or make sure there is an alternative method for search engines to enter and index your site.

Outside Factors

Link Popularity

Link popularity can do a lot for your site. Not only will many search engines rank you higher, but links from other sites will also drive more traffic to you. A growing number of search engines are beginning to use link popularity in their ranking algorithms. Google uses it as its most important PageRank factor in ranking sites. HotBot, AltaVista, MSN and others also use link popularity in their formulas. Eventually every major engine will probably use link popularity, so developing and maintaining backlinks are essential to your search engine placement.

Search engines use sophisticated formulas to gauge how popular sites are based on more than just a measure of how many links point to your site. In general, however, link popularity is measured by the following three factors:

1. **Relevance** – Search engines prioritize incoming links from pages that are relevant to the page in question. If you sell gardening tools, a link from a gardening tool manufacturer boosts your rankings more than one from a antiques discussion forum.

2. **Number of links** – The more, the better. Though lots of irrelevant links are less effective than a few relevant ones, they're better than nothing as they may still generate a little traffic to your site.

3. **Link text** – The text used to describe a link can also affect your rankings. These three links all point to the same URL but use different text:

   > StreetSmartInternetMarketing.com – is somewhat relevant
   > Internet Marketing Tips – is most relevant
   > Click here – is not at all relevant

4. **Page importance** – The more important the page linking to your site is, the more it can do to positively boost your ranking. For example, a link from CNN is much more important than a link from Aunt Eddie's rock collection site.

Most search engines spiders figure that any words other sites use to describe your site are particularly relevant. So, if a lot of sites linking to you use keywords in their link text, search engines will boost your ranking for those keywords.

Search engines won't automatically know every time you develop a new link. Since link popularity is search engine specific and since each site has its own unique database, you need to make sure that sites linking to you are indexed by every engine. You can submit pages with links to your site to search engines, so they can be crawled/indexed and start affecting your link popularity more quickly. It is always a good idea to check and see if the search engine has already registered the link before you go around submitting sites. This will save time and frustration.

To check the link popularity of your site, go to www.linkpopularity.com, which has a free popularity checker.

Click Popularity

Click popularity is the measure of the number of clicks received by each site in a search engine's results page. For example, let's say that 100 users search for "tropical fish." If after scanning the first 10 results, 97 users click on *"Tropical Fish Feeding and Care"* a click tracking technology assumes that the site *"Tropical Fish Feeding and Care"* is more relevant than the others. Next time someone searches for "tropical fish" *"Tropical Fish Feeding and Care"* will appear higher in the results.

The real only way to boost your click popularity is to see what text the various search engines use in your listing and then make it better. Most search engines use one of, or a combination of following: your page title, the first few lines of text on your webpage, part of your meta description, description or keywords you entered when submitting your site to the search engine.

Both click popularity and stickiness allow the search engine users to rank sites rather than web crawling software or site reviewers.

Stickiness

Stickiness is a measure of the amount of time a user spends at a website. It's calculated according to the time that elapses between each of the user's clicks on the search engine's results page, or how long it is until the user clicks the back button in their browser.

An example could be when you perform a search for "chicken recipe." You get the standard results page with 10 results listed in order of relevancy, click on one of the links and surf the website for 2 minutes. It turns that it doesn't quite have what you're looking for, so you try another site that turns out to be junk and spend less than 5 seconds on it before you try another. Click tracking technologies record the time between your clicks and use that time to determine each site's relevance. The longer your visit the website, the stickier the site is (in theory) and the better it will do in the results ranking next time. It is important to note that stickiness is not used by many search engines, as it is hard to track and the results can be easily skewed.

Search Engines and Themes

A theme is defined by search engines as a common topic throughout an entire site. Another way to think about it is that some of your most important keywords are used consistently throughout your site. In an effort to provide their users with more relevant information, search engines developed sophisticated technology that "extracts" website's themes. This technology allows results to be more focused on relevant sites for the topic searched for, instead of individual webpages.

Theme technology is used by some of the major search engine's formulas or algorithms to index and rank sites. They are used by AltaVista, Lycos and Google.

Also, when a Yahoo! reviewer is reviewing sites, sites that have a common theme will receive a higher ranking than one that is all over the place.

Site Design

Your site's design plays a major in role in your visitor's decision to either stick around and look at your content or continue surfing to another site. Graphics, layout, load time, fonts and ease of navigation can all influence the user. To craft a site that retains visitors, make it fast, clean and pleasant. The basic principal is do everything you can to keep them on your site for as long as possible. Not only can that help improve your search engine ranking, but it will help your sales as well.

Aside from attracting and retaining visitors, your site's design is critical for search engine positioning. Directories, such as Yahoo!, manually review your site before accepting it. Directory editors look for sites with good design to add to their indexes. Any editor from a directory will tell you that a site using "This page is under construction," message won't be listed. Visitors don't enjoy "construction" areas either. Don't submit to directories, or even search engines for that matter, until you have your whole site up.

Domain Names

Domain names are another great place for keywords. If relevant keywords are contained in the domain name, it carries more weight with almost all search engines, than keywords found in the text of the webpage. Shorter or top-level domain names with keywords generally carry more weight than really long domain names.

For instance, if all other factors are the same, the domain name InternetMarketing.com would rank higher than MarketingOnTheInternet.com, for the keywords "internet marketing."

More recently, search engines have begun to prioritize the use of keywords in a site's domain name, in their ranking formulas. Google and Yahoo! are two of the search engines that do this.

Capitalizing on Alphabetical Priority

Some smaller search engines use alphabetical hierarchy in their ranking formulas. But more importantly, directories such as Yahoo! and the Open Directory Project list sites in alphabetical order in their directory or categorical listings.

Alphabetical priority is a way of ordering files based on the alphabetical hierarchy of the characters in their names. A site called "**A** Cut Above," would get listed before a site named "**B**ob's Hair Care," because **A** comes before **B** in the alphabet. Numbers and special characters (@, #, & etc.) usually get listed above all numbers and letters in an alphabetical hierarchy system. Consequentially a site titled "**123** EZ Hair Care" would be listed before "**A** Cut Above," but a site with the name "**#1** Hair Care," would usually be listed at the top of the list. It is generally accepted that symbols come before numbers and numbers come before letters in alphabetical listings. Although, you should note that each search engine may have its own unique styling system (pun intended).

Some (not many) search engines and directories even take into account the actual name of the webpage HTML file (mypage.html) which they use for both alphabetical priority and keywords.

Stop the spam – don't try to mislead the directories. You know the game in the yellow pages – who can be listed #1? One company might call themselves "AAA Carpet Cleaning" and another "123 Steam Clean" in a fight to try and get listed at the top of the pile. That doesn't work so well in search engines. Unless your business name and/or domain name is www.AAACarpetCleaning.com don't title directory submissions as such. You risk being rejected on the spot. Remember, directories are reviewed by human editors who can confirm your actual business name.

Since all search engines rank sites a little differently, some website owners elect to create a special optimized landing page for each of the major search engines. So, in the next chapter we're going to concentrate on some of the top search engines and how they individually rank webpages.

25

Insider Search Engine Secrets

If you want to achieve the absolute best search engine rankings possible, you really need to design a webpage specifically for each major search engine. In order to that, you need to know how each specific search engine works and how they determine how your page will be ranked.

Before we get more in-depth in this section, I want to make it clear that there is no guaranteed way to get ranked number one in any search engine. Search engines use a complicated algorithm to calculate how they rank and display their results which they keep ultra secret. That being said, no one knows exactly how to achieve a perfect ranking. So the best I can do is give you an educated guess based on what I know works for me and what I know has worked for other people.

Search engines also change their algorithms all the time and although they aren't prone to make major changes sporadically, they are constantly revising their formulas so as to return the best results possible. Therefore something that worked today might not work tomorrow.

Since a lot of work goes into optimizing a webpage for a specific search engine, you probably want to start optimizing your pages for the most popular search engine and work your way down from there. The following chart shows the most popular search engines in the Us as of July 2006, according to Nielsen/NetRatings.

Rank	Search Engine	Market Share
1	Google	49.2%
2	Yahoo	23.8%
3	MSN Search	9.6%
4	AOL	6.3%
5	Ask	2.6%
6	Other	8.5%

Source: Nielsen/NetRatings

Google

Since Google is the most popular search engine, it seems the logical place to start. Google is the most important crawler-based search engine, not only because it is the most popular, but because it also powers the main results of several other search engines including AOL, Netscape and several smaller search engines.

The best way to get listed with Google is to build links to your website. This is also the single biggest factor in determining what sites are indexed by Google, as well as determining their relevancy. Google also likes sites that look more like news articles, or genuine information. The age of a site, or how long it has been around also has some play.

Crawlers follow links, so if you have lots of links pointing to your website, chances are a crawler will find and include your pages. Google also provides an "add URL" that lets you submit your site your site directly to its crawler, though there is no guarantee your site will get listed. To manually submit your site, go to www.google.com/addurl. According to Google, it updates its index every four weeks, so it may take up to that long to be listed and your ranking may also fluctuate during this time period due to the small changes they often make.

Google, like any crawler-based search engine, doesn't have the ability to index any sites that are password restricted, or database based sites like a search engine.

When someone performs a search in Google, Google needs to do two things before it presents the results according to ranking. First it determines the webpages that contain the search keywords and ranks them in the order of relevance. Then Google determines the importance of each page based on its PageRank algorithm (discussed on the next page). The final results that Google presents are a combination of relevance and importance, which form the heart of Google's scoring system. I should note that there are also more than 100 other factors that Google uses in its ranking algorithm, their keyword relevance and PageRank just happen to have the most influence.

Keyword Relevance

If a surfer performs a search in Google for "internet marketing" Google will look into its index for webpages containing those keywords. Google however goes far beyond the number of times a term appears on a page. It also examines all aspects of the page's content (and the content of the pages linking to it) to determine if it's a good match for your query. Google takes a close look at keyword usage density, and how close the keywords are in relation to each other to help determine rankings. However, some pages which clearly have very close keyword densities, for some undetermined reason achieve a lower ranking than pages with a lower keyword density.

Google ranks based on the keyword relevance according to the following criteria:

- Pages that contain the phrase "internet marketing," will rank higher than pages that contain both "internet" and "marketing" as separate words.

- Pages that contain just one of the keywords will be deemed as less relevant and rank lower than pages that contain both keywords.

- Webpages with page titles that contain the keyword phrase "internet marketing" will tell Google that this page is more relevant than others.

- The closer keywords are placed to each other, the more important the webpage is in the eyes of Google and the higher ranking it will achieve.

- The number of outgoing links and the keywords that are used to describe them. If your links are relevant to the content of your page it helps, as long as you don't have too many links on your page.

- And of course a page that contains the term "internet marketing" several times is likely to be ranked more relevant than a page that contains the term only once or twice. However a webpage that contains the keywords or phrase too many times (more than six or seven) may be thought as keyword spamming, therefore lowering the relevancy.

- Google also uses page titles and headers to help determine the relevance of targeted keyword phrases, so if the keyword(s) appear in headers, titles and near the top of the page, this should increase the relevance.

Google's PageRank Importance

After Google retrieves the relevant pages from its index and ranks them by keyword relevance, it also uses its PageRank algorithm to evaluate them. Google's PageRank algorithm is based largely upon the number and quality of backlinks a webpage has, which is also known as link popularity. Google interprets a link from page A to page B as a vote, by page A, for page B. However, Google looks at more than the sheer volume of votes; it also looks at the quality of page that cast the vote. Votes cast by high ranking or high profile websites (like Amazon, CNN etc.) may be many hundreds of times more important than a link from a Mom and Pop website, and therefore be worth hundreds of times the points relatively speaking. Backlinks are also much more meaningful if the webpage that provides them is relevant to the content of your site.

To see the PageRank of your site (on a scale of one-to-ten) or any website you visit, you can download the Google Toolbar. Simply go to Google, search for the "Google Toolbar," download and install it, then surf. Alternatively, if you don't want to install the toolbar, you can use a PageRank lookup tool such as the one found at www.seochat.com/seo-tools/pagerank-lookup.

Google's highly complex, computer-automated methods make it very difficult to determine how to get the best results. Besides the strategies mentioned above, test your webpage until you obtain favorable results. Once you do, don't change a thing or resubmit your site. If your results aren't what you want, try changing keyword variables one at a time and adding backlinks, then resubmit your site directly to the Google "add a site" page every few weeks until you get the desired results.

Yahoo!

Yahoo! finds most websites through links on other websites, so it's not necessary to submit your site if you want it to show up. However, if you submit your site directly to a Yahoo! directory, you can choose the title and description that is displayed alongside your search results listing. Furthermore, sites that are also included in Yahoo's directory are much more likely to show up and rank favorably in its Yahoo's search results. Yahoo! is particularity relevant because it owns, AllTheWeb, Inktomi and AltaVista.

If you want to get your site listed, you can manually submit your site to Yahoo! There's two ways to do this: you can choose to submit your site to their directory listings, which will show up in both search engine and directory results; or you can simply submit it to be crawled by Yahoo! To submit your site to be crawled go to: www.siteexplorer.search.yahoo.com/submit and enter your URL. You'll need to sign up for a Yahoo! account if you don't already have one.

If you want to submit your site quickly to a Yahoo! directory, it costs a non-refundable fee of $299 for Yahoo! to review your submission in seven days or less. Paying does not guarantee submission, just consideration. It simply gets Yahoo! to give you a "yes, we'll accept it," or a "no we won't accept it, thanks for the $300," in less than a week. If your site is accepted, it will show up immediately.

To submit your site for consideration just go to the Yahoo! express submission form at http://add.yahoo.com/fast/add?+Business, fill it out and submit it.

Since Yahoo! directory listings are reviewed by a human editor, there are a few precautions to take when submitting your site so as to not lose your $300:

- Don't stuff keywords into your description or the submission editors may edit your listing.

- Don't over-hype your site. Editors will notice and may elect to write your descriptions for you.

- Make sure your website is content rich: if it is a bunch of ads (specifically Google AdWords) it will likely get turned down.

- Do not write all in caps, it won't work.

- It's also a good idea to make sure the title of the webpage you submit matches the title you use in your Yahoo! submission.

- Do not simply write your description as a list of keywords. Instead you must cleverly cloak them in a meaningful short sentence or phrase.

- Above all, be completely honest. Submission editors review hundreds of sites daily and will see through any scams.

Once a site gets accepted into the directory, Yahoo! ranks it based on the keyword popularity in the domain name, title and description. Yahoo! also takes into consideration the popularity of the actual website.

If you're submitting your site to be crawled, when Yahoo's spider happens across your webpage, it will rank it according to the keywords contained in the domain name, title, headers, links and copy, in that order.

Yahoo! really likes domain names that are keyword rich. When a searcher searches for a keyword that actually appears in your domain name, Yahoo! tends to give it more relevancy than most other factors. Even if you have to get a separate domain name for this purpose, get it now. It is absolutely crucial for your ranking.

Aside from the domain name, keywords contained in the title you use when you submit your site to Yahoo! carry the next highest keyword relevance factor, followed by the keywords in your description.

Yahoo! also partially determines the popularity of a website by the amount of time a visitor spends on it. If a large percentage of surfers hit the back button as soon as they land on your site, your ranking may very well go down the tubes.

Yahoo! may also place more weight on older sites and rank them higher, but it's not a significant factor, and there's nothing you can do to make your site older.

According directly to Yahoo! this is what they look for in terms of general submission guidelines, and I quote:

"Pages Yahoo! Wants Included in its Index

- Original and unique content of genuine value
- Pages designed primarily for humans, with search engine considerations secondary
- Hyperlinks intended to help people find interesting, related content, when applicable
- Metadata (including title and description) that accurately describes the contents of a webpage
- Good web design in general

What Yahoo! Considers Unwanted

Some, but not all, examples of the more common types of pages that Yahoo! does not want include:

- Pages that harm accuracy, diversity or relevance of search results
- Pages dedicated to directing the user to another page
- Pages that have substantially the same content as other pages
- Sites with numerous, unnecessary virtual hostnames
- Pages in great quantity, automatically generated or of little value
- Pages using methods to artificially inflate search engine ranking
- The use of text that is hidden from the user
- Pages that give the search engine different content than what the end-user sees
- Excessively cross-linking sites to inflate a site's apparent popularity
- Pages built primarily for the search engines
- Misuse of competitor names
- Multiple sites offering the same content
- Pages that use excessive pop-ups, interfering with user navigation
- Pages that seem deceptive, fraudulent or provide a poor user experience"

(source – http://help.yahoo.com/help/us/ysearch/deletions/deletions-05.HTML, September 2006)

Hopefully some of the tips outlined above will help you with your submissions and achieving the desired rankings in Yahoo! This is really only the tip of the iceberg, but will give you a good place to get started and help to achieve an optimum ranking.

MSN Search

MSN used to be powered by Yahoo! but since the end of 2004 it has used its own crawler called MSNBot to index sites. If you play your cards right, you can get listed in MSN in about a week.

MSN places emphasis on the keywords contained in your title and as well the copy contained within the content of your webpage. Therefore if you have something you want indexed, make sure it is easily accessible in text form to the crawler. In the visible page text, include words users might choose as search query terms to find the information on your site. MSN also gives some weight to the keywords contained in the keyword and description meta tags. They also like keywords to be repeated four-to-twelve times throughout the content of the page, but no more than that.

Also, keep your URLs simple and static. Complicated or frequently changed URLs are difficult for MSN to use in determining results.

For example, the URL www.YourDomain.com/index.htm is much easier for MSN to crawl than www.YourDomain.com/web/marketing_internet/123456789_index.cgi. Also, by having a URL that doesn't change, it makes it easier for people to remember your site and the other sites that link to you and any bookmarks that are saved will still work.

According to MSN, you should use only HTML formatted pages and make sure they are coded and work properly. Using descriptive keyword-rich page titles and page content go a long way to help you rank in MSN.

MSN also suggests that you keep your webpages to a reasonable size. The HTML coding should not exceed 150KB in size, which should be way more than enough: the average properly coded webpage is between 20-30KB.

Just as in any crawler-based engine, make sure you have a clearly defined navigation system and at least one link (preferably more) to each page on your site. Otherwise, all your pages may not be added. It also helps if each page is within a link or two from the main page.

MSN also places emphasis on the number of backlinks your site has, so as in Google, it can help get your site ranked higher while driving more traffic to your site at the same time. They also place higher consideration on websites that have a common theme or topic, so if your site is all over the place, you might want to consider some reorganization.

MSN frowns on the following spamming tactics, and their implementation may result in the removal of your site from their index:

- Keyword stuffing, or having irrelevant keywords unrelated to the content on your site in an effort to achieve a better ranking.

- Using hidden links that may be visible to their crawler, but are not visible to others.

- Artificially increasing incoming links by using things like link farms, or FFA (free for all) sites.

If your webpage doesn't show up in MSN, to submit your page for crawling go to http://search.msn.com/docs/submit.aspx. This will not guarantee that your site will be indexed, but it will start you in the right direction. If your site is not listed favorably, check out some of the sites that are, then consider making some changes to your site around the info that is listed above.

AOL

The submission process for AOL, is well, non-existent. AOL search is based on the Open Directory Project, so to get listed with AOL, you need to be listed with DMOZ (ODP). That's just one of the reasons it's so important to be listed with ODP. AOL also gets crawler based and paid listings from Google, so if you're indexed in Google, chances are you'll show up in AOL. If you are listed in the Open Directory Project you can expect to be listed in AOL Search about two-to-four weeks later.

The source of your site's description in AOL's listings depends on where AOL found your site. If it got your site from ODP's directory, it will probably use the description provided there, then re-ranks your listing according to how well you use keywords in your site's title and description. If it gets your site from somewhere else, it prioritizes keyword frequency and location when determining how you'll be listed.

That's it, getting ranked in AOL can be very simple, or extremely complicated. Simply focus on getting listed and ranked well in DMOZ, then AOL should pick up your site up and rank you favorably as well. Since AOL search results are powered, or "enhanced," by Google, a good ranking in Google may also be slightly beneficial.

Ask

Ask (originally AskJeeves) is one of the top five search engines and is gaining even more popularity due to a recent television ad campaign. It's definitely worth the time to try and get your site indexed there.

There is no way to submit directly to Ask.com as it discontinued its site submit program as well as its paid submit program. But if your site has lots of incoming links, there's a good chance that Ask may come across your webpage and crawl it. If you don't have a lot of incoming links, you'll probably have a hard time being indexed. One thing you can do is to email Ask directly at url@ask.com, with your site link, a description and a reason why they should list you. If you beg and plead, you might get lucky and get listed. I know some people who have been successful doing this and some who haven't, so it could go either way.

You'll probably have more luck getting listed by having lots of backlinks to your site, so you might want to concentrate getting linked from sites are already indexed in Ask. Even though Ask crawls your site, it does not necessarily mean it will be included in its index.

Ask's ExpertRank algorithm provides relevant search results by identifying the most authoritative sites on the Web. With Ask search technology, it's not just about who's biggest, it's about who's the best.

Ask results are more community oriented than keyword oriented and they like sites that are community-based authorities in their topic. They call this Subject Specific Popularity, or SSP. They determine this by checking the total number of outbound and inbound links to and from your site.

If a site has many outgoing links to sites that have many incoming links, it's considered a hub, which is not so good. If a site has many incoming links from sites that have many outgoing links, it is considered an authority, well trusted and tends to rank well. Results are then calculated based on this ranking platform.

Once Ask determines how much of an authority your site is, it uses a vector analysis tool to determine if the search phrase matches the keywords contained within your webpages. If it is, it will use a combination of the authority of your site, and how well the keywords match to determine the ranking.

Ask also takes into account how long your site has been around, although the difference it makes is marginal. Since there's nothing you can do to increase the age of your site, I wouldn't worry about it too much.

This is some of the things Ask likes:

1. Sites that load quickly (within 15-20 seconds).

2. Sites with a good navigation system, properly formatted HTML and sites that are spelling error free.

3. Sites with quality content which are regularly updated and free to access.

4. Sites with useful and credible links that work. Broken links will diminish your ranking.

5. Sites that have links from sites that are relevant to your sites keywords.

6. Links from other sites that serve as authorities.

Ask isn't always the easiest to get ranked in, but you should strongly consider giving it a go. If you continue to grow your site, add more content and get links from other sites you will most likely get indexed by Ask and be ranked favorably when people search for your topic.

AltaVista

AltaVista, like most other search engines, uses a crawler (called Scooter) to build its database.

If there are a lot of hyperlinks from other pages to yours, they as always increase your chances of being found without taking a lot of direct action. Do a quick search (www.av.com) and if your site's not listed, you can submit it for crawling at www.altavista.com/addurl/default. You'll need to have a Yahoo! account to do so.

Even though you submit a page through AltaVista's "Add URL" form, it doesn't guarantee that your page will be listed. You only need to supply the web address and the crawler will take what it needs from your page. If accepted it may take up to four-to-six weeks to be indexed.

AltaVista's crawler goes down about three pages deep into your site, therefore all pages need to just be a link or two away from your main page. If your links go deeper than that, you'll need to manually submit the deeper pages for crawling at the link given above.

AltaVista ranking algorithms tends to reward keywords contained in the HTML title of your site. If a keyword is not in a title tag, it will likely not appear anywhere near the top of the search results. AltaVista also likes it when keywords are near one another and when they're near the top of the page. After the title, the first couple of lines of text are the most important part of your pages. If the words and phrases that match a query happen to appear in the HTML title or first couple lines of text on one of your pages, chances are very good that the page will appear high in the list of search results.

AltaVista strongly dislikes sites with numerous keywords, or sites with keywords that are unrelated to the content. Also keywords that are hidden (not visible on the actual page) that don't match site content are a bad idea.

Exceptionally large pages also present a problem to AltaVista as they will only index the first 64KB of content on any single page, but it stops there. Although AltaVista stops indexing the content, it will still crawl the links throughout the rest of the page. It's just another reason to keep page size small and put the most relevant info at the top of your page. Slow loading pages are also frowned upon.

AltaVista likes sites with uncommon keywords, a good navigation system, plain HTML pages with only text on them and, as well, place emphasis on themed sites.

As in Yahoo!, AltaVista tends to rank pages that are placed higher in the directory structure (of your site, not the search engine) as more important than pages that are buried deeper. Also a site or webpage is ranked better if it has quality backlinks from relatively important sites.

The Open Directory (DMOZ)

The Open Directory (www.dmoz.com) is a volunteer-built directory or guide to the web. Getting your website listed in DMOZ - the Open Directory Project (ODP) is extremely important because this is the directory that is used by many sites (including Google) to categorize your site. Some of the advantages of being listed in ODP are:

1.   Improvement of Google PageRank ranking.

2.   You get automatically linked to other sites that feed from ODP.

3.   There's a good chance the site description you submit with your website's address may show up in Google's search/directory results.

4.   More, higher quality, traffic to your site.

5.   AllTheWeb, Hotbot and Lycos give a sizable boost to DMOZ pages/sites.

6.   AOL and Netscape also use DMOZ data for their results.

7.   The main benefit of being listed in DMOZ is that it will result in hundreds of links pointing to your site from other smaller directories and search engines.

To submit your site to the ODP, locate the category you want to be listed in then use the "add URL" link that appears at the top of the category page. Fill out the form, and that's it -- you've submitted. Submitting may be extremely easy, but getting listed isn't. If your site is eventually accepted it may take anywhere from a few weeks to a year or more to go through.

DMOZ can be extremely difficult to get listed in and many people have spent a year or more begging and pleading with no results to show for it. The reason it takes so long to get listed in DMOZ is because it runs on a stream of volunteer editors. A reviewer for DMOZ only needs to review a site once every four months. So if you're number 27 on their list, you could see why it may take a while. Other editors take their volunteer jobs much more seriously and may plough through 100 submissions in only a couple of weeks.

It's best not to submit your site again during this time period, or it may take forever to get listed, if at all. From what I've heard, if your site is on the list and you resubmit it, it can go back to the beginning of the list.

According to DMOZ's forum, only 31% of sites are submitted to the right category. So, make sure you pick the right category and you may be listed more quickly. If you're unsure what category to list in, look and see where your competitors are listed to get an idea.

DMOZ does not like and will not list sites consisting of: ads, links to other websites, affiliate links, affiliate ads, lots of advertising, offsite links, spelling errors, poor grammar, long download times (more than 15-20 seconds), broken links, bad words, hatred, or anything else that's not content based or generally comprises a crappy webpage.

Each page needs to be complete with a proper title, description and keywords. There's no room for broken links, under construction pages or anything that is not highly content based and likeable/useable to the general web surfer. If you have lots of links on your site, according to ODP, its best to put them on a separate links page.

Providing contact information can also help you get listed, and that doesn't mean having a "contact us" form. Provide your address, phone, fax, email, mother's maiden name, credit card number and so on.

If they still don't list your site, most of the time it's because your site lacks quality content or content in general. It is highly recommended that if you are considering submitting to DMOZ, take the extra time and care in preparing your website. The benefits from a quality listing in DMOZ will eventually come more from a ranking boost in other search engines, than the DMOZ site alone. For more information on submitting to DMOZ, you can read up on it at www.dmoz.org/add.html.

Search Engine Results Chart

To sum up this chapter the following chart from www.searchenginewatch.com simplifies where each search engine gets its results. If you know this important information, you can easily determine where you should concentrate your efforts to get listed, and get listed in a favorable light.

Search Engine	Type Of Search Results	Provider Of Search Results	Paid Results	Directory Results
AllTheWeb	Crawler	Yahoo	Overture	None
AltaVista	Crawler	Yahoo	Overture	Open Directory
AOL Search	Crawler	Google	Google	Open Directory
Ask Jeeves	Crawler	Teoma	Google	None
Gigablast	Crawler	Gigablast	None	None
Google	Crawler	Google	Google	Open Directory
MSN Search	Crawler	MSN	MSN	None
Netscape	Crawler	Google	Google	Open Directory
Teoma	Crawler	Teoma	Google	None
Yahoo	Crawler	Yahoo	Yahoo	Yahoo

Source: http://searchenginewatch.com/showPage.HTML?page=2167981

The information provided in this chapter and the proceeding chapters should give you a good place to get started in optimizing your website for the major search engines. It's completely up to you whether you want to try and optimize and submit your webpages yourself or pay someone to do it for you.

Here's what I recommend: if you have the time, try optimizing your site yourself (with your webmasters help if you need) and submit it to search engines and directories, develop quality backlinks and see how it turns out. If it does well – great, if not you might want to consider hiring an expert.

If you don't have the time, but have the money, then hire someone to do it for you. Beware of companies claiming top ten results or your money back. Some of these sites are legitimate, but nobody can guarantee where your site will get listed. All they can do is try, and if what they do doesn't work, try again. Most of the time they should be able to get you somewhere close to the top, but it takes a ton of man hours, analytics and gets quite expensive. If you're going to pay a quality company to search engine optimize your site for you, expect to pay $1,000 - $10,000 per webpage, to get your site in the top ten for just a couple of keywords.

Search engines are constantly evolving and improving their ranking algorithms so something that worked when I wrote this book, may no longer work. To keep up to date on current trends, you can visit www.searchenginewatch.com for additional or revised information.

Section 5

Low Cost Website Promotion

26

Driving Traffic to Your Website

Have you ever heard of the Field of Dreams, "If you build it, they will come" method? Could anything be farther from the truth? Sure this may work if you're building a super 8th Wonder of the World skyscraper, but what if you pitch a tent in Antarctica? Basic common sense states that if you want to get people to your website, they need to know it exists, and if it exists, where to find it.

If you want people to find it, you must promote it in places where people will see it. Not only that, the people who see it must be interested in looking at it. And to make money, the people who are interested in looking at it must be at least partially willing to take some kind of action involving their money.

To do that you need to know your target market inside and out, including what they do, how they do it and where they do it.

Determining Your Target Market

Before you start selling your product or service; even before you start designing your marketing plan, you need to determine who your primary target market is.

Your primary target market should consist of a very specific group of people who are most likely to buy from you, and who are the easiest to reach. Don't try to market to everyone, only market to people who want what you have. Don't waste time trying to convince people that don't want what you have to buy it. Concentrate on the people that do want what you have, it's much easier.

The easiest way to find your target market is to look at those that have purchased what you have to offer from someone else in the past. That way you don't need to waste your time and money educating them on your product or service. Instead concentrate on educating them on why your product or service is better and why they should buy it from you.

To help identify and market to your primary target audience you need to look at their demographics and psychographics. Demographics include things like age, gender, income, location and lifestyle. Psychographics is includes hobbies, clubs or organizations that your customers belong to, where they shop, what they read or watch on television, as well as their core values. You really need to know your target market inside and out; live and breathe as they do and spend a few days in their shoes. Figure out how they want to be presented to and then present to them in that way.

Driving Traffic – The Fast Lane

Once you determine who your target market is, what they do and where they go, you need to figure out how to get them to your website.

Driving traffic to your website can be easy if you have a lot of money to spend on it. Some of the largest websites literally spend millions of dollars each year just to get people to go to their site. I'm just guessing here, but if you're reading this book you probably don't have a multi-million dollar internet marketing budget. And the great thing about internet marketing is that you don't need one.

When most people hear the term "internet marketing" they immediately think of it as ways to get traffic to their site, and although that does not encompass everything that internet marketing is, it is certainly a large part of it.

In the real world, businesses rely on traffic, high visibility and easy access – on the internet things are much the same. The good news is you don't have to have hundreds of thousands of people coming to your site to make money. It makes more sense to have 100 visitors a day who stay in touch and visit regularly, than to have 10,000 visitors who never look seriously at what you have to offer and quickly pass you by. It's the quality of traffic that matters, and it matters a lot. If you have 10,000 visitors, but only three of them buy something, they're not very targeted, not very high quality and not very good for business. But if you have targeted 100 visitors, and seven of them buy something, you're much better off; and it's probably easier to get 100 quality visitors than 10,000 random visitors.

Since this book is about internet marketing, we'll primarily concentrate on the online ways to get traffic to your site, but I thought it'd be worth mentioning something about the offline world:

Offline Marketing

I know it may seem like common sense, but the fact is that most companies do not advertise their website everywhere they can. Your website address really needs to be on every piece of material that comes from your business. Your customers can come from anywhere, at anytime and you need to be ready.

Below is a list of some of the obvious and not so obvious places, you should be advertising your website. Some of them cost you nothing, most of them cost you very little, and a very few cost a lot.

Newspapers	Fax Cover Sheet	Mouse Pads
Journals	Invoices	Calendars
Magazines	Checks	Key Chains
Classified Ads	Product Packaging	Bumper Stickers
Public Speaking	Business Cards	Refrigerator Magnets
Letterhead	Mugs	Press Releases
Pens and Pencils	T-shirts	Flyers
Word of Mouth	On Hold Message	Bus Stop Benches
Window Stickers	Answering Machine Message	Free Bulletin Boards

Clothing	Outdoor Display Signs	Direct Mail
TV	Radio	Infomercials
Billboards	Inside Your Business Location	Envelopes

This is just a small slice of the offline advertising pie; there really are countless ways to promote your site - you can even have your website engraved into the bottom of your shoes. That way, everywhere you walk in the sand, snow or mud will leave a free ad for your site!

It also amazes me, not only how much business spends on print advertising, but how many of them do not include their web address in their ads. This can even save you money – advertise with smaller ads. Instead of trying to make the sale right there in the ad, give the readers a reason to go to your website, collect their email addresses and then you can continually market to them at little or no cost.

Put your site on everything. If you're already paying to have things like order forms or envelopes printed, it usually doesn't cost anything extra to add your website. This way everyone with whom you or your business has contact has easy access to your site. Many of these items pass through tons of hands and you never know who might see a piece of your material and become a beloved customer.

Online Advertising

There are countless ways to advertise your website over the internet. Many of them cost money, but there are also many that don't cost anything except a little of your time. There have been some extremely successful businesses that have been built with only a few dollars in their advertising budget. The following is a list of what I consider the top five ways to promote your business online and drive targeted traffic to your website.

1. **Email joint ventures** – This is the absolute best way because it is quick, and easy and can get you tons of target traffic which can make you a lot of extra money.

2. **Article writing** – If you write ten articles and place them on ten websites with a link to your site, within a few weeks you'll have thousands of inbound links to your site.

3. **Search engine traffic** – Both free and paid search engines are a good way to get lots of traffic. It usually takes a little while to get free traffic from search engines, so if you're just starting out, you might want to pay for it.

4. **Online advertising** – This encompasses things like banner ads, ads in ezines, text ads, PPC ads and more.

5. **Press releases** – Sending out a press release to the media is another great way to promote your site. Distribution methods are both free and paid.

I'll end this chapter here. The following chapters will focus on specific ways to promote your site, some of which are free, others are cheap and some cost a pretty penny.

27

Paid Advertising

Advertisers must be very creative in the way in which they market their products or services on the internet. Internet users are bombarded with countless different types of advertisements from the time they start searching and/or surfing the internet to the time they finish.

Free internet ads can be very effective, but there comes a point that to get wider exposure, to break into the consciousness of thousands of people, you may need to resort to paid advertising. You can pay high traffic sites or internet publications to include a graphic or link that will channel large numbers of people to your site. There are several popular forms of paid advertising, with new approaches cropping up all the time.

There are a variety of ways to get traffic to your website, some of which don't cost you anything and others that do. In this chapter we're going to focus on relatively low-cost methods, but nonetheless paid internet advertising.

Banner Ads

Banner ads are the pioneers of internet marketing. The first banner ad appeared on www.hotwired.com (now www.wired.com) back in October 27th, 1994 in the form of an ad for AT&T. Since that time banner ads have taken over the internet in a variety of forms.

A banner ad is a graphical promotion used on websites as a form of advertisement. Banner ads can come in any size you want, however the accepted standard is 468 pixels wide by 60 pixels high. Due to the widespread acceptance of this size, the same banner ad can be used on most websites without having to reconfigure the size and layout. Although banner ads can be used to advertise your phone number, address, or anything else you like, the real purpose behind banner ads is to get someone to click on it and jump to your website.

There is a great deal of controversy about the effectiveness of banners. Some people swear by them, others swear at them, saying they don't work worth a darn.

Although click-through rates have gone consistently downward, the same can be said of banner ad prices. The average click-through rate hovers somewhere around 0.5% range for banner ads. But, with a good banner design and placement it is still possible to achieve a good return on investment, by combining below-average ad rates and above-average response rates.

Banner ads are sold in any one of three ways: cost per 1,000 impressions (CPM), pay per click (PPC), or pay per action (PPA). If you've forgotten exactly what CPM, PPC, and PPA are, the in-depth explanations can be found in Chapter 4.

Buying a PPC banner is usually more expensive than the CPM basis, but can be much more effective because people actually take some kind of action by clicking though to your site. One of the drawbacks to PPC banner advertising is that one person may click on an ad more than once and you get charged for each click. However some ad providers track IP address, and only charge one click per computer per day. Most places though don't do this for the simple reason that it means less money in their pocket.

The effectiveness of cost per impression banners can vary quite a bit, depending upon their placement on the webpage and you typically (not always) pay the same whether the banner is displayed prominently at the top of the page, or hidden in a bottom corner. Most CPM banner sites rotate the banners throughout the site (Run of Site – ROS) and throughout the page. Banner ads to reach general audiences are typically priced at $1 to $10 CPM, while targeted sites may get CPM rates of $30 - $50 or more. Even though it may not seem like much, banner ads can be quite expensive. Do the math with me:

If you're paying $10 CPM and the click-through rate is an industry average of 0.5%, then it costs you $10 to get 5 people to your site, or $2 per person. If 2% of the visitors to your site make a purchase, then your customer acquisition cost (CAC) is $100, ($2 / 2%). That means for every transaction you do you need to pay out $100 in advertising fees. Some websites don't even manage to convert 2% of visitors into customers, especially when they originate from a banner ad.

Consider the following tables for a minute:

Banner Advertising Cost with a 0.5% Click-through Rate:

Click-through Rate	Conversion Rate	Cost per CPM	CAC
0.5%	1%	$10	$200
0.5%	1%	$50	$1000
0.5%	2%	$10	$100
0.5%	2%	$50	$500
0.5%	3%	$10	$67
0.5%	3%	$50	$333
0.5%	4%	$10	$50
0.5%	4%	$50	$250
0.5%	5%	$10	$40
0.5%	5%	$50	$200

Let's say you employ a good sized portion of the banner strategies you are about to learn about, and experienced double the average click-through rate, or a click-through rate of 1%.

Banner Advertising Cost with a 1.0% Click-through Rate:

Click-through Rate	Conversion Rate	Cost per CPM	CAC
1.0%	1%	$10	$100
1.0%	1%	$50	$500
1.0%	2%	$10	$50
1.0%	2%	$50	$250
1.0%	3%	$10	$33
1.0%	3%	$50	$167
1.0%	4%	$10	$25
1.0%	4%	$50	$125
1.0%	5%	$10	$20
1.0%	5%	$50	$100

In order for banner ads to be effective, you need to combine above average click-through rates, with below average banner prices and sell either a high-ticket product, a product with a high markup (like an info product) or have a strong back-end in place so you make money on the second, third, fourth and even twentieth sale.

Pay per action banners are usually the most expensive, since you pay only for a desired action. This can be a product sale, having someone sign up for an email list or any other action you want. PPA banners can be very similar to an affiliate program and use the same type of tracking. More information on affiliate programs is coming up in Chapter 34.

Banner Exchanges

Just like link swapping, some companies have banner swapping programs. Most banner swapping programs are free and some might require you to pay a monthly administration fee so they can cover their costs.

Many of the free companies make money by the in-proportionate ratio of banners you display on your site, vs. your banners being displayed on other sites. Let's say you need to place a certain banner on your site for a total 10,000 impressions, but you only get 8,000 impressions of your banner on someone else's site in return. This is how these sites fund themselves. They sell the extra 2,000 impressions you lose, for a profit.

Some banner exchanges are pure and simple; I'll put your banner on my site, if you put mine on yours. There's absolutely nothing wrong with this if both sites are of a similar interest and get comparatively the same amount of traffic.

Some sites will track your stats and some will allow you to upload multiple banners so they can be rotated throughout the sites where are placed. This way you can determine what works best if you're paying per impression. It's also always a good idea to use your own ad tracker so you can follow the click-throughs to your site and see how many actually lead to a sale.

Some banner exchange companies will actually design the banner for you as part of their program. Although I suggest you design, (or have designed) your own banners. If you are going to let the banner exchange company design it for you, make sure it is on target. Some of these companies use software that automatically creates your banner untouched by human hands and unseen by human eyes, until it gets to yours. As with any type of advertising, the design, wording and call to action of your banner is quite important.

Since the purpose of a banner is to stop, interrupt really, the surfer's train of thought, clicking on a banner is an impulse decision. People need a reason to make an impulse decision so you need to give them one. The following are some tips to help generate the highest click-through rate possible:

- Have a call to action. Always say "click here" on your banner, or some variation thereof. I know this sounds overly simple, but it is often overlooked and can easily double your click-through rates.

- Add a button. Placing the words "click here" into an actual or obvious button on your banner improves response.

- There's no room for subtlety in banners. Your banner should scream your message.

- Try posing questions: "Want to save 15% on your car insurance in 15 minutes?" Questions work better than statements, particularly when they're used to tease your audience. Studies have shown that by changing a statement to a question you can raise your click-through rate by 16%.

- If appropriate use humor. Make sure it's actually funny and get some others opinions first. Quite often something that might be funny to you, other people may not get.

- Use bright primary colors. Brighter colors attract visitor's eyes. Blue, green, and yellow elicit the most click-throughs. Stay away from transparent colors either in the foreground or background – they tend to get lost among the colors of most websites so stick with solids.

- Use simple animation. Moving images and blinking animation attract visitors to your banner. Strategic use of movement grabs attention more effectively than static banners. Don't make them too wild or complicated so the message gets lost, the senses are overloaded and/or the file size is too large.

- Offer a reward or free gift when someone clicks on your banner. It will help motivate people to click. Contests also work well, especially if you're giving away money. Money is the biggest motivator.

- Run a series of banners. It may take more than one message to tell your story or to go after a particular market. Run a series of banners and vary your message. Keep you message consistent and catchy to make your visitors want to read further. After the fourth impression of the same banner, most people tend to subconsciously block it out in their mind.

- Keep the copy short. Think billboard advertising – the average person spends six seconds looking at a billboard and you have less than a third of that time on the web. Write compelling copy. Use action words that motivate.

- Use italics if you can. Although they don't have a huge impact, they can increase click-through rates by a few percentage points when compared with standard typefaces.

- Create curiosity. A large number of those who click on ads do so because they are curious. Studies show that curious clickers very widely by demographic and other characteristics, so targeting based on curiosity can be very effective when you have a general interest product or service.

- Use wide banners or tall skyscraper banners. They're clicked on significantly more than smaller, skinnier, or square banners.

- Make your banner file size is small, so it loads quickly; 10-30kb is typical for a 468 by 60 pixel banner.

Some Tips on Implementing Banner Ad Campaigns

1. First, determine if you think it would be worth it to participate in a banner ad campaign. Consider the banner costs, compared to an average click-through rate of half a percent, your sites' conversion rate, profit margins and customer's LOV (lifetime of value).

2. Determine where and on what sites you want to consider placing your banner ads, taking into consideration the cost, banner placement, payment types (PPC, CPM, PPA) and if it's a targeted site or not. Find some websites that complement yours.

3. Contact the site on which you wish to place your ad and ask if they have a rate card and get info on their payment options. You can also see if they offer any specials or discounts if you purchase in bulk, or even simply ask for a better deal. A lot of the time they will give you one simply because you asked.

4. Read the submission guidelines. This usually covers things like:

   - Maximum file size
   - File types accepted (commonly .gif, .jpg and flash - .swf)
   - Accepted banner sizes
   - Deadlines for submission and review
   - How many banners can you submit for rotating campaigns? How often do they rotate the banners?
   - How do they determine where your banner is placed on each page?
   - Do you pay for placement or is it random?

5. Keep track of all your banner statistics. Even though the company you are advertising with may do this for you, it's also a good idea to track it yourself.

This way you can track and determine results like your conversion rate, ROI, CPC (cost per click) and click-through rate for each banner.

All in all, banner advertising can be a key part of your online marketing campaign. Depending on all of the key factors mentioned above, it may or may not be a financially feasible part of your marketing campaign, if it can make you a profit. If it can't, don't sweat it, there's tons of other ways to cost effectively market your business online.

Newsletter and Ezine Advertising

Ezine advertising is one of the most effective forms of advertising on the internet. There are literally hundreds of thousands of ezines and newsletters on the internet, each of which has one of three main purposes: to build a relationship with your subscriber database, to make money from advertising, or a combination of both. Since this chapter is on advertising, we're concerned with the paid advertising component of newsletters and ezines.

The main advantage of ezines as advertising vehicles is that they are delivered to a very targeted group of readers. Usually, the quality of the subscribers will be higher in ezines that focus on single, very narrow topics such as crocheting or knitting. Ezine ads generally fall into one of three categories:

1 - Classified Ads

Classified ads are among the cheapest newsletter ads and are usually found at the bottom of newsletters. Sometimes free classified ads are given away as an incentive to subscribe to the newsletter or ezine. They are also the least effective due to their poor placement and limited copy. The best results with classified ads are obtained in the largest newsletters, since response rates are usually fairly poor.

2 - Sponsor Ads

These ads are priced higher than classified ads and are usually found at the top of the ezine or in the middle (within the content). They allow for more words and are more effective than classified ads, but are also usually more expensive. Sponsor ads are generally more effective than classified ads simply because their placement is better and they can contain more content. Some ezines only have one sponsor ad per issue and some have a handful depending on the publisher's preferences.

3 - Solo Ads

Solo ads are by far the most effective ezine ad type. Solo ads fill up an entire email with only your advertisement. That means that the content is sent on your behalf to the subscribers. No other content is included, so you get the reader's full attention and your ad gets the biggest exposure. Since a solo ad is usually seen as an endorsement from the ezine publisher, your message will enjoy a great deal of credibility. Solo ads are more expensive than sponsor ads, but are also many times more effective. Needless to say, reserve them for your products with the highest profit margins.

Another way to run solo ads is to partner in a joint venture. This way instead of paying a fixed fee to run your ad, you reach an agreement with the ezine publisher to split the profits 50/50 (or any other mutually agreed percentage split). The benefit of doing it this way is that you only pay for what you sell. If you don't sell, you don't pay; and if you sell well, you and the list owner both come away quite happy.

Before you spend money on ezine ads, it is a good idea to do some research: ask publishers what their typical click-through rate is and make sure their ezine is highly targeted to your primary target market. The conversion rate will depend on what's on the website you send them to, but the more highly targeted your ad and the publication it's in, the higher you can expect your conversion rate to be.

If you're aiming towards a sponsorship ad, it's also a good idea to check to see if the ezine publisher has a policy of never running ads for two similar products in the same issue. Your ad will be much more effective if it's the only one of its kind in that particular issue. Also ask the publisher if they have ever had an ad placed in their publication for a similar product or service to the one you are offering. And find out what the success rate was like.

Since ezines are published on different schedules (some weekly, some monthly or bi-monthly) the impact of your exposure is affected. More people likely read a monthly newsletter more thoroughly than a weekly newsletter and will be more impacted and exposed to your ad. For solo ads, there is a proportional relationship between the time period in which different mailings are sent and the overall response rate to the ad.

Another way to advertise in ezines is to write an article and allow the publishers to use it for free with your resource box. That way you also gain credibility and build trust, and any leads you generate will be more qualified than those arising from an advertisement. Articles may also be placed on websites for back issues of the ezine and can have a shelf life of a few years or more.

With any type of ad, always be sure to track it with your own ad tracking software, so you can follow your visitors through to the sale. If you're running ads in subsequent ezines, don't forget to test a different variable in each issue. If you don't have an ad tracker, www.1StartCart.com has a good one, or check out www.TopAdTrackers.com for some other options.

Ezine advertising is a great way to deliver highly targeted traffic to your website. If you pick the right ezines and the right type of ads, you will experience an above average click-through rate for the product you sell, and with a good sales page, an above average conversion rate as well.

Text Ads

Text ads are another one of the very effective ways to advertise any product or service on the internet. A text ad consists of a few lines of copy together with a link to a website, or a phone number. Text ads can be found everywhere including webpages, emails, newsletters, classified sites, blogs, search engines and anywhere else you can squeeze one in on the net.

While lacking some of the advantages of graphical ads, text-based ads have some powerful advantages of their own. They download almost instantly and are not affected by ad-blocking software. They are also growing in popularity because they sometimes disguise the fact that they are ads at all. Some of the good ones are hidden right into the content of a webpage or email. This way they look like part of the information and appears to receive the endorsement of the author.

Text ads are usually priced the same way banner ads are and sold on a CPM, CPC, CPA or flat-rate weekly, monthly or annually basis. Text ads in newsletters and on websites are usually specified as a maximum number of allowed characters, or specific number of lines that only allow so many characters each.

Text ads have become a key part of the internet. So much so that companies like Yahoo! and Google have PPC advertising campaigns based solely on the application of text ads that make them billions.

Email Lists

Renting a List

Sometimes when you don't have a list of your own yet, or want to grow your list, renting a permission based opt-in list may be a viable alternative to send an email to. A permission based opt-in rental list is a list of prospects or a targeted group of subscribers who have opted-in to receive information about certain subjects.

Under no circumstances should you ever purchase a CD of millions of email addresses. These emails have been harvested from the internet and if you contact anyone on these lists, you will be spamming them. Also avoid opt-out lists where recipients are placed on a list involuntarily and then invited to unsubscribe if they want to.

It's important to note that the lists are always rented, never bought. The list owner is the only person who ever sees the actual list. You rent the one-time use of the list, send your promotion to the list owner, who in turn sends it out to the list.

Since you only get the one-time use of the list, instead of trying to directly sell the recipients a product or service, pull out all the stops to try and collect their email address. Since most people are unlikely to buy from the first contact, this allows you to contact them again and again until you eventually sell your product or service to them. Try some of the things we talked about in Chapter 19, like offering a free gift or ethical bribe, then sell them later. This way, not only can you try and sell one product to them later, but over the span of their lifetime with you, you can sell to them again and again.

The average list rental will usually cost between $0.01 and $0.50 per name with an average of about $0.20 per name. Additional specifications, including postal/zip codes, ages, gender and job types carry an additional cost of about $0.05 per name. A typical response rate from a rented list hovers around the 0.5% mark; of course it depends on the list, the copy and the offer, but 0.5% is average.

List Brokers

It's not always a simple and easy task to find the right opt-in email list to rent for your business. In fact, most of the time it's a very difficult task and takes lots of research, patience and time. That's where a list broker can help. Their job is to help you select and acquire the properly targeted list at the right price. They will even sometimes negotiate for you with the list owner. And the great news is that it won't cost you a thing. The broker earns an industry standard commission of around 15-20% from the actual owner of the list. Most brokers have a minimum order value of $1,000 (or 5,000 names at $0.20 a name) to make it profitable for them.

Since list sales reps usually work on commissions, they may sometimes try to sell you more names than you want or need, instead of the best names for your campaign. However, you should remember that it is list quality, not quantity that counts.

Here are some tips on choosing a list broker:

- Make sure you have a specific definition of your target audience for them to work with. Having a budget in mind will help as well.
- Find out if the list is single or double opt-in. How did they opt-in?
- Ask the list broker if they will review your offer/copy. Although they will most likely not be a copy editor, they should have a good idea if it will be successful based on previous offerings.
- It would also be worth it to insist that there be a warranty built into the contract that will protect your business should the rented list fall foul to spam or data protection legislation.

Perhaps the most important thing about purchasing email lists is to test them first. That means sending a test email to 5-10% of the list before purchasing it to test your response. Be wary of list owners that won't allow you to test their list. Most will charge you for it (or include the initial rental charge if you do decide to rent the list) so don't expect it for free. It's also not a bad idea to send a couple of test emails testing different elements of your email before you blast it to the entire list.

If you're just starting out, or looking to grow quickly, purchasing a list can be a very viable option. Always remember to research list owners to make sure they are reputable. If they have testimonials, or email/phone numbers of past clients you can call, all the better. Just remember, you get what you pay for.

Other Ways to Advertise Online

Sponsorships and Partnerships

This is a paid effort from an advertiser to tie its name to a company, an event, or a venue that reinforces its brand in a positive, yet not overtly commercial, manner. Sponsorship programs are a different way of promoting your business. "This [contest] is sponsored by [sponsor's name and website]." You don't usually run a banner or text ad (although you can), but you connect yourself in more subtle ways. Sponsorships and partnerships are really more about branding, not immediate sales.

Interstitial Ads

Interstitial means in-between, thus interstitial ads are ads that are shown in the transition between two pages of a site. When you click on a link, instead of going to the page you expected, you are interrupted and sent to an intermediate page, forcing exposure to some kind of advertisement before you can continue.

Another emerging interstitial is the popup ad. Although less intrusive than a full interstitial webpage, it's still something that many web users frown upon. More information on popups is coming up next.

I do not recommend these interstitial type ads. They are seen as an annoyance and an intrusion on the internet, are highly ineffective and more often than not, just tick people off.

Popup Ads

Popups are loathed across the internet, and for that very reason, use them at your own risk. The do have a place if you're using them for your own purposes on your own webpage as we discussed in Chapter 14. But to advertise by way of a popup, pop-under, or pop-over on a third party site is not only ineffective (financially speaking) but also make your business look bad and can actually do more harm than good.

Certainly, there are many more types of paid advertising, such as paid search engine ads coming up in the next chapter. These are some of the most common and most effective. Try different things until you find something that works, keep using it, but never stop trying and testing new things. You never know, you might find something better.

28

Paid Search Engine Advertising

Instead of looking for customers, what if they found you? That's the theory behind paid search engine ads. Searchers are actively looking for the products and services you offer and most major search engines carry paid placement listings. In fact they love them, mainly because it's their primary source of income. Advertisers are attracted to paid search engine advertising because it is simple: they can get their site listed on the results page in a matter of minutes, they have significant control over their ad campaign and they also receive better feedback on its performance.

Achieving a high (top 10 or better) ranking in the free, organic search engine results is an exceptionally valuable achievement. However, with thousands upon thousands of sites competing for the same top spot, it can be extremely difficult to rank favorably. In contrast to organic search engine listings, PPC listings don't require an extensive content development and link building campaign. Paid search engine ads simply allow you to buy your way to the top, in just a few minutes. Often, the best approach is to bid on the search phrases you can't achieve in the free search listings.

Paid search engine ads are often referred to as paid placements or pay per click (PPC) ads. Since Yahoo! Search Marketing (formerly Overture which was formerly goto.com which was formerly go.com) invented and patented the P4P (Pay 4 Performance) search engine ad listings, they have become commonplace and highly attractive to marketers. With PPC search engine advertising you pay only when someone clicks on your ad, no matter how many times it is shown.

PPC search engine advertising is huge. In fact, research firm, Piper Jaffray, forecasts sales in paid search engine ads of over $14 Billion US in 2006, which will continue to grow at an astounding rate of 37% each year. Given such a scenario, paid listings are an option that should be explored by site owners who wish to quickly build visibility. They may also be a long-term advertising option for some.

There are numerous PPC programs available on all kinds of search engines. The main 3 that we'll discuss and which have the greatest market reach are those offered by Google, Yahoo! and most recently, Microsoft. Most of the others may be industry specific, or be so small in comparison that they hardly seem relevant. A list of some of the other pay per click search engines can be found at: www.payperclicksearchengines.com.

If your site is new and has not yet been indexed by the major search engines, or does not have a favorable ranking, it might be a good idea to pay for the ads until you can get things on track. This form of search engine advertising means that you are guaranteed to appear in the top results for the terms you are interested as long as you are willing to pay for it.

How PPC Search Engine Advertising Works

For most of the PPC search engines, the advertising listing procedures are straightforward. You must have a website that is converting sales, then you need to sign up for an account and put money into it. Then you choose your keyword phrases and bid on how much you're willing to pay. The highest bidder for a phrase gets top spot, until they are outbid. For every searcher that clicks on your link, you pay the amount that you bid and agreed to pay.

Google AdWords, Yahoo! Search Marketing and Microsoft adCenter all have relevance requirements. That means you have to target the right type of searcher with your ad and the corresponding keywords. Then your ad must get clicked on regularly enough or it will be removed. If you don't generate money for the search engine (your ad has a low click-through rate), there's not much use for them to have your ad on their site, so they simply disallow you from bidding on those particular keywords and put someone else's ad in place of yours.

Organization

If you don't have any experience with PPC search engine campaigns, it is increasingly important to plan a strategy in order to achieve optimum performance. Although each click may not cost a lot in its own sense, it is quite easy to quickly blow through thousands of dollars.

Furthermore, some PPC search advertising can be quite expensive, with bids ranging up to $100 per click, so there is either a need for an excellent conversion to sales rate, or a high ticket sales item. With a $100/bid, and a standard 2% conversion rate, your product would need to be priced at a $5,000 markup just to break even or you would need a super strong backend in place.

The key to effective PPC campaigns is in your keyword strategy and the quality of your visitor analytics. Many people set up their PPC advertising campaigns without a lot of planning, which is a mistake right from the beginning. Campaigns need to be constantly tracked so that unproductive (negative) keywords can be filtered out and high performers improved upon. Even though the ad services track clicks for you, it's important to track the results yourself as it safeguards against click fraud.

On occasion, an advertiser will find themselves prohibited from bidding on keyword phrases because their ad's click-through rate was poor. You definitely want to try and avoid that problem by writing quick compelling ads. Popular keywords are associated with particular solutions in consumer's minds, so make sure your solution is the right one. The only surefire way to do that is to test.

To maximize your PPC advertising performance, you must bid on the right keyword phrases, write persuasive, moving ad copy, and have a well written page that they click-through to. If you know how to attract the prospect and deliver him or her seamlessly to a solution he or she needs, you'll be rewarded with a good sales rate. The number, style and type of words you can use in your ads are restricted, so writing attractive, persuasive text ads is much harder than you'd expect.

Placement

Paid listings are usually segregated from organic results and labeled to highlight that they are ads. The exact position of the paid placement listings can vary. However they are usually found at the edge of a webpage. Sometimes, they appear above editorial listings, other times, they appear to the right or left, or at the bottom of editorial content.

Top Listings

One of the most attractive features of PPC search engine ads is that you can pay to be number 1; although you might not want to be. It stands to reason that the top listing will get the most clicks. The thing is that being number one gets you a lot of junk or unqualified clicks from people that are clicking not necessarily because they are interested in your site, but simply because your site is listed first. Unlike the free listings in search engines, you actually need to pay for every click, so you'll end up going through a lot more money than the number two ranked site, while your conversion rate suffers.

By the time people make it to the second and third listings they are more qualified because they have a better idea of what they are looking for. While the number 1 site might do more overall sales, they might end up paying twice as much as the number 2 listed site. Let me give you a quick example:

#1 Site gets 1,000 clicks, and does 13 sales = conversion rate of 1.30%
#2 Site gets 680 clicks, and does 11 sales = conversion rate of 1.62%

If site 1 is paying $0.50 per click their cost per sale is $38.46
If site 2 is paying $0.45 per click their cost per sale is $27.82

Therefore, all other factors being the same, site one ends up paying 38% more than site two for the same sale just because it is listed first.

If you're selling an expensive item and it's still quite profitable for you to be number one then go for it, but if you want to get the best bang for your buck, you might want to consider taking second place this once.

Keyword Selection

Just as in choosing keywords for your website, choosing keywords for PPC search engine ads is equally important. It's something that you'd be well advised to research a little before you jump into it. You need to make sure you choose the correct keywords that will transform into the highest numbers of sales. This is something that will most likely take a little trial and error to find exactly which ones will work best for your business, and it's important to make sure you have a good tracking system in place.

Some of the more popular keywords like mortgage, loan, personal injury and so on, have very high (expensive) PPC rates. Instead of using such a general, expensive term as one of your keywords, your results will be more accurate if you use more descriptive two or three word phrases. Something like "San Diego mortgage broker" will get you much more qualified clicks and it will be a lot cheaper than simply using the word "mortgage." Even "San Diego mortgage broker" isn't as specific as it could be. The more specific and exact your keyword phrases are, the less you'll pay and the more accurate and qualified you click-through traffic will be.

Keyword suggestion tools like those provided by Yahoo! and Google can help you choose more specific search phrases.

http://inventory.overture.com

https://adwords.google.com/select/tools.html

If you try "mortgage" into the Overture tool, its top 10 suggestions are as follows:

Searches done in August 2006	
Count	Search Term
950579	mortgage refinancing
584130	refinance second mortgage
567677	mortgage
391225	mortgage calculator
196116	mortgage company
166158	home mortgage
154253	second mortgage
136670	mortgage lead
136637	mortgage rate
91602	mortgage loan

In this example you can see that the word "mortgage" is actually third on the list, simply because advertisers understand that it is much too general. If you type in "San Diego Mortgage Broker" you'll see that it will give you even more specific phrases you can use. If you use more specific keywords, you'll get less clicks, but you'll also have a much higher conversion rate and it will cost you a lot less money.

Searches done in August 2006	
Count	Search Term
1152	mortgage broker san diego
83	mortgage broker in san diego
48	broker diego lender mortgage san

It takes skill and experience to cull out the good keyword phrases. Keyword tools like those above won't give you every searched phrase, so it's a good idea to do your own research in determining which keywords potential customers may be looking for. Don't forget to include the plural versions of your keywords as well.

Both AdWords and Overture have keyword rules and they may not allow you to bid on keywords that aren't used very often, even if those keywords are highly productive in terms of profit.

Writing Your Ads

The title or headline is the first part of your ad, so it is very important that it be attention grabbing, yet relevant to the keywords you have selected. Make sure you test different headlines during the same time of day/week while keeping the rest of the copy the same, so you can tell what is effective and what is not.

Also research what your competitors are using for their titles and headlines. Remember, you need to learn quickly what works and what doesn't, otherwise you may lose your bidding privilege for certain keywords.

The wording or copy of your PPC listing is a tricky matter partly due to the limitations of space and partly due to wording restrictions. You need to use natural promotional language that is compelling enough to get the visitor to click on the link to your site. It always helps to give them a reason, focusing around the word "Free," such as "14 Free Internet Marketing Tips." Some of the character limitations include using all caps, excessive use of certain symbols such as $, !, *, and any words that are excessively promotional in nature, or certain limited keywords.

Even your domain name listed below the title/copy can influence the reader's perception of the quality and relevance of your ad. If the web address they will actually be going to is www.YourSite.com/promotions/google/adwords/ads/1.htm, the PPC ads will allow you to shorten the displayed URL, to www.YourSite.com, even though it will still point to the more complicated page. If your site appears to be promotional in nature, or unrelated to the search keywords, you might want to consider changing it.

Here's a quick ad sample for you to consider:

Auto Insurance Quote
Instant, free quote in mins.
Save 25% or more!
www.InsuranceQuote.com

Something else you can consider is to pause your campaign during the times when your prospects aren't searching for your product or service and you receive a lot of junk clicks. I usually wouldn't recommend this unless you have highly sought after keyword(s) that have a high PPC cost and are prone to receiving a lot of clicks that don't go anywhere.

Google AdWords

Google leads the way with its increasing share of paid search engine ads, primarily from its pay per click service, AdWords. Google is particularly important because it receives over 29 million searches each day, more than twice that of any other search engine.

When a user searches Google's search engine, ads for relevant keywords are shown as "sponsored links" on the right side of the screen and sometimes above the main search results. To show the searcher that your ad is relevant, Google will display the search keywords in bold in your ad if they are present.

AdWords is available on a self-serve basis, allowing you to manage the details of your campaign over the internet at any time. You simply decide on which keywords you would like your ad displayed along with and how much you're willing to pay for each new customer who clicks on it.

Google's text advertisements are short, consisting of one title line and two content text lines. Here is how much space they give you for content:

Headline – max 25 characters
Description line 1 – max 35 characters
Description line 2 – max 35 characters
Display URL – max 35 characters
Destination URL – max 1024 characters

Google AdWords charges a fee for each click on your ad receives and allows you to set the price you want to pay for it. With their system, you set a maximum cost per click (CPC), which is the maximum bid amount you want to spend per click. Their "Traffic Estimator" gives you an estimate of the traffic you can expect to receive according the keywords you selected, your maximum CPC and the maximum daily cost you have set for the campaign.

When you first start using Google AdWords, or setup a new ad campaign, you want to start by bidding high. Google's ad system determines placement by both the cost per click and the click-through rate. To earn a high CTR, you first need to generate some clicks and the best way to do that is by bidding high. Once you achieve a consistently high click-through rate, you can lower your bids. If you set your daily budget too low, your ad will only be displayed intermittently. Preferably, you want your ads displayed regularly when someone searches for your keywords.

To setup an AdWords account you need to pay a $5 (depends on the country/currency you select) activation fee, and there are no monthly minimums. Minimum CPC's start at $0.01 cents and vary by keyword. The AdWords Discounter ensures you pay the lowest per click possible to keep your position. For example, if your maximum bid was $0.97 and the next closest bid was $0.88, you would only pay $0.89 per click to keep in the number one ad position. Once you sign up for an account, there's no delay in getting started, and your ads appear within minutes, connecting new customers with your site immediately. To sign up go to www.adwords.google.com.

Google divides your ads up into ad groups, where each ad group has its own set of keywords that you choose. If you have two websites for example, you might have one ad group for each site. Ideally, you want to keep the ad group keyword list short. Instead of having a single ad group with a large list of keywords, create many ad groups, each with a shorter list.

Another one of the features Google offers is the ability to allow multiple ads to be created and rotated within a single ad goup. This makes it easy to see which version works best, and to test different variables.

Google offers several different keyword matching options you can choose from including:

Keyword Matching - Shows your ad when a search includes your selected words.

Phrase Matching - Shows your ad when a search includes your selected phrases.

Exact Query Matching - Shows your ad when a search contains your exact keywords and no others.

Negative Keyword Matching - Will not show your ad if a search contains certain words you select not to include.

Negative Keywords

Negative keywords are the opposite of regular keywords. If someone performs a search that includes one of your negative keywords, your ad will not be displayed. For example, if you sell products or services at a premium, you might want to include negative keywords like:

- cheap
- free
- discount

The more negative keywords you use, the better your click-through and conversion rate will be and the more money you'll untimately save and make.

Through methods such as employing negative keywords, using exact matches, targeting by region and adjusting keyword bids, you can easily control your ad spending and achieve a higher click-through rate.

Google AdSense

Google's ads can also be syndicated out to other sites within their partner network including AOL, Ask, Netscape, EarthLink, AT&T, Worldnet, CompuServe, ABC.com and the many other AdSense sites. This program, called AdSense, is the other side of Google advertising. It allows regular websites to host Google ads that are related to the content of the site. Google automatically determines the subject of the pages and displays relevant ads.

Google AdSense is a tool for people who have websites and want to create some advertising revenue. If you have a site that has lots of information about a certain topic, you might want to consider placing Google's AdSense ads on your site. For more information or to signup go to www.google.com/adsense.

It's simple to do so, just sign up for an account, and Google will give you a script to place into the code of your site. The code supplied by Google will automatically determine which ads fit best with the content of your webpage, so as to only display relevant ads. Each time one of your visitors clicks on one of the ads on your site, Google pays you a percentage of the cost per click that the advertiser pays. While no one knows exactly what percentage of the advertisers cost that Google pays, from my experience it seems to be somewhere around the 50% range.

It is important to make sure that you have quality content on your site, so the ads that Google displays are relevant to the content. If they aren't targeted, then people won't click on them and you won't make any money. If your webpages are all over the place, Google will need to guess what to display, and there's a good chance that it'll be irrelevant. In general, niche websites fare better than more general sites. Popular niche sites that have a high per click cost (for the keywords the advertiser bids on) will make you more money than a site with lower per click cost keywords.

If the purpose of your site is to sell any type of product, or to promote affiliate programs, placing any type of advertisement on your site will distract visitors from the products or affiliate links.

All in all, Google AdSense can be a good way to make money and many people do quite well, but you need to have the right type of site that you can easily drive traffic to for an amount of money that is less than what you make from the AdSense ads.

Yahoo! Search Marketing

Yahoo! Search Marketing is a fairly new creation of Yahoo!, although Yahoo! is by no means new to PPC search engine ads. In 2003 Yahoo! purchased Overture, which was the original PPC search engine program, and recently restructured and renamed it Yahoo! Search Marketing.

Yahoo! is the second most important paid search engine ad provider. Yahoo! Sponsored Search advertising also allows instant exposure on Yahoo! as well as its vast array of search and contextual partners including AltaVista, AllTheWeb, CNN, Excite, MetaCrawler, and many others. Due to the large distribution of the Yahoo! ads, studies suggest that you might be able to reach up to 80% of all internet users.

When a user does a search in Yahoo's search engine, PPC ads for relevant words are shown as "sponsored links" on the right side of the screen, and sometimes above the main search results.

Human editors review your keywords and your site, so you may only bid on search terms if your website has substantial content to back it up. It takes 1-2 business days to for keywords to be reviewed, so it will take at least that long until your ads are up and running. But, if you're setting up a brand new account with Yahoo! the keywords you choose (and bid on) in the setup process will appear in the search listings right away (there is no review period).

If your ads don't maintain a certain click-through rate Yahoo! will force you to rewrite your ads until they pull better. If they don't generate click-throughs, then they don't make money for Yahoo! and they don't like that for obvious reasons. Sometimes you can bid on common misspellings of words if they are common enough, and sometimes you can't. If you bid on any misspellings, it's not visible to the searchers, so in this case it's ok to do.

It only takes a credit card and a $5 deposit to open an account and your click-through charges are deducted from this amount. There is both a Fast Track signup option as well as a self-serve option. The Fast Track costs $199 and comes with a variety of benefits that can help you get set-up quickly and properly. The self-serve option is free (does not include $5 deposit) and doesn't come with any extras. If you're signing up for the first time and can afford $199, take the Fast Track option. This way Yahoo! will help you with your keywords, titles, descriptions, and budget and get you started off on the right foot.

Should you have a budget of over $10,000 per month for online advertising, you can contact the Yahoo! sales team for a customized package that better suits your business.

All minimum bids in Yahoo! are set at $0.10 and maximum bids are capped at $100. There is a minimum monthly spending budget of $20, so even if you don't generate at least $20 in clicks, you still need to pay a minimum of $20. So it's probably best to setup your ads and account so you spend at least that much. Yahoo! allows up to 40 characters for titles, and descriptions cannot exceed 190 characters. For more information on Yahoo! Search Marketing or to sign up, go to http://searchmarketing.yahoo.com.

The account interface/control panel offers billing, transactions, listing management and report production. A nice feature is that you can place exact bids, and know right away what your rank will be. That way if you want to be listed number one, two or three, you'll know right away how much you need to bid. Among the tools Yahoo! offers, their free keywords suggestion tool is the best one on the web. It can be found at www.inventory.overture.com.

Overall, I find Yahoo! easier and simpler to use then Google, so you can get more done in less time, but Google is used more frequently and thus is more popular. Bids in Yahoo! tend to be less than those in Google, and I personally experience a better conversion rate with Yahoo's clicks than Google's across all of my sites.

Microsoft adCenter

The long awaited self-serve internet advertising center, Microsoft adCenter (formerly MSN adCenter) opened for business on May 4, 2006. Microsoft's MSN Search was the last of the big three search engines (Google, Yahoo! and Microsoft) to develop its own system for delivering pay per click (PPC) ads. Until the beginning of 2006, all of the ads displayed on the MSN search engine were supplied by Overture (now Yahoo!).

According to a study by Nielson/NetRatings Competitive Site Reports, MSN reaches two out of every three web customers and MSN Search reaches over 40 million people a month and had a 9.6% market share as of July 2006. Using Microsoft adCenter, search marketers can specifically target the segment that is most interested in their offerings, producing greater ROI.

Microsoft adCenter allows advertisers to target their ads by restricting them to a given set of demographics and by increasing your CPC (up to your maximum bid) whenever the ad is seen by a user of a certain demographic. Microsoft adCenter also allows advertisers to target their ads based on day of the week, time of day and/or a specific geographic location.

At the time of writing this book, neither Google nor Yahoo! can target an audience that precisely. The way the theory goes is that the more targeted and refined the audience, the more successful the marketing. Although Microsoft has the smallest audience out of the big three, they are currently the cheapest overall per click and have the most tightly targeted audiences. As an advertiser that means a better ROI and a better conversion to sales rate. Their advertising platform also features built-in reports that help to fine-tune your campaign so it performs to its maximum potential.

Similarly to Google AdWords, Microsoft adCenter allows you to bid against others and uses your maximum bid, along with the advertisement's click-through rate to determine how frequently an advertisement is shown. Each time someone clicks on the ad, Microsoft gets paid the amount of the winning bid. Additionally, this system is set to maximize Microsoft's revenue to the fullest. Here's how it works:

Advertiser A is willing to pay $1 for every click on their ad, which is clicked on by 5% of those who view it. Advertiser B is willing to pay $2 for each click on their ad which is clicked on only 2% of the time it is viewed. Over 1,000 impressions (views), *the first ad would generate $50, ($1 x 1,000 x 5%) for Microsoft, while the second would generate $40, ($2 x 1,000 x 2%). Even though the second advertiser is willing to pay more than the first advertiser for each click, the first advertiser's ad would be preferred by Microsoft's system because they'll end up making more money.*

There is a $5 signup fee for adCenter and the minimum bid is only five cents. You get charged at first in $50 increments (or every 30 days, whichever comes first); the $50 increment slowly goes up as your time in the program increases. There is no minimum spending limit, so you only pay for clicks you actually get. To signup visit http://www.adcenter.microsoft.com/Default.aspx.

If you have trouble with Microsoft's system, their self help system is much like it is in any Microsoft Office application, where it opens a new window and shrinks the current window alongside which makes it very easy to use. If you still need help to get up and running, phone support is free and of decent quality.

At the time of writing, Microsoft adCenter is only a few months old, and although it's headed in the right direction and out-targets Google and Yahoo, there are still a few very minor bugs to be worked out. Your ads also don't receive anywhere near the impressions (and overall clicks) that they currently do with Yahoo! and Google. Only time will tell how they fare in the long run, and what Google and Yahoo! do to catch up with its sophistication. Since Microsoft is new, its prices are lower and targeting is precise, which makes their system very attractive to the average online advertiser.

29

----

eBay

Don't underestimate the power of eBay. Before we get started, here are some quick eBay facts you should be aware of:

- In 2005 eBay did $42 billion US in sales, more than Sears and Wal-Mart combined.

- There are currently 162 million eBay users.

- 45,000 new people join eBay each day.

- 14% of internet ecommerce is done on eBay.

- eBay is in 28 countries.

- eBay is the #6 most visited website on the net.

- More than 724,000 people have quit their jobs to sell on eBay.

- More than 2 million new items are listed on eBay every day.

When I started to write about eBay, I was only planning on writing a few paragraphs within a chapter. It wasn't until I started writing that I realized just how big a part of my online business that eBay really is.

eBay is great for three reasons: First, it gives you access to a very large market for very little money that you can sell your products and services to. Second, it allows you to get more traffic to your website. And third, it's a lead generating machine. If you have a product or service (with a website) that you wish to sell on eBay, you can put a link in your eBay listing that goes back to your website where prospects get a chance to:

- sign up for your email list
- find out more about you or your business
- browse your other products

If you have any type of information product, or any other product for that matter, why not sell it on eBay? eBay charges an insertion fee starting at only $0.20 to list an item on it's website, which goes up from there depending on the starting price, if you set a reserve price, a "buy it now" price and any number of other options. Where else can you market and sell an item for less than 5% of the total costs?

Don't expect to sell your product on eBay for full price. People on eBay don't buy anything at full price; they're looking for a deal. The only time items sell for more than retail on eBay is when they are extremely high demand as in the following example:

If you remember in 1996 when the "Tickle Me Elmo" doll was released, it created a pandemic. Parents actually fought other parents to get one of these toys for their kids for Christmas. It was even reported that some parents paid as much as $1,500 USD on eBay for the doll which sold for just $28.99 USD. It's makers, Tyco, did an excellent job of creating a very high demand for an otherwise ordinary product. Shortly after Christmas, there were plenty of the dolls around for regular price. The same thing happened with the Xbox 360 when it was first released.

Basic psychology suggests that when an object is a rarity, it is all the more appealing, and people will pay through the roof to be the first one to have it. That's a very rare situation and chances are that your product's not in high demand, especially if it is an electronic or information product that you can reproduce easily. Only expect to sell your stuff for a fraction of its regular selling price on eBay.

Let's say that you have an ebook that you sell on your website for $97. On eBay you might expect to get $10 - $20 for it. If it doesn't cost you anything to produce, that's $10 - $20 in your pocket right? Yes - but that's not the point. The point is that by selling the ebook on eBay you hopefully gain a satisfied customer, who you eventually may be able to sell your $497 audio CD course to, or maybe your $2,000 seminar, or any other number of more expensive back-end products.

eBay can even be used to generate leads for service based businesses. Even if you have a carpet cleaning business, you could do something simple like sell a $25 off coupon for $1.99 on eBay to attract new customers.

This is called front-end – back-end marketing. You sell a cheap product up front to gain a customer, then over the years you sell them many other more expensive products on the back-end. Sometimes you may even lose money on the front-end product (which is called a loss leader). That's all right as long as you have a strong back-end marketing campaign set up. This is how most television infomercials work… have you ever called one? The have an absolutely, amazingly low-priced product, but when you call to order it, they try to upsell and cross-sell you like crazy: that's where they make the real money.

One of the questions I often get asked is, "If I sell my product on my website for $100, but sell it on eBay for $20, why would anybody want to buy the product from my website? Wouldn't I lose money?

Well, sure you'll have people that will come to your website, be ready to buy your book, but check to see if it's available on eBay first; then buy the $20 eBay ebook instead of the $100 one from your website. That's a sacrifice you must make on the front-end to make tons more money on the back-end. Another thing is that most people won't look on eBay for a cheaper deal unless it's a really expensive product. It's also quite easy to avoid this situation with electronic or digital products. Take an ebook for example, simply change its name and cover graphic and sell it on eBay as a brand new product. That way the business you lose on your website will be minimal and the number of new customers you gain could be huge.

One more thing: Have a separate eBay user ID for your personal and business needs. It looks more professional and makes accounting and business in general, much easier.

The are tons of books and ebooks that claim to show you how to make a fortune selling on eBay, so I'm not going to go into too much detail in it here and waste a whole lot of time. I just want to open your mind to some of the potential that eBay has to offer your business.

Getting Started – Selling on eBay

Before you start selling your product on eBay, always take time to do a little research. Make sure there is a market for your product. And take a look at similar items, noting the categories other sellers list their items under, how much they are asking for them, what descriptions they use and the photos they provide.

If you're new to eBay, getting started selling on eBay is a fairly straightforward and simple process. Simply go to www.eBay.com and click on the "register" link, then follow the instructions. Once you've registered, or if you're already a member, log in and click on the "sell" tab at the top of the screen. Then from there just follow the simple step by step instructions, which are simplified below:

Auction Format

eBay is famous for its classic auction-selling format, but it is not the only way to sell your item(s). The options that are available after you click on the sell tab are:

- **Online Auctions** – allows bidding with a "buy it now" option
- **Fixed Price Listings** – lets buyers purchase your item at a fixed price
- **Ad Format Listings** – posts an ad to generate leads for your item

Online auctions are the formats most often used on eBay, and are what eBay is really all about. This allows users to bid on your item and the highest bid wins so long as it meets the reserve price. If an item does not meet the reserve price, it does not sell, simple as that. Online auctions also allow you to set a "buy it now" price, so users can choose to buy your item outright for the price you specify in advance.

Fixed price formats are just as they sound. You sell your item(s) for a fixed price. There is no bidding, if someone wants it for the listing price they simply click on the "buy it now" button.

Ad or classified ad format allows you to post an item on eBay but no bidding or selling takes place on eBay. The way it works is people who are interested contact you through a contact form on the eBay site. This is most often used for real estate, or other high ticket items such as yachts or airplanes.

You also have the ability to do Dutch style or multiple listing auctions that allow you to sell multiple identical items in the same listing. This is available both in the traditional auction format and the fixed price format. When filling out the quantity field in the auction listing, simply list the quantity of the items you want to sell.

Choosing a Category

After you select the correct auction format, eBay asks you to choose the category you want to list your item in. This is especially important since many eBay users browse whole categories in lieu of performing a keyword search. If eBay users can't find them, then they can't bid. If you're unsure of what category to choose, type some item keywords into the box at the top of the screen (when listing your item) and eBay will make some suggestions. If you're still not sure, take a look at other auctions for similar products to find the most logical categorical locations for your items.

eBay also allows you the option to select a second category to list your item in if you wish. Most of the time there's not much point in choosing a second category, unless there's more than one category that your item fits equally in. It can also be useful for more expensive items to gain additional exposure and hopefully additional bids. I should note that eBay charges you double final value fees if you choose two categories. The final value fees are percentage based fee you pay to eBay when your item sells.

Choosing a Title

This is especially important. Your title needs to catch potential buyers' attention so they can click on your item and bid on it. Also, when an eBay user performs a search on eBay, eBay uses the keywords contained in the title to return relevant results. If the proper search keywords aren't contained in your title, your listing will not be displayed and you won't get any or many bids. Although it is possible for eBay searchers to search the body of the listing and browse by category, 95% of items are found on eBay through the keywords contained in the title.

eBay allows you up to 55 characters, including spaces to accurately describe an item, so don't waste precious title real estate with words like "wow" or "L@@K!" People aren't looking for these terms. You are much better off using every character of your title to describe the item. Think of every related term someone might look for when looking for an item like yours and include as much information as you can. I usually do a search and see what keywords other people that sell similar items are using, then create the best combination for my auction.

For a little more money you also have the option to select a subtitle for your listing. This appears under the main title in eBay's search listings and can give browsers a little more motivation to click on your item. Depending on what you're selling and how much it is worth, it's up to you if you want to add a subtitle. If you were selling a new, orange Wilson rubber basketball, there's not too much more you could say in the title, but if you were selling a car, you could use the subtitle to describe its condition, features, mileage and a whole lot more. The subtitle keywords are not searchable unless the user searches under "include title and description."

Here's a quick example of a proper keyword-rich title:

"2004 John Deere x575 Lawn Garden Tractor 54" Mower Deck"

The above title is actually quite clever because not only does it accurately describe the item, manufacturer, year, model number and blade size, but it also encompasses the most common keywords for this type of item, including:

- "Lawn Mower"

- "Lawn Tractor"
- "Garden Tractor"
- "Garden Mower"
- "John Deere Tractor"
- "John Deere Mower"
- "John Deere Lawn Mower"
- "John Deere x575"
- "2004 Lawn Mower"
- "54 Mower Deck"

There are really a whole bunch of other keyword combinations that it covers as well. And by starting with a number (the model year), it makes the listing stand out a little from the other ones that usually start with words. Also, if you count carefully, you might notice that the title takes up exactly 55 characters (including spaces), which is the maximum number allowed by eBay.

Describing Your Item

Always take some time to accurately describe the item you are listing. Give detail – the more detail and description you give, the more your item is likely to sell for. Always be sure to list any potential features and benefits that may be of value to the consumer. Research your competitors, checking out what information they have in their descriptions that you don't. What strategy are they taking with their copy? Browse their listings and make sure yours are better. Your listing is really your product ad or sales letter – what would you look for in a product like yours?

When writing your description you have the option to list in HTML format (like a webpage) or text format. If you choose to list in a HTML format you can make up your own webpage type listing design and copy it to eBay. If you're going to go this route and plan on using eBay much, you can create or have created a template which you can use for all future listings. Or, if you prefer you can choose to use one of eBay's template (called themes) and just fill in the text, title and pictures for a small fee. And of course there is always the un-themed, non HTML, text only auction format which can also be effective depending on your product.

In my personal experience, creating your own HTML webpage for your listing seems to generate the most bids and the highest final bid price. For super simple items (like the basketball referenced earlier) there is no need to use a theme or design a webpage. There is a finite amount of information to list and people don't need a whole lot of sales pressure, either they want it, or they don't, there's not much in-between.

Pricing

Depending on the listing format you have chosen you have several pricing options. If you are going to go with the classic auction listing you can choose a starting price and let bidders take it from there. You also have the option to set a reserve price, which is a price below which you won't sell your item.

In an auction format you also have the option to have a "buy it now" price. This is would be the price you would ideally and realistically want to sell your item for on eBay. So again if you want to ideally sell your item for $20, you can put that as the "buy it now" price, and eBayers can either choose to bid, or purchase your item at the posted "buy it now" price.

In fixed price auction formats you sell your items at a fixed price so there is no bidding. If someone wants to buy your item at the price you list, they click on the "buy it now" button and buy it.

There is also an option that allows you to accept "offers" from people in both auction and fixed-price listings. If their offer is acceptable to you, you simply accept it and process the transaction.

A Dutch auction allows sellers to offer multiple identical items for sale. Multiple item auctions can have many winners - buyers can specify the number of items they're interested in and the price they want to pay. If there are ten items up for auction, the ten highest bids win them.

See what similar products in your category sell for and make sure your prices are competitive with theirs. Test different reserve prices, starting prices or buy it now prices to see what works best for your product and market. I usually start almost all of my auctions at $0.99, so I can generate as many bids as possible. I've found that the more bids I can generate for my items, the more it usually sells for.

Auction Duration

When you're done deciding on the pricing aspect of your listing, you need to choose how long you want the auction listed on eBay. Seven days is the standard default length, but you can choose to have your auction run for one, three, five, seven or ten days. If you want to try and sell your item quickly, choose a one or three day format. For more expensive items in the auction format seven or ten days is usually better. For very expensive items like a car, you want to get as much as you can for it, so it goes without saying that the longer your item is listed, the more exposure it will get and hopefully the more it will sell for. There is a small additional fee for a ten day listing (it's about a quarter), but it's really inconsequential for the extra exposure you'll gain. The way I see it, the longer your item is listed on eBay, the more people will see it and the higher the bids should go.

Pictures

A picture is worth a thousand words – I'm sure you've heard that before and on eBay it couldn't be truer. Always make sure that you include detailed pictures of what you are selling. The more expensive the item, the more pictures you should have. If you're selling a book, you only really need one picture, but if you want to sell your car, you should have at least ten-to-twenty or more. Digital cameras are a must have for eBay selling - if you don't have a digital camera, get one. You can buy something good enough on eBay for a hundred dollars or so. When taking pictures, it's usually best not to use the flash as it tends to wash out the item you are taking a picture of. Natural light is best, so open a window, or go outside if possible.

You can either host your pictures on the eBay servers (which you need to pay for, although the first one is free) or use your own web hosting service. If you want to host them with eBay, simply upload them from your computer. Since I usually create HTML listings, I usually host the pictures myself. It doesn't really matter which way you want to go, but if you're new to eBay, it's easier to let eBay host them for you.

Other eBay Options

eBay offers several ways to increase the visibility of your auction many, of which are listed below:

Gallery Picture – adds a small version of your first picture to the search and category listings.

Gallery Plus Picture – display a larger picture in search results when buyers bring their mouse over the "enlarge" icon.

Subtitle – adds a subtitle to give buyers more information.

Bold – bolds your listing on the search results page.

Border – adds a border to your listing.

Highlight – adds a colored highlighted band to your listing.

Featured Plus – showcases your listing in the featured area at the top of listings results.

Gallery Featured – adds a small version of your first picture to listings and showcases your picture in the featured area of the gallery view.

Homepage Featured – listings appears in featured listings and your item is likely to appear on eBay's home page in rotation with other items.

Gift Services – puts a gift icon next to your listing. It also provides cost and details about gift wrapping, adding a gift card and means that you will ship to an address other than the buyers, on behalf of the buyer.

With all the options available, what do you choose? Honestly that's up to you, but let me give you some pointers. Always include the gallery picture. If you don't, you'll only get about half as many people to click on your eBay listing and the bids will be lower. If you're selling a very expensive item like a house or car do them all, it will more than be made up for in the final bid price. If you're selling a relatively inexpensive item (under $5-$20) like an ebook, it's not usually worth it to do any of them except the gallery picture. For anything more than $20, it may be worth it to add some extra options to increase your exposure. The more you do, the more people will view your listing, and the more money and bids you'll get. Use your discretion. I rarely ever use the home page featured, but quite often use the bold, highlighted, and featured listings. eBay is always looking for ways to help you make your listings more prominent and charge you for the privilege. Depending on what you're selling, you'll probably want to consider some of these extra options.

Payment Methods

Next eBay asks you to select the forms of payment you will accept. The forms of payment that you accept may determine whether or not someone chooses to bid. The more payment options you have, the more bidders your item will attract and the more successful you'll be. Credit cards (through PayPal) and PayPal are an absolute must. If you accept pickup for physical goods, cash is good as well. Checks and money orders can be accepted at your discretion, but then you need to wait until it clears before you can ship the product out. There are also a slew of other options including COD's, BidPay, escrow services and wire transfers that you can use. PayPal is the accepted standard and really the only must have "payment option," but the more the merrier.

Shipping

As an eBay seller you have control over the shipping, including the price, how it will be shipped and who pays for it. Traditionally the buyer pays for the shipping on top of the winning bid and this is the way I recommend doing it. It's better to have shipping as an additional charge, rather than include it in the price for two reasons. When people are bidding, often they bid based on the actual selling price of the item, not the total price with shipping. Usually when shipping is included, most people don't take that into consideration in their bid amounts. The second reason is that the price that shows up in the eBay search results or category listings will be lower, thus enticing more people to go to your auction and bid.

Shipping costs can be listed as a flat fee, or can vary by location. There are also interactive shipping calculators you can include in your listing so buyers can calculate their own shipping costs. It is always a good idea to specify where your item is located. Buyers prefer to deal with local people in case there any problems, or if they want to pick the item up.

In your eBay listing, always quote shipping as "shipping and handling." Most buyers know it costs more that the actual freight charges to ship an item and will be more understanding if you tell them upfront in your listing that you are charging them for the shipping, handling, packaging and any other related charges. Of course, it's best to charge as close to your actual shipping costs as possible. Some sellers try to make money off the shipping, which is unethical and contrary to eBay's policy.

I recently purchased a product where I paid $23.99 for shipping and handling. When I received the package, it said on the envelope that the seller paid $3.12 to send it to me. Given the fact that the bubble envelope it came in costs $0.59, I was quite peeved that they made $20 off of me. I felt cheated - ripped off - and can't see myself doing business with that person again.

Some eBay sellers that sell $0.99 ebooks charge $4.01 for shipping, even when the ebook link is automatically emailed to you upon payment; which is not allowed as stated by eBay's "reasonable costs" shipping policy. The point of these examples: don't try to make money from shipping and handling. Honestly charge approximately what it costs you to send it to the customer and you'll have many more happy, lifelong customers.

You also need to specify what countries you ship to and if you allow pickup. If you ship outside your own country you need to clearly state that the buyer may be charged additional duty and tariffs by their country. Depending on how your business is set up and what type of business it is, you may need to charge sales tax to buyers in your own country, state or province. If you do, make sure that it is very clearly stated in your listing. And if you allow local pickup, state that as well. People like to pick things up because it feeds more to the concept of "instant gratification" and it eliminates the possibility of fraud.

Being the seller, you need to figure out the best shipping method for your product. For small items, you can't beat the price of the local post office; for larger items any shipping company such as FedEx, UPS or DHL can do the job. You can usually get an online estimate of the exact cost and shipping time. In your actual eBay listing you'll get more and higher bids if you offer the buyer several shipping options (and display them with prices), such as ground, air, and overnight shipping.

Also one last quick thing, if you're not shipping items within 24-48 hours of the auctions end, you need to clearly state when you will ship the item in the listing and when the buyer should expect to receive it. I've purchased several items that the seller hasn't shipped for two-to-four weeks after the auctions end, either because they are out of stock, lazy, or on vacation. It doesn't leave a happy buyer and can get you negative feedback lickety split. What happens if the item is a gift and you're expecting it within two weeks, but don't get it for four?

Having a Return Policy

Some eBayers allow returns and some don't. Some charge a restocking fee and some don't. It's up to you what you want to do. Usually you'll fetch more money for your listings if you have a strong return policy, however having a return policy on eBay isn't as important as a return policy in a store, or even on your website for that matter. Unless I'm selling the exact same product I sell on one of my websites, I usually don't bother with a return policy. It's not something that's really expected on eBay and doesn't seem to hurt the bid amount or final selling price. When selling personal (non business) items I no longer want, I simply don't allow returns because I don't want the item back.

Buyer Requirements

This section allows you to set certain requirements for bidders or buyers of your items. Here's what I recommend, set eBay to block buyers that:

- Are registered in countries you don't ship to
- Have a feedback score of -1 or lower
- Have received 2 unpaid item strikes in the last 30 days
- Are currently winning or have bought 2 of your items in the last 10 days

The reasons should be self explanatory, except for the last one. The reason I select the last one, is someone who is out to get you for whatever reason, can bid on and win all of your auctions, not pay you, and cause you to lose out on tons of business and some of the listing fees. If this happens to you, you can get most of your listing fees back in the form of a "Final Value Fee" credit, but not all of them.

Review and Submission

Simply review your listing, make sure it is correct, then click on the submit button, and congratulations, you're all done.

Feedback

eBay has developed a feedback rating system to rate buyers and sellers. Feedback is made up of comments and ratings left by other eBay members you've bought from and sold to. These comments and ratings are valuable indicators of your reputation as a buyer and seller on eBay. They are included, along with an overall feedback score, in your member profile. Feedback cannot be erased - the feedback you give is permanent, so be sure to make only fair and factual comments.

As a buyer or seller on eBay, you have the option to leave positive, negative or neutral feedback, along with a quick comment. Here's how it works, you receive:

- + 1 point for each positive comment
- 0 points for each neutral comment
- - 1 point for each negative comment

For example: BobbyBoy(110) means that the eBay member with the user ID "BobbyBoy" has received positive feedback from at least 110 other eBay members. Even though BobbyBoy may have a feedback score of 110, he may have actually received more positive feedback than that, but it may have been cancelled out by negative feedback that he's received.

For example, he may have 121 positive feedbacks, 11 of which were cancelled out due to receiving 11 negative feedbacks. This would then result in a feedback score of 110, (121 positive – 11 negative).

Thankfully, eBay also expresses positive feedback as a percentage. For the above example, the math is quite simple: divide the positive feedback by the total feedback and multiply by 100%, so (121 positive feedback / total feedback(121 positive + 11 negative)) x 100% = 91.7% . Therefore BobbyBoy(110) has received positive feedback 91.7% of the time; which means that if you do business with him, you have a 9 out of 10 chance that the transaction will be successful.

You should really have as close to 100% feedback as possible. There are sellers that have done 10,000+ transactions on eBay that manage to have a 100% positive feedback score. Most eBay members have feedback of 98% or better and many people are reluctant to do business with anyone with a lesser score than that.

Feedback also actually makes quite a difference when you're selling on eBay. If you have a consistent record of positive feedback, prospective buyers will bid more often and be willing to pay higher prices for whatever you're selling. You may also want to hold back on selling higher-priced products on eBay until you have a more established track record. An easy way to get a lot of feedback quickly is to buy and sell a lot of cheaper items. This can mean buying some $0.99 ebooks or selling some of the junk around your home.

It's always a good idea to check feedback before you bid on an item – just check the seller's member rating by clicking on the number next to the their eBay username, or through the eBay "view feedback request form." Usually, a high feedback score and high percentage is a good sign, but you should always check their member profile to read comments and look for negative remarks to see what the problems were.

After you make a sale or purchase, remember to leave feedback for the eBay member you bought from or sold to, so that others can benefit from your experience.

30

Writing Articles

One of the best ways to generate massive amounts of traffic for your website is by writing articles. Yes, something as simple as writing an article and getting it spread all over the web can get you tons of traffic. And the best part is that it's all free. In four simple steps, here's how it works:

1. You write an article or have one written for you.
2. Post it on the internet and send it to ezine publishers.
3. Let it spread across the net.
4. Sit back and watch your traffic grow.

Ads and even press releases will come and go, but articles can have a useful shelf life of years and continually generate new traffic. Strangely enough, many people associate being published (even online) with expertise. Not only are articles read by thousands of people, but the people who read them are also more prepared to purchase your product or service, much more so than after viewing a text, banner, or other graphic ad.

Writing articles for online publications and print magazines is not only cost effective, but something that you can start doing immediately. They create a <u>ton</u> of inbound links to your website, which in turn boosts your search engine ranking and gets more people to your site.

If you write only ten articles and place them in ten well-known article directories, within a few weeks there could be thousands of copies of your articles all across the net; all with a direct link to your site.

Writing Articles

Your main objective when writing an article must be to provide valuable information to others. If you don't accomplish this, the rest won't really matter. Your article should be a high quality, informative, relevant and beneficial to your potential customer audience.

There are many different types or styles of articles that you can write. Remember that you are writing for the readers in your target market. It doesn't make any sense to write an article about cars, when you sell hot air balloons. Always keep in mind topics your readers will want to read about or you won't convert very many sales or opt-ins. Here are a few suggestions for article formats:

1. **How to articles** – These usually include step by step instructions for solving a particular problem, or performing a certain task, such as painting your kitchen.

2. **Tip sheets** – Tip sheets are mainly made up of a list of problem solving steps or tips, such as how to drive traffic to your website.

3. **Hot idea lists** – These are made up of a group of thoughts or ideas that are in a list format. This could include things like a list of "Top Ten Converting Headlines" or "Five Thoughts on Customer Service."

4. **Industry trade articles** – This can include news and currents events or trends related to your industry.

5. **Interview experts** – Tape it, transcribe it, add a title and voila, instant article. Always make sure experts are relevant or related to your primary audience.

6. **Niche market articles** – This would include everything else that is related to your business, which your readers might find valuable and interesting.

There are a great number of electronic magazines and newsletter publishers who don't have the time or the inclination to write their own material. You write the article, they get content, you get published and everybody's happy. But keep in mind, if you want them to publish your article it must be newsworthy and offer something that is of real value to the reader. If you use statistics or references, make sure they are accurate and traceable.

Your article should be short and to the point. It must act as a free sample that entices your reader to go to your website for more. Here are some quick tips on writing articles:

- Write in easy to understand layman's terms and always use fifth grade English.

- Whenever possible, write from personal experience. People love to hear other people's experiences (How did they do it?) and it also holds their attention longer.

- Be extra careful to avoid spelling and grammatical errors. Otherwise you may lose any credibility as an expert.

- Don't make your article sound like a sales pitch. The valuable content of the article, along with your resource box is as much of a pitch as you should need.

- Including affiliate links in your article can make it seem biased and lessens the credibility, but can make you extra money. It's a trade off that you need to decide on for yourself.

- Articles should be about 500 words in length, plus or minus 200. Longer articles offer more content and will get read and passed around more than shorter ones.

- You can also put special tracking links into your articles so you can see how much traffic they generate. Just be sure they're not a long obscure link. Something like www.YourSite.com/articles/ would work just fine.

Try to also make your article search engine friendly. You can do this by writing your article around a target keyword phase. You can find keyword phases that will produce the best results by using the Yahoo/Overture keyword suggestion tool at www.inventory.overture.com. The more times the keyword you write about is searched for, the more traffic you will get to your website. Remember though, that your first priority is to write an article your audience will want to read.

If you don't believe you can write a very good article or don't have the time, then pay someone else to write it for you. Elance (www.elance.com) is an excellent place to find potential article writers. You just post an ad describing what you need done, people will bid on it and then you select one of the bidders. For a relatively low fee, someone will ghostwrite quality articles for you. You can then slap your name on it and promote it as your own (which is perfectly legal). It usually costs about $100 for ten 400-500 word articles.

Another super easy way to quickly write an article is to take something that you have already written, like an ebook or special report and find few paragraphs on a specific, relevant topic. Clean it up a bit, add a title and in ten-to-fifteen minutes you'll have an expert article.

Remember to never promote a website until you want someone to see it. That means it needs to be online, tested and working perfectly. No under construction, check back laters, or coming soons.

Your signature or resource box is all the promotion that is needed, and often all that is accepted by publishers. A resource box is similar to a signature or SIG file. It is small paragraph (no longer than six lines) that is found at the end of your article. It usually includes your name, the name of your business, a short tagline and a link to your website. That way when readers like your article they will follow the link to your website and you'll get instant, high quality traffic. Here's an example of a signature that I may use to promote this book:

Justin Michie is the author of "Street Smart Internet Marketing," the most comprehensive, intensive online marketing manual ever! To grab your copy for under $20, go to www.StreetSmartInternetMarketing.com now, and receive hundreds in free bonuses.

Always remember to copyright your articles so that no one else can steal or use them illegally (© 2006 Justin Michie).

Once You Have Written an Article

Once you've written the article you need to get it out on the net. There are three steps you need to take to spread your article across the internet.

1. Post the article on your website.
2. Send it to ezine/newsletter publishers.
3. Post it to ezine/article websites and/or directories.

Whenever I write an article for my newsletter, I also post the article on my website a couple of weeks later and then eventually post it on other websites and send it to ezine publishers. After I post the articles on my website, I always allow others to use it for their website, newsletter, or ezine as long as it remains unaltered, and they leave the my resource box attached. The more exposure the article has, the more exposure my website gets, and consequently the more sales I do.

Your first step is to make the articles available to your customers. You can send them in a newsletter or bulletin, as well as post them to your website. Allow your articles to be freely published, that way they will spread virally. Viral marketing is a marketing phenomenon where people pass along a marketing message like wildfire. When a large percentage of recipients forward something to a large number of friends, the overall growth snowballs very quickly, like a contagious virus.

Next, send your articles to the editors of relevant ezines and websites. Once you have your list, send a personalized letter to the editor of each ezine every two-to-four weeks with a new article for their consideration. Don't email them any more than once every two weeks, you don't want to annoy them and risk having your articles remain unpublished. An email announcing a new article could look something like this:

Subject: Justin Michie – new article for your consideration

Dear [first name],

Here is a new article I've written for consideration in your publication. I'm sure the readers of your [ezine name] will find the unique information on [topic] extremely useful to them.

Please feel free to publish the article I've pasted below, along with my resource box. I'd greatly appreciate an email notification of your intent to publish and a courtesy copy of the publication.

Thank you for this opportunity,

Regards

[Insert sig file here]

Personal details:
[list]

[Article title]

Article size: [# of words]

[Paste article here]

When you're emailing an article to an ezine publisher, never send it as an attachment. There's a fairly good chance it won't get opened (if it even gets past the spam filters) for fear it may be a virus. Simply copy it into the body of your email, or reference a web URL where it can be found.

The next step is to get your articles into the hands of as many article websites and directories as you can. Both ezine publishers and website owners who are looking for informative articles regularly use these services to find free content. The following is a list of some of the more popular sites that accept article submissions.

www.ezinearticles.com
www.articleplanet.com
www.goarticles.com
www.articledashboard.com
www.articlealley.com

For an updated and more complete list, go to www.ssim.biz, and enter "ssim" as your username and "member" as your password.

If you follow these simple steps you will be employing one of the best free internet advertising methods available. When used effectively you can expect increased credibility, increased link popularity, more traffic and more sales.

31

Ebooks

An ebook is simply an electronic form of a book. They are usually in .pdf format, or compiled with an ebook compiler into an executable .exe file. The benefits of publishing an ebook are threefold: First, it gives you instant credibility and makes you an authority figure in your area of expertise. Second, it generates tons of traffic flow to your website. And third, if you're not giving it away, it's a source of income.

Some ebooks are only 30 or 40 pages long, and others are 700 or more. In my opinion, it's best to write something between 50 and 100 pages. Most people don't have time to read an ebook that's much over 100 pages and any less than 50 pages doesn't appear to provide enough value if you're planning to sell it for a profit. If it's a free giveaway, then you could probably get by with 30 pages or so, but it must be a good 30 pages.

There are three main categories of ebooks, which are:

1.   Ebooks without resale rights
2.   Ebooks with resale rights
3.   Free ebooks

Ebooks Without Resale Rights

Ebooks without resale rights have one huge advantage over other types of ebooks, which is that they usually sell for a lot more than ebooks with resale rights. It's not uncommon to find an ebook without resale rights that sells for a few hundred dollars or more. Of course, the information contained in an ebook in this price range is highly sought after and extremely valuable. They must be content rich, very informative and very well written. You can even embed your affiliate links into the content when it's appropriate, to make a little extra income from click-throughs.

A major supplier of non resale rights ebooks is www.clickbank.com. They will help you sell your ebooks for a commission and they also have an affiliate program available so you can sell other people's work and they can sell yours.

If you're customers are going to spend good money on an ebook, they'll probably want to have a very good idea of what the ebook is about and why they should buy it. That is why you need a strong sales page, with a high conversion rate to compel your visitors. If you go to www.StreetSmartInternetMarketing.com you'll see that I have a long and strong sales page, even though it's only for a $20 book. When a prospect reads your sales page you want them to need to buy your ebook like their lives depend on it. I also give away 3 free chapters as a preview of the books content and quality. By giving away free chapters, it also allows me to capture the email address of the prospects, which I use to start an autoresponder campaign where I reinforce why they need to buy this book.

Ebooks With Resale Rights

Ebooks with resale rights are everywhere, and are usually quite inexpensive to purchase. They are sold over and over by anyone who buys them and wishes to make a profit reselling them. They have the same snowball effect as a well written article, and will spread across the web very quickly. Just like when you write an article, you can have a resource box attached to your ebook with a hyperlink back to your website, both at the beginning and end of the ebook.

From the ebooks that you sell, 5%-10% of the buyers may choose to resell them for a profit and then 5%-10% of the people that buy from the resellers will also resell them, and so on. Eventually the ebooks you do sell will spread like a virus and will be passed from person to person and website to website all over the world, all with a hyperlink back to your website.

But, you need to give people a more compelling reason to pass it along other than the few dollars they can sell it for. Here's what I do: I allow them to replace some of (but not all) of the affiliate links with their own so they have two income streams from one ebook. You can also let people re-brand your ebook with a link to their site or affiliate links so they're more likely to distribute it. But you need to make sure it still links to your site at all costs.

Free Ebooks

Free ebooks are just that; ebooks which are free. These are usually lower quality and shorter (30-50 pages) than ebooks with or without resale rights. Although they are free, I always recommend if you're writing one to make sure it does contain some valuable information (don't give away all your secrets for free though) and is very well written. Free ebooks are like a preview of the quality of your other paid materials, and if it's not up to par the reader will assume your other materials aren't either.

These can be short books on any subject related to your business. Perhaps it can be a book of hints and tips, or a compilation of articles branded with your company details and an encouragement to pass it on.

For an example of a free ebook that I use as a list building mechanism, go to www.99InternetMarketingTips.com.

How to Write an Ebook in 30 Days or Less, Working Only 1 Hour a Day, in 8 Simple Steps

An ebook is one of the most powerful ways to promote your business while educating people with the knowledge and expertise that you already have. And if you're just starting out, writing an ebook will not only promote your business, but it will also help you make a name for yourself and/or for your company. They are also a great source of income. Here's how to write one:

1 - Establish Your Reason for Writing:

Make a list of the reasons for which you want to write an ebook. Do you want to promote your business? Do you want to bring quality traffic to your website? Do you want to enhance your reputation? Do you want to sell it for a profit? Do you want to brand yourself or your business?

What are your goals in terms of distribution? Do you want to use it as a free gift or a giveaway? Do you want to sell or give it away with resell rights? Do you want to allow other people to alter your affiliate links? The more you know before you start writing, the easier the actual writing will be.

2 - Determine Your Target Audience:

Another important step is to figure out who your target audience is. Your target market will dictate the elements of your ebook including the subject, style, tone, diction and length. If you already have an established online business, you should write to your current target market. If not, figure out the age range of your potential readers, their gender, culture, social background, and education. What they are most interested in? What else do they read? What do they do for fun? Where do they live? What is your preferred target audience truly interested in that is related to your business? What problem does your book solve for them, or what problem does it help them with? Aim for specificity.

3 - Choose Your Topic:

After identifying the market you're writing to, you need to decide exactly which subject you want to write about. It's a good idea to choose something you have an interest in or knowledge of. The more you know about your subject, the easier it will be to write about. It's also important to make sure that you choose a specialized but popular enough topic to ensure that there is a considerable audience for your product before you expend time and energy.

4 - Select a Title:

After you've chosen your subject, you'll need a title for the ebook. The easiest way to choose a title is to jot down 10 or 100 possible title choices, rearrange them, let it sit with you for a few days, rearrange again, repeat and eventually you'll find a title that will grow on you. You'll probably find that the title you end up choosing will be a combination of the original titles you started with. A catchy title will help you sell your book, but remember to balance catchiness with clarity. Almost all non fiction books will also have a subtitle. The job of the subtitle is to help clarify the main title, and describe what the book is actually about.

5 - Coordinate Your Plan of Attack:

Before you get down to the actual writing of your book you need to develop a plan or an outline of what you're going to write about. Start by picking 8-12 main topics or subjects that fall under your main topic. These will be your chapters. Then decide on 4 or so points that you want to write about under each topic. Write it out on a sheet of paper, and now you have an outline.

Next, write the sales letter or sales copy for your ebook. You might be wondering, "Why write the copy first?" It really makes the actual writing of the ebook a whole lot easier. Trust me on this one, I wasn't so sure I believed it when someone first told me about it, but once I actually tried it, it really made things a whole lot easier. By writing the ad copy first, you'll know exactly what you need to talk about when you start writing, and have a better sense of where you're going.

Your sales copy should be full of compelling benefits that anyone who reads your ebook should expect to receive. When you start writing, make sure they receive these benefits - it's that simple.

How could your target audience benefit from reading your book? What will it do for them? When you're writing your sales copy think about your potential buyer. What are their problems or challenges? List the benefits of reading your book, include compelling copy, features, testimonials and a small blurb about you (the author).

If you've done any research on the internet on how to write an ebook, you'll see courses that claim you can write one in 7 days, or even 24hrs. Most of these courses are a bunch of baloney and assume that you know everything about everything that you're going to write about, and that you can sit down at your computer and write forever. No one in their right mind can sit down and write for hours. Some people have jobs, kids, appointments, dinner, sports, other activities and need to sleep at some point. Also, no matter how much you know about your topic, writing ebooks usually involves some research, editing and revision.

To give you an example, I've spent many more hours researching for this book than I have writing it, not because I don't know anything, but because I don't know everything. And I wanted to make sure that I gave you as much information as possible, within a reasonable read. For what I did know, it was just a simple matter of sitting down, writing, revising and editing it. For what I didn't know, it might have taken me a few hours of research for every hour or so of writing I did.

The point of all this – you need to schedule research into your writing plan. So assuming you have twelve chapters, here's a suggested schedule breakdown:

Day 1:

<u>30 mins</u>: This is your first day and you should spend it going through these 8 steps. Decide why you want to write an ebook, who your target audience is, and what you'll write about. Jot this down and write a minimum of 10 possible titles and subtitles for your ebook.

<u>30 mins</u>: Choose 8-12 topics you want write about that fall under the subject of the book. Under each topic, find at least 4 main points that you'll write about concerning the main topic. This is your table of contents.

Day 2:

1 hour: Research your first topic and sub-topics. Make comprehensive notes as you go, including sources.

Day 3:

1 hour: Write 5-10 pages about your first topic. Break it down into the 4 or so main points.

Days 4, 6, 8, 10, 12, 14, 16, 18, 20, 22, 24:

1 hour: Research topics 2-12

Days 5, 7, 9, 11, 13, 15, 17, 19, 21, 23, 25:

1 hour: Write about topics 2-12

Day 26:

20 mins: Review and edit chapter 1

20 mins: Review and edit chapter 2

20 mins: Review and edit chapter 3

Days 27, 28, 29:

20 mins each: Review and edit chapters 4-12

Day 30:

30 mins: Write a brief introduction to your ebook (yes, it's best and easier to write the introduction last).

10 mins: Check and confirm all links contained in your ebook as well as make sure sources are correct.

10 mins: Send instructions and specifications to a graphic designer for ebook cover, or use an ebook cover generator software. This needs to be done last, so you have time to think about your title and subtitles.

10 mins: Save, export or convert your ebook into a .pdf or .exe file.

Day 31:

Congratulations – you're now an author!

6 - Write the Copy:

Your ebook can be as long as it needs to be, but stay focused. If you need 200 pages to give all the information, by all means use 200 pages. But, if you can say it in 20 pages, don't use a page more. Don't use any filler content or fluff, it's annoying and not appreciated by anyone. It's often harder to write shorter ebooks, but the effort will be appreciated by your readers. The longer it is, the more interesting you have to make it to keep your readers' attention.

Some of your readers may be familiar with your topic and may just be looking for additional information, or perhaps another idea - don't write for them; write for the beginner. There are far more beginners, and the more experienced readers will skim through what they already know. Always write in a casual, conversational tone rather than in a formal tone as used in textbooks. Readers respond better when you're having a conversation with them, rather than lecturing to them.

You need to keep your writing engaging and hold your reader's attention. Often written or graphic illustrations, comparisons, anecdotes, testimonials, little stories, photos, graphs, advice, tips and maybe even a little bit of humor (if appropriate) will keep the reader turning the pages.

Next, decide on an easy to read design. Even though most people have the ability to print out your ebook, most people prefer reading it on their computer screen. For that reason keep sentences and paragraphs fairly short, concise and to the point. Pick a font that's easy on the eyes and stick to that font family. Using multiple fonts will tire out your readers before they get through the introduction. Use at least one and a half line spacing, double space if you want and use a minimum of a 12 point font size.

There was a test done some time ago, on the best font to use in copyrighting. Arial was determined to be the best and Times New Roman came in a close second. It's up to you to use what you want, but stick with one if the standards so you don't need to worry about licensing. I like Arial because it's rounder and I find it easier on the eyes, especially on a computer monitor.

Use lots of white space, or what artists refer to as "negative space." This will give your reader's eyes a chance to rest in the cool white oasis' you create on the page. If everything is packed in together and the white space is minimized, your reader's eyes will begin to tear, then blur and finally they'll quit reading. It also looks a lot less intimidating than a page plastered full of text – like this one!

Try to use lots of bulleted and numbered lists. This not only makes your information easy to absorb, but also gives reader's eyes a break by creating white space. Also don't use full pages for new chapters titles just in case people print it out, it wastes paper and leaves them flustered.

Now that you have the foundation, you can begin writing. A standard, readily available and flexible application like MS Word is a good choice to write in. Save your document regularly. MS Word has an auto recovery feature that is useful if you don't save the document on a regular basis or your computer crashes. As a precaution it's also always a good idea to back up your work on another media such as a CD, DVD, friend's computer, or memory stick and keep it in a safe place.

If you're not a very quick typist, alternatively you could record your ebook on a tape recorder and then hire a transcriber to type it out for you. Or you could also invest in a speech recognition computer program like Dragon Naturally Speaking, and a computer microphone, then dictate it to your computer. It will automatically turn your words into type, with about a 99% accuracy rate. If you're going to go this route, buy a USB computer microphone, it's little more expensive but offers a higher speech accuracy rate.

If you're ever unsure about a fact or statistic in your book, look it up from several sources to be sure it's correct. If someone notices an incorrect fact, your credibility can diminish.

When you're finished writing, editing and reviewing, have someone proofread your work before you put it out for the world to see. Often when you read your own writing, you read what you meant to say, not what you actually wrote. Also don't forget to run a spell and grammar check - you are judged by something as minor as correct punctuation, so don't mess up a great book. Once it's on the net it's permanent and there's no turning back. Don't forget to include your resource box with a tag line and hyperlink to your site.

7 - Design the Cover:

Even though you're writing an ebook, it still must have a cover. Studies indicate that by just having a picture of your ebook on your sales page, you can increase sales by over 300%!

I'm sure that you have heard the saying "don't judge a book by its cover." The fact is that people do judge a book by its cover. An ebook with an exciting professionally designed cover can outsell an ebook with a boring plain Jane cover 5 to 1. If you can, have a professional graphic designer create an attractive cover and 3D book graphic for you. Try to avoid generic, free ebook covers or software generated covers. It will make you look cheap and could impact sales negatively. If you don't have a graphic designer, Elance or even eBay are good places to look for a great deal.

8 - Choose Your Format:

Most ebooks are available either as an executable (.exe) file format or a Portable Document Format (.pdf) file. Each has its own advantages and disadvantages and depending on your target audience and plans for your ebook, either one could work. I'll let you know the details, my recommendations, and you can decide for yourself.

EXE files need to be compiled using an ebook compiler and can only be read on a PC. There are tons of ebook compilers available on the internet at sites like www.ebookpro.com and www.ebookmaestro.com. Unlike PDF files that require Adobe Reader to open, they don't require any special software to be installed. Executable files also offer many features (depending on the compiler you're using) that aren't available in PDF files, such as ebook disabling or authentication using password protection. Some ebook compilers can program an EXE file so it is only accessible on one computer and can't be passed around among friends. This usually requires an internet connection and is an annoyance and inconvenience for your visitors. It is also possible for EXE files to become infected with a virus and spread from computer to computer, so some people may be cautious opening one.

PDF files can either be created using Adobe Acrobat or several other third party applications. PDF files are the industry standard document format and although you need Adobe Reader to open the files, almost everyone has it; and if they don't it's available for free from www.adobe.com. PDF files can also be viewed both on a Mac and a PC and are almost impossible to infect with a virus. Currently there is no way to prevent PDF files from being passed around, other than password protecting them, but the password can easily be passed around with the file. Here's what I recommend:

For inexpensive, or free books a PDF file format is a better way to go. Even if people pass your ebook around freely (and less than 5% do), chances are the extra exposure and money you make from affiliate links is still worth it. It actually pays to be ripped off. PDF files are also the readily accepted standard for ebooks and used over 90% of the time.

For an expensive, targeted ebook with highly specialized information, you may want to consider using an executable file format so your ebook can't be passed around. If your ebooks is that valuable, you might want to consider printing it or recording it to audio CDs and charging more.

32

Press Releases

Free publicity is the tried, tested and true, most cost-effective marketing tool there is. If you had to pay for a few minutes on a TV or radio station, it could cost you thousands of dollars. Press release PR is not only free, but it also gives you much more credibility than a paid ad ever could.

The goal of a press release is to connect with the media. If you want a interview, TV or radio appearance, a brief mention about your website, or a news story written about you, a press release is a good place to start.

A well written release can dramatically increase your sales, your exposure and greatly enhance the image of your business and/or products. A well executed media strategy has the potential to get your site free regional, national and international exposure. A story or an interview about your website, or even a brief mention in the press can have a major impact on the amount of traffic you get to your website.

Before you write a press release, ask yourself the following questions:

- What do I hope to achieve from my press release? (increase sales, awareness, publicity etc.)

- What information will my press release provide?

- Is it newsworthy? Is it timely? Is it unique?

- Who is my target audience?

A press release is really a news story. A good story must have the following four attributes:

1. **Key message**: This is the most important part of the story.

2. **Timeliness**: The chances that your release will be published, or picked up by the media improve when your release is about a current hot topic.

3. **Uniqueness**: Your message must be unique, newsworthy, or contrary to the industry norms. If you don't give the media an immediate reason to pick up your story, it won't get picked up. Simple as that.

4. **Angle or spin**: This is perhaps one of the hardest parts of creating a press release. The who, what, where, when, why, and how are very important here. How do you present your story to make it interesting to the masses?

Is Your News Newsworthy?

The goal of a press release is to inform people through the media about news. Just because you are excited about something does not mean that anyone else will be. Think about your market - will they find your story interesting? Even though you may be pumped about announcing a new website or a new product, it's not necessarily a newsworthy event. There are thousands of new websites and products launched everyday. Who cares about yours? What makes it so special? Most importantly, why should the media who has been there, done that, care and pick the story up?

You need to answer the question "so what," or "who cares about that?" If it's not newsworthy, you don't have a reason for a press release. Identify a problem, then illustrate why your solution is the right solution. Give real life examples if you can. Communicate the real life benefits can that can be expected from your solution. Focus on the aspects of your news item that truly set you apart from everyone else.

Provide the media with useful information about your business, product, service, event, study, etc. But don't use press releases to try and make sales, it doesn't work and it won't get picked up.

Why Timeliness is Important

If you can, try to tie your press release in with current news, or things that are happening in the media. This way more people will come across it in their web searches, it will rank better in search engines and be picked up by more media outlets. Another popular method for obtaining press coverage is to ride piggy-back on a breaking news story by alerting the media to your expertise on that particular subject. What can you release a press release about?

- **Launch of website** – Only if it is newsworthy, meaning different, unique or altogether a new concept. Unique does not mean offering good customer service or offering the lowest prices. How does your site really benefit people in ways that others don't? Does it offer a unique service not previously available or sell a revolutionary new product?

- **Contest or sweepstakes** – Highlighting winners is huge news, especially if what they win is big. Launching a contest that is different (not the standard ballot entry to win a trip or money) such as the X Prize is also a very newsworthy event. In case you're not familiar with it, the X Prize was a reward of $10 million dollars for the first non-government organization to launch a vehicle into space twice within two weeks.

- **Charity donations** – Be aware that some people may see this as boastful, but why shouldn't you be? Just make sure that you tie it in to a current event, or go deeper than giving money away so you can brag about it. Giving proceeds to charity from a sale or event are something else you can write a release about.

- **Receiving a major contract, grant, or award** – Mention the details and reference your website for additional information.

- **Releasing findings** – A special report, survey, study or polls are big news, especially when results affect your market.

- **Events** – Having a big party or event? If it's the largest of its kind, or unique, why not let people know? Does it benefit charity? If it does, that's means for releasing another press release.

- **Book release** – Let people know what your book can do for them. What are the perceived benefits of buying your book? How will it affect the average person's life?

Of course there are other things such as corporate milestones, mergers, new products or services, hiring (and firing) of a high profile employee, sales milestones, accelerated corporate growth and so on that you can release. Just make sure people outside your company have a reason to care.

Press Kits

A press kit is a more complex and complete form of a press release. It's up to you whether you will want to create a press kit. Although it is not necessary, it is convenient to have in case someone in the media wants additional information about you or your company for a news story.

Press kits usually contain:

- An introductory letter
- One or more press releases
- A fact sheet containing the facts about you or your business
- A biography of you and your accomplishments
- Your company's promotional material
- Your business card

Press kits can even come in the form of a website which simply has the introductory letter on the main page and links to the other features, or it can be a physical folder or binder containing the above info. Online kits can also contain audio and video clips, such as those from a radio or TV interview. Have a separate section of your website for the press, and don't require them to sign in, or register to view your information.

Writing Tips

Write in an active, informal, neutral style. Avoid a marketing (I want to advertise) tone. Use strong action words (verbs). Don't use unnecessary adjectives, flowery language, or redundant expressions; instead try using more basic, clear words free of industry jargon. If you do need to use adjectives, use vivid and compelling ones. Use as many words as you need to accurately tell your story (300-800 is standard) but not a word more. Make each word count and be there for a specific purpose.

Write for the media - when a media outlet picks up your press release, they may run it with little or no modification, or they may use your press release as research for a larger feature story. The point is, write the story the way you want it told.

Avoid hype, including excessive (or any) use of the exclamation point. If you absolutely must use the exclamation point, do not use it more than once (!!!) ever. Also never write in uppercase. Nothing should be in uppercase except the "FOR IMMEDIATE RELEASE" headline at the top of your release.

If you are submitting your release online, do not use HTML. If you need to link to a website, link to it in full form (http://www.YourDomain.com), so that it is available to click or copy if and when received in people's email inboxes.

If you place your email address anywhere in the body of your press release, it will probably get picked up by an email harvesting program and you'll receive truckloads of spam. Either make sure you have a good spam filter and set up a special email account (media@YourDomain.com) for the purpose of the press release, or write your email out longhand (email_at_domain.com). I recommend combating the spam and setting up a special email account, that way you won't miss any inquiries you might otherwise get.

Stick to the cold, hard facts. Tell the truth. Avoid fluff, embellishments and exaggerations. Avoid too good to be true scenarios. Even if it is true, tone it down a bit, otherwise people will be skeptical (journalists are naturally skeptical) and won't believe you.

Some Other Press Release Tips

- Make sure your press release is short, concise, to the point and accurate. Keeps sentences and paragraphs short, with about three or four sentences per paragraph, and four-to-five paragraphs total.

- Include quotes if you can. Employees, customers and industry experts are a good place to get quotations. Keep in mind that the media are more inclined to use outside objective comments than ones directly from an employee of your company.

- Avoid directly addressing the consumer or your target audience. Do not use "I," "we" or "you" outside of a direct quotation.

- Be sure to check and double check your spelling, grammar and punctuation. Have someone else read it over for you, a professional editor if you can. It's less than $20/hour for an editor on www.elance.com.

- Use a legible font (Arial, Times New Roman, Verdana) and ideally keep the release to one page. Legibility overrules creativity.

- Make use of bulleted points, they simplify and are easy to understand.

How to Write a Press Release in 4 Simple Steps

Step 1 – Titles:

For Immediate Release

The very first thing at the top of your press release should say in big, bold, capital letters, **FOR IMMEDIATE RELEASE.** This lets the reporter know the news is authorized for publication on the date they receive it. If your press release is not to be released to the public yet (ie. not for immediate release), then it should not be released to the media. They literally receive thousands upon thousands of press releases and they're not going to hold onto yours until it is ready to be released. Never send it out until it's ready to go out.

The Headline

The headline or title for your press release should be written in bold, but not all caps and should be kept to ten words or less. The purpose of the headline is to suck the press into your announcement. The title of a press release is just like the subject of an email. It must be catchy, but informative and clearly state the purpose of the communication. It must grab the reader's attention and entice them to continue reading the release.

Step 2 – Summary Paragraph:

Include a one paragraph summary of your release if you can. Elaborate on the news in the headline in 2-4 sentences, to give readers a general idea what your release is about. If you fail to include a summary paragraph, you may reduce the overall effectiveness of your press release.

Step 3 – The Body:

First Paragraph

Begin the text of the release with the city and state/province followed by a dash (-) and then the date, since the media doesn't always use press releases immediately. The first sentence should simply state the news you have to announce. It also needs to draw readers into the body and content of your release within a matter of seconds. Do not blow it with a weak lead. The rest of the first paragraph needs to tell the story in a snapshot. Answer the who, what, where, when, why and how questions of your news. The rest of your press release will provide the detail.

Middle Paragraphs

The rest of the news release expounds on the information provided in the lead paragraph. It can include quotes from staff, customers or outside experts in your field. It broadens the detail about the news you have to tell and can include key points, product/service release or commencement dates, prices, distribution, or specific details about the topic of the release. In short, the body provides the details of your story.

Last Paragraph

The final paragraph of a news release traditionally contains the least newsworthy information. It is also good practice to restate and summarize some of the stronger points offered in the body of the release.

Step 4 – Finishing Up Your Release:

About

This is a short and simple paragraph where you include a quick background sketch about you or your company and describe your product and/or services. This might include a quick synopsis of the activities of your company, information about your products, your location (if physical), years in business and any other pertinent information. Be sure to keep it short and concise, but detailed.

Contact Info

After your release has been written and hopefully read, you need to let people know how to contact you. Always provide a contact name, telephone number, address and email address. Also provide a link to your website where they can find additional information, or where they can request a printed press kit, or view the online equivalent.

The End

Finally, close the release with "###." This is a universal style convention that lets the reader know that they have reached the end and there are no more pages.

Distributing Your Press Release

So now that you've got your press release, you've got to get it out there. You can either pay a company to send out your press release for you, or you can send it out yourself. Hiring a company to do it for you has some advantages: namely the company has experience and the right media contacts to get your release seen. But then again, you pay for their experience. However, some places like www.prweb.com also have an option that allows you to distribute your release for free.

If you have the time but not the money and want to do it your own, there are places where you can buy a list of media contacts that you can use over and over. You can also go to your local library and look in the free media info broadcasting and cable yearbook (ask the librarian), or you can usually find out most necessary information and who to contact via the World Wide Web.

Some places that you can hire to send your press releases for you are:

www.prweb.com
www.ereleases.com
www.xpresspress.com

I prefer to pay a company to send it for me and almost exclusively use prweb.com. It's easier, more convenient, saves time and they do a better job than I could. But, if your budget's tight and you have the time to do it yourself, there is nothing wrong with sending it out yourself. Just keep a detailed list of your media contacts for future use.

Also if you're submitting your release yourself, make sure you never send your press release to more than one contact per news outlet; it will annoy the heck out of them and they are more than likely to ignore your release. Also, once you submit your release, don't bother to follow up with the media. You need to consider that many media outlets receive a 10 foot pile of press releases every week and don't have the time and ability to publish them all. They also don't have the time or desire to tell you what's happening with yours.

Here are some things to keep in mind before sending out your press release:

- General assignment newspaper reporters usually turn around stories within 24 and 48 hours. However, feature writers work on stories weeks before they are published. Who are you sending it to? What is your audience? Remember timeliness.

- Monthly publications (magazines) choose editorial content many months in advance of the issue date. If there's a particular publication you're interested in, ask them for their editorial calendar so you can appropriately schedule your release.

- Some television and radio stations may elect to plug your website if your press release is extraordinarily newsworthy or unique. Some may also want to have a representative of your company appear on one of their programs. Radio interviews are most often held over the telephone, while TV interviews are almost always in person. If you're going to be interviewed, be prepared. Ask if you can get a list of the questions that will be asked, or points that will be discussed ahead of time. You can even submit a list of interview questions that they can ask you if you like.

All in all, sending out a press release via the internet can be a great way to not only boost traffic to your site, but get you free publicity. And free publicity is much more credible than anything you could ever pay for. Just remember to make sure your press release is newsworthy and something that others will care about.

33

Other Low Cost Tips

On the internet a lot of people expect a lot of things for free. But when it comes to advertising, you can rarely ever find anything of value that's free, and most of the things that are free, are either hard to do or take a lot of time. However, with a little time, effort and creativity, there are still a few free or almost free ways to promote your site, which we'll discuss in this chapter.

Newsgroups

Newsgroups are places on the internet where people go to discuss a particular topic of interest to them. People post messages to a newsgroup and read them much like sending an email. The first post in a newsgroup usually states the topic or question up for discussion and subsequent posts are answers or comments in response to the topic or question. Newsgroups are not in real time, so it can take a few hours, or even a few days until you receive a reply to your posting. Some web browsers, email software, or software specifically designed for handling newsgroups can be used to read and check for new posts on a regular basis.

Before you go out and start posting to newsgroups all over the place, do a little research. You won't have time to post to all newsgroups that apply to your business, so choose a few, so you can check back every few days and keep posts consistent.

Most newsgroups don't allow you to post advertising messages, so be sure to read the rules and regulations of the newsgroup and strictly adhere to them. Since newsgroups cannot be used to post blatant advertisements, you must use them subtly. Here's how: Answer people's questions as a perceived expert. That's it. But don't forget to include a good signature file with your name, a link to your website and maybe a quick one liner subtle ad such as "check out my blog at www.MyBlog.com." It also helps to end your post with a quick "hope that helps" before the signature line. That way it looks more like you're there to try and help, instead of get free advertising. Always be sure that the message you post provides an actual benefit.

Most newsgroups use what is called a moderator whose responsibility it is to make sure all articles are on target, informative, and adhere to the rules set forth by the newsgroup. If your posts are found to violate the rules, they will be removed and you could be banned indefinitely from the newsgroup. Don't forget that once you post, your words are out there forever for the entire world to read – so choose them carefully.

The results you get from your newsgroup marketing are directly proportional to the time and effort you invest. The more time you spend posting, the more exposure you will get, the more traffic you'll draw to your site and the more sales you'll make.

Discussion Forums

Discussion forums are very similar to newsgroups, so we don't need to spend too much time on them. The major difference between discussion forums and newsgroups is that discussion forums are all web based. (i.e. you post through a web based form and view posts in your internet browser) whereas newsgroups are not.

Again, as with newsgroups, read the rules and follow them closely. Take a look around at what forums are out there and then pick a few that you can do the rounds with once or twice a week. Answer questions, or post new topics, just don't forget the important signature file with a link to your site.

You can even place a discussion forum on your website to gain new visitors and give them a reason to keep coming back. If you do decide to do this you're in charge, so you need to moderate the forum, or find someone to do it for you. Always be sure to keep the discussion alive by posting new topics and replying to others posts.

Discussion forum marketing is an excellent way to get more website traffic, both directly from your postings and the higher search engine ranking you will achieve in some search engines by having more outside links to your website.

Chat Rooms

Chat room marketing is the use of online chat rooms to promote your product or service. Chat room marketing is very similar to newsgroup and discussion forum marketing, but with a few twists. Again, before you start talking about your product or service, remember to read and understand the rules of the room.

One big difference between chat rooms and discussion forums or newsgroups is that chat rooms are in real time. This means that you are chatting live, either one on one or as a group which makes this method of communicating with potential customers a much more personal approach than many other types of advertising.

Chat rooms are organized by topics of interest just like newsgroups and discussion forums, so it is your job to find the right chat room(s) where your target audience would gather. Remember, to build a presence and reputation among users you should visit the chat room regularly, so don't sign up for ten different chat rooms, unless you plan to spend every waking hour chatting. On that note, chat rooms can become quite addictive and get off topic easily, so keep that in mind. When I do use them, I like to set a specific time limit so I don't overdo it. Most chat rooms will require you to sign up and create a profile. Always include your signature in your member profile with your name, email, website and one liner ad.

Start up a conversation with people who have questions about the topic you are the expert in, then if possible, indirectly introduce your product or service and how it can be of help to them. Give them your email address or website in case they think of any more questions, or want additional information. You can also try using some of the chat room emotions (or emoticons) and acronyms like the smiley face (:) or ☺) if you want. I've never been a big fan of doing this, as it seems childish and unprofessional – but that's just my opinion.

Even though chat rooms are live and you may be feverishly pounding away at your keyboard, that's no excuse for bad spelling and grammar. Keep it clear and clean. Even though chat rooms are free, they can be very time consuming and depending on your products and services it may or may not be a financially viable option for you.

You can also host a chat room on your site which will get you more visitors and give them a reason to come back again. Then if you like you can host free seminars in your chat room about your subject of expertise, and/or you can schedule experts to participate in discussions. You can charge money for doing this, or use it to gain free publicity. Don't forget to work in how your product or service can help, but don't make it a sales pitch. If it's not informative and helpful people won't come back for the next one.

If you choose to have a chat room on your site it can operate in two ways. It can only be for special discussions or chat events which you or an expert would host. Or, you can have an open forum where people can chat in moderated free form with each other. The problem with the open forum method is that it can wreck havoc on your company's image if a user chooses to criticize or flame your site or business during the chat. You can include flaming provisions in the chat rules, but that doesn't mean people will abide by them and it's hard to regulate unless you choose to monitor it constantly.

You can even host other people's chats as an expert, which you could charge for, use as a bartering exchange, or do it purely for the publicity.

Chat rooms are a free way to grow your business and also a way to monitor what other people are saying about you. It is also a good way to keep on top of new trends and get tips and ideas from other like-minded people. When used properly they can be a very success-oriented marketing tool. So get out there and chat!

Bartering

Bartering is the exchanging of goods or services without the exchange of money. You can literally barter for anything including accounting, consulting, legal services, travel, food, electronics, office supplies, printing and much, much more. Bartering is a $15 billion a year business, primarily because it saves many businesses a pile of money.

There are two types of bartering, direct bartering and exchange bartering. Direct bartering is when you directly swap your product or service for the product or service of someone else. Exchange bartering is where you trade your product or service for credit or points that you can use in the future for goods or services that you need. Each point is usually worth about a dollar.

Direct bartering usually occurs between people who know each other and have something that each wants, so they make arrangements for a fair trade. You can even try contacting another business whom you have not had any previous experience with to see if they may be interested in forming a barter arrangement.

The key to a successful trade is in the offering. You already know what you want, just make sure that what you're offering is of equal or higher value and of interest to the other party. For example if you're a marketing consultant, contact a small business owner who may have little or no marketing experience, but don't contact a huge corporation which has many marketing executives on the payroll. If you're going to go this route it is better to try this with smaller businesses and always make sure that you speak directly to the decision maker. Cold calling/emailing is hit or miss, so prepare to be turned down often.

When you're direct bartering make sure both parties have a clear view of what they're giving and what they're getting. It is always best to have something in writing so there are no misunderstandings. You'll also find that in direct bartering, negotiation is a skill that will come in useful. You want to get as much as you can out of the deal, with the other party feeling like they got as much as they could.

Exchange bartering is when you go through a barter broker who makes all the bartering arrangements. You put the services or products that you wish to barter with up on the exchange and when someone takes you up on your offer they pay you the dollar amount in credits or points. Then when you need something and you find it on the exchange you can redeem the credits or points that you have received to pay for it. No cash exchanges hands, except maybe a small commission or fee to the bartering broker.

To give you an example of how a barter exchange works, suppose the owner of a restaurant wants to advertise on a local radio station which is a member of their barter exchange. The restaurant owner has accumulated $2,500 in exchange credits or points from meals that it has put up on the bartering exchange. The regular rate card price averages $50 per ad, so with $2,500 the restaurant owner can run 50 ads. The owner then trades in its $2,500 in credits or points to pay for the commercials. If it only costs the restaurant owner $0.25 on the dollar for the meals it bartered with, they're only really paying $625 for $2,500 worth of radio commercials. You can easily see why it's smarter to barter!

One important thing when bartering is that you must be honest. People will know if you manipulate your prices, and if your products or services are shoddy, word will travel quickly. Everything must be posted at fair market values, which are the same rates that you would charge cash paying customers. You can even offer a slight discount for people in the bartering exchange – that way they'll feel even more satisfied by doing business with you.

I should also note that most governments require that you report bartering gains as if you had received that amount in cash, it might be a good idea to check with your accountant on this to make sure you follow all tax laws in your area.

Bartering is a good way to get inexpensive and/or free advertising. If you become part of a barter exchange you get free promotion through the exchange site which exposes you to an audience you may not have been exposed to and you also get services or products that you need for a fraction of the price.

On the internet, the terms of a barter agreement are often limited only to the creativity of the participants. Some bartering arrangements won't even cost you a penny. If you sell advertising either in an ezine, newsletter or on your website, you can put unsold advertising spots up on the barter exchange. Since it's all electronic, it doesn't cost you anything to fill the spots except maybe a minute or two of your time. You can also use electronic products with a high perceived value and selling price such as ebooks, audio recordings or home study courses. Banner and link exchanges are also a form of bartering.

Linking Exchanges

A link exchange is where you exchange links with another site. The benefit is two-fold: First people visiting the site you are link exchanging with, may follow the link on their site to yours. Second, having reciprocal links to your site can increase your search engine ranking in some search engines. There are a few different ways to get links to your site, several of which are outlined below:

Free for All Sites

Free-for-All (FFA) sites are similar to a link exchange site, but instead of exchanging links, they are created to capture your email address and offer you a link in return. You usually choose a category for your link, as well as a text description to be placed on their webpage. I don't recommend FFA sites, for a few reasons:

- First, some search engines such as Google consider these sites an artificial and illegitimate way to increase link popularity (or in other words: spam), and may ban your site for participating.

- Secondly, they're in the business of capturing email addresses and will likely flood your email inbox with junk you don't want.

- Thirdly, the quality of links is very poor and hundreds of new links are added daily, making you a very small fish in a very large pond. Therefore, it is highly unlikely, unless you submit to them daily, that someone will actually follow a link from their site to yours.

Link Exchange Programs

Link exchange programs are made up of website owners who agree to place links to one another on their respective sites. The way it works is this: you sign up with them and they give you a bunch of links (say 20) to place on your site. In exchange, your link will usually be placed on an equal number of other sites. Most of these sites have a monthly membership fee of $5-$20 and up.

I don't recommend becoming part of a link exchange for the following reasons:

- Some link exchange programs require that you place the links on the home page of your site. Whether it is a text or a graphic link, it clutters up the main page of your site and makes your site look a lot less professional.

- As with FFA sites, many search engines consider link exchanges artificial link popularity and can ban your site because of it.

Informal Link Exchanges

Since FFA sites are out, and search engines discourage the use of link exchange programs, many webmasters choose to develop high quality links through a simple informal link exchange. An informal link exchange involves contacting the owners of another website that is related to your business and asking them if they want to set up a link exchange with you. This is the best kind of link to get because:

- They are in a similar but non-competing business and share a target market with you. So their customers can easily transform into your customers as well.

- You're more likely to receive actual targeted traffic to your site.

- Because the links are highly targeted it can positively affect your search engine ranking more than regular links.

Newsgroups, discussion forums and chat rooms are also great places to look for people to link exchange with. Don't expect every webmaster you contact to agree to link to your site, and be prepared to contact lots of webmasters before you see any results.

Link Tips

On my websites, I almost always have a special page for links. That way they don't clutter the other pages and they are all grouped together – so if someone wants to look at some other information related to my website, but not found on it, they have a nice convenient place to go.

Text links can actually be better to use than a banner or graphic because they contain visible keywords that graphics do not. If you want, you can use graphics and text descriptions together but don't forget to include alt tag keywords. Text links, depending on how they are used, can also be perceived by surfers as additional help, instead of a link or link exchange.

Be wary, having links on your page can cause surfers to leave your site to go to another. Solving this is simple; have a new window open with the link anytime you have a link to an outside site. Although, by the time they click on the link, you should either have them, or not have them – if you don't have them, it's probably too late to make an impression anyway.

Word of Mouth Advertising – Viral Marketing

When your customers talk... people listen. Word of mouth advertising is the most powerful and effective type of advertising there is, but it also happens to be the only kind of advertising you can't go to an advertising firm and buy. It has to be created, stimulated and nurtured with truly creative techniques.

How many times have you made a decision to do business with, or not do business with a company based on what someone told you about them? Probably more than you realize. Every business, either knowingly or unknowingly, generates word of mouth; it's your choice whether or not it will be positive or negative. Though it may seem inconsequential, word of mouth can make or break your business.

The reason that word of mouth advertising is so valuable is simple: Nothing you could ever say about yourself, your product or your business, can ever have as much impact and credibility as something somebody else says about you.

Believe it or not, artificial word of mouth advertising is still the most effective form of TV commercial. It's called 'Slice of Life' and you're probably very familiar with it. Ever see a commercial that shows a scene with a person telling a friend or acquaintance how good a product is or how it has changed their life? That's artificial word of mouth advertising.

Most businesses take whatever word of mouth advertising they can get, and for some businesses, it's the only advertising they do. If a customer has a bad experience with your company they'll tell everyone they know. If they have a good experience with you, they may tell one or two people. One of the best ways to build word of mouth advertising is to generate exceptionally positive experiences. It's the little things, when combined with other little things, that have a huge impact on the experience people have with you.

The foundation of generating positive word of mouth is by making sure you offer quality products and services.

How many times have you been treated rudely by customer service personnel at a place of business? What about business people that tell you they will call you right back, or that they will send the information out to you right away, or that they will do this, that, or another thing, but consistently don't follow through on their word? Do your best to follow through with what you say you're going to do. Don't make unreasonable promises you know you can't keep. If something unforeseen comes up that prevents you from living up to your word, try to let the other party know about it in advance. Don't just try to meet your customer's expectations - exceed them. In other words, under promise and over deliver.

Solicit feedback from your customers. Have comment forms and do surveys, find out what they like, what they don't like. Take these opportunities to improve your products, services and customer support. Providing friendly caring service gives that little bit extra and generates positive word of mouth for your business.

If a customer is not satisfied, do whatever you can to make them happy, within reason. You may even be able to turn a disgruntled customer into one of your best word of mouth advertisers.

Classified Ads

Classified ads are small adverts that are usually no more than three or four lines long. They are traditionally placed in the classified sections of newspapers and magazines. On the internet however, these ads can be placed in ezines, newsletters, special classified ad sites and the classified sections of other sites.

It is very difficult to make a sale directly through a classified ad because they are so small and just a few lines of text, even on the internet where you generally get much more space. What classified ads are great for is getting leads. Whether your goal is to get prospects to a sales page on your website, or call an 800 number for a 24hour recorded message, classified ads are a relatively inexpensive way to generate leads, whether you are online or offline.

Classified ads are also a great and inexpensive way to test headlines. Simply place the headline in the paper as a classified ad, add a phone number or website and track the results. Then try another headline the next week, and so on. The same principal can be applied to online ads just as easily; easier actually, just have them go to a webpage and track which ads pull the most.

How Effective are Classified Ads?

The results from submitting classified ads to ezines tends to be most effective, and submitting to classified sites tends to be least effective. When you submit an ad to a classified site, it must compete with hundreds of other ads (depending on the size of the site) and may be pushed out in a matter of hours to make room for new ads. This is largely due to automatic submission software which can submit thousands of classified ads in a very short space of time.

One of the most effective ways to get some traffic, from the few classified ads sites that are still visited by "real people," is to advertise a free gift. Then get their names and emails and you can market to them for as long as they remain on your list.

Tips for Ads

Classified ads are unique and to the point because you have only a few short lines to elicit a response from the reader. It is very important that you test and track different ads to see which pulls the greatest response. A good classified ad should include:

- A heading or title which includes at least one major benefit.

- Should explain how your reader will benefit from responding to your ad using as few words as possible.

- A strong call to action (go to our website, call this number).

- A re-direct for your link to the webpage you are advertising (having a direct link to your site can harm your search engine ranking).

- Some kind of contact information, including your name, website and possibly your email and phone number. If you're going to post your email address, always use a secondary address. Besides receiving emails from prospective clients, you will likely receive loads of spam.

Posting Your Ad

There are tons free classified ad sites, and a bunch of paid ones as well. Obviously the paid ones are much better quality than the free sites, but then again, you need to pay to use them. I suggest that at some point you try some of the paid sites, track your results and see whether they are worthwhile.

For the free sites, you can either post ads by hand, which is very time consuming, you can hire an online submission service, or use an automatic submission program. If you're serious about classified ad marketing, use an automatic program so you don't waste your time and can get on with the rest of your business. Online submission services and automatic submission programs both work the same way; they take your site and submit it to hundreds of classified websites automatically and quickly. Most submission sites will charge a one time submission fee, or have monthly submission plans, where they will submit your site periodically for as long as you are a member. If you're using an automatic submission program, it can be web-based or something that you run from your computer. If you buy the program, you can submit ads whenever you like as often as you like. If you go the route of the online program, you again can pay a monthly fee, or pay on a *per diem* basis. Whatever method you choose, to get the most out of free classified advertising, you should resubmit the ads about once a week.

Your results will depend on how good your ad and offer are. A poorly written classified ad is not going to get any results, no matter how many sites you submit it to. A good classified ad must appeal to the reader and as such, it must say exactly what you want it to say in the least possible number of words to keep your operating costs down. And finally it must produce the results that you hope to achieve.

Your first objective is to grab the reader's attention – if your ad doesn't do this, the rest of the ad is useless, no matter how good it is. To do this you need to assume that the reader is scanning the page on which your ad appears in the company of many other ads. Your ad must have something that gets the reader to stop scanning and look at your ad. Therefore the title, or the first few words of the ad are of utmost importance and it's worth taking a little time to write them properly. Then the body of the ad should state how it would benefit the reader to take your desired call to action.

When I write classified ads, I write down everything I want to say, then go through it combining phrases, crossing out words and condensing it into only a few lines. I always do this in a word processor on my computer so it is easy to cut and paste. When you're all said and done, you should be left with a few lines that are simple enough for everyone to understand.

When it comes to online advertising, classified ads are usually overlooked, simply because of their simplicity. Although they're not great for outright selling, they are a good way to generate leads that you can eventually turn into sales and subsequently lifetime customers. That being said, always be sure to treat your leads as you would your best customer, and who knows, they may become your best customer some day.

Blogs

The blog is taking the online world by storm and is quickly becoming an internet fad as more and more people start their own blogs everyday on free sites like www.blogger.com or www.wordpress.com. If you want to start your own blog, simply go to one of these sites, sign up, add some content and voila, you've got a blog.

A blog is simply an online diary or journal where people communicate their personal thoughts, along with web links, and/or other interesting information on an ongoing basis. A blog is essentially a mixture of what is happening in the blogger's life, and what is happening on the web. They are forums for voicing opinions and developing communities with common interests. There are really no set rules as to what defines a blog, but it is generally accepted to be a web document containing some personal thoughts of the writer combined with any other number of elements. Blogs are sometimes referred to as "web logs," however this can cause some confusion as "web log" can also refer to a web server's log files.

To smart marketers, blogs offer more than the communication of thoughts on the internet. Blogs are becoming an increasingly popular advertising medium and another source of revenue for marketers. There are two ways to market with blogs, the first is to use your own blog to build relationships, customer loyalty, branding, and subtly mention your products or services in them. The second way to market with blogs is to place ads on or in other people's blogs.

One of the reasons that blogs are popular with marketers is that they often rank high in search engines because the content is usually updated daily.

Blogging

Since blogs are personal, a company or a business can't technically have its own blog. However, the president, CEO, owner, or an employee can have their own personal blog. The business the blogger is part of can then use the blog to advertise their products or services subtly throughout the blog, or less subtly as graphical or text ads on the blog page.

A blog is also an excellent way to popularize products and services. It serves an informal medium for reaching potential customers. And blogs are an excellent tool for viral marketing, or free word of mouth publicity.

Search engines look for change. If the search engine sees that you have new information, they will see that they need to visit your website more often to keep their listings current. To achieve the optimum search engine ranking, you should ideally update your blog 4-6 times a day. Since that's often not possible, you can settle for once every couple days, or use an RSS feed to add content.

Rich Site Summary, or RSS feeds, allow you to post content on your blog automatically from any website with an RSS feed or vice versa. Types of content could include news feeds, events listings, news stories, headlines, project updates, excerpts from discussion forums etc. You'll need to ask your website designer to do this for you, as it does get a little technical.

Blog Ads

Blog ads work because blogs serve as watering holes for like-minded people. Bloggers are vocal and influential, so people read them with passion and tend to give them more influence in their lives than they probably should. Blog advertising is appropriate for new products launches, service offers, newsworthy material and other things of relevant value.

Blog ads require different creative tactics than most of the rest of the internet. There are three ad options: They can be graphical in nature, solo text ads, or text ads intertwined into the actual text content of the blog. Like the blog itself, successful blog ads rely heavily on content. Humor and sarcasm tend to work well, as do ads with a timely newsworthy hook and/or some thought-provoking text.

Some of the best blog ads are placed right into the blog, so as to appear to be part of the blog itself. These types of ads don't actually appear to be ads to the casual reader, so they give some extra credibility that you couldn't get from an ad.

Blog ad pricing is all over the place, but is usually priced by CPM, and can be priced by PPC, and rarely by PPA. Prices usually go up from $5 CPM to $50 CPM, or range anywhere from $0.10 - $1.0+ if you pay per click.

Blog ads have become so popular that there are blog advertising agencies that will design and place ads for you on targeted blogs. Some of the more popular sites are listed here:

www.blogads.com
www.weblogs.com
www.adbrite.com
www.feedburner.com

Getting started with a blog of your own does not take a lot of technical know-how and almost none if you use a site like www.blogger.com. Today blogs are spreading across the internet like wild fire and there does not seem to be any sign of abating.

Section 6

Affiliate and Joint Venture Marketing

34

Affiliate Marketing

What is Affiliate Marketing?

Affiliate marketing can be one of the best ways to increase your passive income without the worries and responsibilities that go along with running your own business or selling your own products. Or, if you have your own products, affiliate programs easily allow you to advertise your products or services on thousands of websites while only paying for actual results.

Affiliate programs (also known as associate or reseller programs) are the process of marketing products or services on behalf of other companies and being paid a commission. Compensation is based on performance measures, typically in the form of sales, but can sometimes include opt-in signups, registrations, free trials and more.

Affiliate programs are really just another form of partnering and networking. The way they work is that you're paid a commission when your affiliate link leads to a sale or some other action. The strategy is also known as performance based marketing. Forrester Research estimates that over 20% of internet revenues are driven by affiliate marketing, so it's no small thing.

This basic premise made Amazon a billion dollar company. Though Amazon wasn't the first, they have one of the most successful affiliate programs on the internet. Amazon pays people a commission of up to 8.5% on purchases made when someone clicks on a link from your website to Amazon's website and buys Amazon's products.

Now millions of small businesses are taking advantage of the same concept. It's like having an army of commissioned salespeople working for you, and you don't pay anyone a nickel unless they sell something.

The products or services you can sell range from digital downloads and membership websites to home gym equipment and vitamins. Pretty much any product that can be sold in a store can be sold online and an affiliate can earn a commission for putting the buyer and seller together.

Affiliate marketing is really a form of PPA, or pay per action marketing. Paying only for performance shifts much of the advertising risk from the merchants to the affiliates, although merchants still assume some risk of fraud from partner sites.

Some sites, with recurring access or membership fees will pay you a commission each month, as long as the person you signed up via your affiliate link remains a member. This is especially attractive as it allows you to make a steady monthly affiliate income and a lot more money over time, than being paid a one-time flat fee. Since the payout over time is larger and recurring, the companies who use this affiliate model are more likely to have people promote their affiliate programs than their one time fee counterparts.

Signing up for an Affiliate Program

Since this book is more about marketing your business, product or service on the internet, I'm not going to go into great detail about signing up for other people's affiliate programs and marketing their products for them. Althought, I wouldn't be doing you justice if I didn't give it some space in this book.

If you're looking to sign up for an affiliate program there are a couple of routes you can take. You can go to an affiliate directory and browse through many programs options, or you can find a site complimentary to yours with an affiliate program and sign up for it individually.

To sign up for an affiliate program, you simply complete the site's application form and submit it to them. Some sites will give you instant approval and others require a person to review and approve your application before it is approved. Once approved, you'll get a special coded affiliate link that you can copy into all of your promotional efforts. Some of the more popular affiliate directories are:

www.cj.com
www.clickbank.com
www.affiliatesdirectory.com

Something else that you may want to consider is how many affiliate programs you actually join. Some studies suggest that sites that make the most money from affiliate programs are affiliates of only a small handful of programs. If you're an affiliate of a 100 different programs, you can't concentrate promotional efforts on each of them individually. Furthermore, if you advertise for hundreds of different affiliate networks on your site, you may wind up earning only a few dollars each per month from each network. If the minimum payout is $25, or $50, it may take you a long time before you accrue enough to be paid, like once or twice a year.

Choosing an Affiliate Program

While the payment scheme a particular affiilate program offers is paramount, it is not necessarily the largest contributing factor in how much commission you'll make. The most important thing is to make sure that the affiliate programs you sign up for promote match the content of your site and more importantly your target audience.

It doesn't do any good to have an affiliate link on a health site for computers, even if it pays ten times more than any health related affiliate programs. If the people that visit the site aren't interested in buying a new computer, they're not likely to click on the link and actually buy something. Also, with unrelated affiliate links, you can't embed them into the content of your site, you need to post them as ads which is less likely to get them clicked on.

After you've narrowed down a few affiliate programs that fit with your website, start looking at the commissions they offer, their conversion rates, their product prices, the promotional material they offer, the payout scheme and some other options mentioned above. Ideally, you want to find the best combination of high commissions on high ticket products, on a website with a good conversion rate. The more promotional material (pre-written emails, banner and other graphical ads, text ads and articles) they offer to advertise their product, the easier it will be for you.

One Tier Verses Two Tier

One tier affiliate programs pay commissions on one only level. For each sale an affiliate makes, they will receive a commission. For example, if you offer your affiliates 50% commission and your product sells for $50, for every sale your affiliate makes, they will receive a $25 commission.

Two tier affiliate programs pay commissions on two levels. Affiliates will receive a commission for each sale they make, and they will also receive a commission for each sale their recruits make. Two tier affiliate programs usually divide the commissions over two levels. For example, if you want to give your affiliates a total of 50% commission for each sale, you would offer 30% commission on their first level sales and an extra 20% commission for second level sales. If your affiliate makes a $50 sale, they would receive a $15 commission. If one of their recruits makes a sale, they would receive an additional $10 commission.

You can easily see that two tiered programs are usually better, as they can potentially make you more money. Just be sure to take the time to weigh all options when comparing affiliate programs.

So, what do you do once you've signed up for an affiliate program? You sit back and get rich. No, not really, you need people to click on the links and buy or sign up for stuff. And to do that you need to drive traffic to your site, or get the affiliate links out there and clicked on some other way.

One of the easiest ways to promote your affiliate links is to write an ebook. That way you could have your affiliate links throughout the ebook and on a resources page. When someone clicks on them and buys something, you get the commission. Then sell the ebook with resell rights, so it gets spread around as quickly as possible. Then you simply sit back and wait for the commissions to pour (slowly) in. You can also have affiliate links throughout the copy of your website, write and distribute articles with the links in them, market the links via your email list, have them in the signatures of all your outgoing emails, post them in your newsletters, or place them anywhere else you can think of.

If you have an information based website, blog or an opt-in email list and don't have any of your own products to promote, become an affiliate and promote other people's stuff. It's easy. There's no product development cost, no dealing with customer's questions, no order processing, no shipping, no advertising development costs, no nothing. Simply promote the affiliate links, drive traffic to them and let the money pour in 24/7.

35

Creating an Affiliate Program

If you're marketing your own product on the internet, you can dramatically increase your sales with an affiliate program. An affiliate program will enable you to recruit an unlimited number of individuals to sell your products. The key to obtaining affiliates is to offer a nice commission for each sale. The higher the commissions, the more affiliates you'll recruit.

The best way to have a successful affiliate program is to give affiliates what they want. This includes:

- High payouts
- To get paid on a recurring basis
- Sales being tracked correctly
- Real time access to stats
- Email notification of every sale
- Promotions that are proven to work
- FAQ's, tutorials, ads
- Sales pages with high conversion rates

Affiliates will constantly measure you and your program against other affiliate programs, so research your competition and make sure you are the best.

Since there are thousands of affiliate programs on the internet, you must sell your affiliate program just like your products if you want to be successful. In other words, your affiliate sales letter should be written like a product sales letter. You must persuade your visitors to join your affiliate program by packing your affiliate sales letter with benefits. Tell them exactly what your affiliate program will do for them, how much commission they will receive and make the sign up process dead simple.

Commission

One of the first decisions you'll need to make is the payment scheme you're going to use. The more you pay, the more people you'll have signup for your program, and actually promote it.

Most digital products (ebooks, software, downloadable audio/video) which don't have any reproduction cost usually have a commission split 50/50 of the sale price. A 50/50 split is generally accepted as fair and no one can really argue with it. Both the developer and the affiliate both may encounter some costs in the production/advertising, but one doesn't really outweigh the other by much.

With physical products the commission may be based on the scale of profit. Therefore, if a $100 CD course and transcripts cost $20 to reproduce, the affiliate and creator may split the profit 50/50, or $40 each.

Higher ticket items may have a lower commission than lower priced items, but are still highly desirable for affiliates due to the larger profit margin per sale.

Keep in mind that the commission can be dependent upon the product, and just because you have multiple products in your affiliate program does not mean they all need to have the same percentage commission. Take this book for example; due to the fairly high production cost (compared to electronic based information products) I pay a 35% commission, whereas I pay up to a 50% commission on some of my other products. But that brings up another important factor, which is the ease of sale. A larger percentage of people that go to the sales page for this book will convert into sales, as opposed to people who click on an affiliate link for lawn tractors. The reasons are quite simple: one is the $20 price, the other is the compelling benefits for buying this book. If you buy an expensive lawn tractor, you can simply cut your lawn quicker. If you buy this book, you can potentially transform your entire life; and it's only $20. For more info on reselling this book simply go to www.ssim.biz/reseller.

Will your program pay commissions on one or two tiers? Two tier programs are usually more effective in recruiting affiliates because the offer is more attractive. In the mind of the affiliate, they can recruit affiliates and let them do the selling while they sit back and let the money come in. But this is not always the case, since usually less than 5% of affiliates actively sell the programs they are members of.

If you have a membership program, will commissions be recurring or one-time flat fees? While recurring commissions are most attractive to affiliate promoters, they also usually cost you the most money over time. Though, it's less money upfront, which can be attractive to you as well. Do a little research and see what your competitors do, then do it better.

In summary, if you're selling a $20 ebook, it's almost expected that the sale be split 50/50; but if you sell a $300 CD course and manual, most affiliates would be happy with a 70/30 split in favor of the developer.

Payment / Refunds

It's up to you how you want to pay your affiliates, and it does help if they reside in the same country that you do. If they do, then checks are an option. If not then you can pay by bank transfer or through PayPal's mass pay function. PayPal works well since it is compatible for out of country affiliates and it is very easy and painless to setup. For more information on PayPal, check it out at www.PayPal.com.

If your affiliates do any volume of sales, it might be worth your while to setup up a separate bank account where all the sales from affiliates go. That way it's not overwhelming to your bank account when it's time to pay. If your affiliates did $50,000 in sales in July (which is split 50/50), you want to make sure that you don't spend any of their money by accident and fall short when it's time to pay. Transfer it to a separate bank account and you'll never have to worry about it - it also makes your accounting easier.

Most people pay their affiliates on the 15th of the month for the previous month. So, affiliate commissions for the month of January would be paid on the 15th of February. That way if there are any refunds, most of them will occur before the affiliates are paid, which should be automatically deducted from the payout amount by the software that you use.

In your affiliate agreement you need to clearly state what happens in the unlikely event of a refund. The way 99% of programs work, is that if there is a refund from an affiliate's sale the affiliate no longer gets the commission, because the sale was refunded. Otherwise the affiliate or a friend of theirs could buy a whole bunch, collect the commission and refund the sale, therefore scamming the system.

Affiliate Contracts

Having an affiliate contract that all affiliates must agree to before they can become an affiliate has never been a bad idea. It's always good to get everything out in the open, and this way if there's any kind of problem, the solution should be in the affiliate contract. If everything is spelled out in writing ahead of time, then your affiliates should know what's expected of them and there's not much room for discrepancies.

Your contract should address everything including how much and when you pay your affiliates, how you pay them and under what circumstances they may forfeit their commissions. The contract should also have guidelines as to what form of advertising the affiliate may do (not sending out spam etc.) and what type of advertising they may use. I usually only let affiliates use ads that I have created for them, instead of letting them use/create their own. Not only does this keep everything consistent, but it also protects me against any claims of false advertising. It's also a good idea to use the affiliate contract to limit your company's liability for actions taken by an affiliate, state terms of termination of contract, and have a confidentiality clause.

Something else that you may want to have in your contract is the minimum payment amount. To avoid wasting resources issuing cheques for very small amounts, set a minimum payment amount of $25, $50 or $100 before you pay affiliates.

It's completely up to you if you want to get a lawyer involved. If everything is stated clearly in plain, clear language and there is not much room for interpretation then there isn't really a need for legal advice. However if your affiliate program is extravagant and complex or deals with super sensitive information then it might be a good idea to have a lawyer look it over for you. There are plenty of places on the web to get an affiliate contract template; simply customize it to your exact purpose and that should be good enough in most cases.

Tracking Software

The whole affiliate process needs to be tracked by some kind of affiliate tracking software. Most affiliate programs track users by their IP address. When someone clicks on an affiliate link, the affiliate program adds a cookie to the user's computer, which allows them to track the visitor and tell if they make a sale.

So, when you're ready to set up your affiliate program, there are basically two options. The first option is to purchase an affiliate software program and install it on your server. Affiliate software will track your affiliate sales and enable your affiliates to view their stats. This option requires that you run your affiliate program and you are responsible for accepting payment and sending out commission checks.

The second option is to use a third party web-based, affiliate tracking company to run your affiliate program for you. These companies will track your affiliate sales, enable your affiliates to check their stats and some will even send out commission checks for you.

I use the affiliate software that is built in with the 1StartCart shopping cart system. It will automatically track all commissions for me, tally up the numbers, and notify me when it is time to send out checks. It also allows affiliates to login and track their stats in real time and get access to your promotional material. And it integrates 100% with my shopping cart and autoresponder because they're all part of the same system. The best part is, it doesn't cost me anything extra – it's included for free with my shopping cart. If you're interested in making more money with your affiliate program, you can find out more at www.1StartCart.com.

www.Assoctrac.com is another affiliate tracking program. Assoctrac offers real time tracking, affiliate login, ad trackers and automatic auto-response messages. www.Clickbank.com is another popular affiliate program which also allows you to accept credit cards and can automatically pay commissions to affiliates. They charge a setup fee, and a flat fee plus a percentage per sale, but no monthly fees. For some other options, you can login to the members site.

Here are some questions to ask when choosing affiliate software:

- Can it handle two tier programs?
- Will it work with multiple websites?
- Can affiliates place codes on their links for tracking?
- Can different commissions be paid to different affiliates? And for different products?
- Can you send email to all affiliates?
- Does it notify you and your affiliates by email of new sales?
- Does it integrate with your shopping cart software?
- Can affiliates login to your members section or area?
- Is there a section for promo material, FAQs and tutorials for members?

Take your time and select the best affiliate option for your business. If you're just starting your own affiliate program, it's a little easier to start with a third party affiliate program. This will save you time and money upfront as they're much easier to use, and don't require any technical ability. This will enable you to concentrate on making more sales and developing new products.

Tips on Finding New Affiliates

The most important aspect of any affiliate program is its promotion. Here are some quick tips to get new affiliates:

- Make sure that your affiliate program is listed in as many affiliate directories as possible. This will be the first place most people look when they want to sign up for an affiliate program.

- Publicize your affiliate program. There are many companies that do not publicize, or advertise their affiliate programs. If nobody knows about them how will people sign up for them? At the very least, always have a link on the bottom of the main page of your website (and every other page), where users can click to find out more information about the affiliate program you offer.

- Find complimentary sites that already attract your target market and contact them to see if they might be interested in signing up for your program.

- Always place a link on your webpages that link to an affiliate program sales page. You need to sell your program. Provide the benefits of doing business with you, and how easy you make it for your affiliates to make money.

- Have a very strong affiliate signup sales letter. This sales copy is just as important as a sales letter for any of your products. Emphasize the benefits, and give an example of the financial rewards. For an example of an affiliate sales page, click on over to www.JustinMichie.com/affiliates.

- If you have a two tier program, as a secondary focus, ask your affiliates to sign up new affiliates and give them the tools to do so.

- Something else you can resort to is hiring an affiliate management company (similar to an advertising agency) to find new affiliates for you.

- Lastly, promote your affiliate program absolutely everywhere you can.

Ways to Increase Affiliate Sales

The stats on affiliate programs aren't pretty. Only about 5% of people that join an affiliate program make sales on a regular basis. I know it sounds crazy, but you want to write as many checks as possible every month. The more checks you write, the more your affiliates are selling and the more money you make. One of the best ways to increase affiliate sales is to keep in constant contact with them, so you can encourage more of them to go out and sell more.

When an affiliate first signs up for your program, add them to an email autoresponder series. Get them excited about selling your product. Give them encouragement, teach them new strategies and techniques and provide other resources. Some ways to help increase your affiliate sales are outlined below:

Promo Ebook

To further increase sales, you can also create an ebook that is directed towards your target audience and allow it to be freely distributed. This ebook should be packed with valuable information and, at the same time, used as a sales tool for your product. Customize a copy of your ebook for each of your affiliates (with their affiliate links in) and allow them to freely distribute it.

Opt-in Email List

Something else that you can do to help keep your affiliates motivated is set up an opt-in email list. This allows you to stay in constant contact with them, which can almost double you affiliates sales. It also allows you to send them sales letters, articles, and notify them of any other new promo material available to assist them in making more sales.

FAQs

Have a frequently asked questions (FAQ) page in the affiliate's members site. Not only will it help make it easier for them to sell, but it will also save you time answering any common customer support questions. Make sure your FAQs cover your site thoroughly and answer the wide variety of questions which are specific to your affiliate program. As your affiliate program grows, you'll receive tons of questions from your members. Whenever you receive the same question more than once, always post the answer on your FAQ page.

Training Tools

It is absolutely critical that you provide your affiliates with all the tools they need to sell successfully. Nobody knows more about your product than you do. Provide your affiliates with banners, headlines, endorsement letters, testimonials, sample ads, graphics, articles where they can insert their affiliate links and anything else that will assist them in making sales.

Contests

You can run contests for the top affiliates, or have prizes for affiliates that reach certain levels or are the most improved. This can either be monetary, in the form of your products/services, or any other kind of compensation.

Conversion Rate

You want to make sure that your sales page has a high closing or conversion rate. If your website doesn't close a large percentage of sales, your affiliates won't be too happy and you won't make much money. Remember to continually test each element individually.

Affiliate Fraud

Some affiliates have been known to use a stolen credit card to make sales and get a commission. When the credit card holder files for a chargeback, you lose money, and in plain English, get screwed. One common way to avoid this is to make sure that your affiliate program tracks the IP addresses of people making sales. If the IP addresses are the same and an affiliate is either new or all of a sudden starts doing thousands in sales, you know there's something fishy going on. Also, most affiliate programs track the number of unique visitors that click on the affiliate's link. If they have had ten visitors and all of them have purchased something, you might want to check it out. Another thing to watch out for is multiple purchases from the same credit card.

You can also limit the countries that your affiliates can live in. You might not want to send a check overseas to someone who might have used a stolen credit card number. It's far too hard to do anything about it. I know I probably lose a lot of potential legitimate affiliates doing it this way, but I also don't want to get taken for thousands of dollars.

Affiliate marketing is a simple way to make money like crazy using other people's time, expertise and effort. If you don't already have an affiliate program get, one. Once you set it up, it is one of the easiest ways known to man to sell your products. Simply promote it with a strong marketing campaign and the sales will roll in. And the best part is, you don't pay anyone until you get paid first.

36

Joint Ventures

If you are a business owner who wants to significantly increase your market reach, break down entry barriers to a new market, or simply generate skyrocketing profits in a short amount of time then a joint venture may well be in your future.

Hopefully, by now you've heard of joint venture marketing (JVM) and have at least a basic understanding of what it's all about. In all honesty, joint ventures (JV's) are what business is made of. They are one of the simplest and quickest ways to make a lot of money in a very short amount of time. Joint ventures work so well, that fortune 500 companies do them all the time - McDonalds does them, Wal-Mart does them (they do it together), and so should you.

JV partnerships can be one of the most rewarding and profitable methods used to influence your online business in a financially positive way. If you're not utilizing this strategic weapon, chances are your competition is (or will soon be) using this to their competitive advantage, quite possibly against you. According to the Commonwealth Alliance Program, businesses estimated that in 2005, 25% of their total revenue (40 trillion dollars) was the result of joint ventures.

A joint venture is defined as a cooperative arrangement or partnership that will mutually benefit two or more companies or individuals that have complimentary products and/or services.

Let me give you an example of a simple JV:

Company X sells home study computer courses on various topics including: word processing, email, the internet etc. Company Y sells computers online at an average of about 100 per week. Company X thinks that Company Y would be a good JV partner, so they call them up and agree to form a mutually beneficial partnership. Company Y is going to let company X send a sales letter to all of their previous customers from the last four years (100 per week x 52 weeks per year x 4 years → 20,800 customers) in return for 50% of the net sales. Company X sends out a well-written sales letter and receives an industry average response rate of 2%. Since their average sale is approx. $50 their total sales are ($50 x 20,800 x 2%), or

$20,800, which they split 50/50 with company Y.

$10,400 is a lot of money, especially for only a few hours work sending out a simple sales letter to someone else's email list… but what if we could somehow increase the response rate? What if we could double it? Then double it again? Is an 8% response, or better, unheard of? Absolutely not! That's what *endorsed* JVM is all about. You know at the start of this chapter where I said that JV's are one of the easiest and most successful ways to make money in business? Well… I didn't tell you the complete truth! Endorsed joint ventures are without a doubt, are one of the best ways to make a lot of money quickly and easily in any business.

There are many different types of joint ventures, but since this is an internet marketing book, we're going to concentrate primarily on electronic or online joint ventures.

An endorsed JV is when the company or individual that you are partnering with endorses or recommends your products or service to the customers on their mailing list. This is one of the only ways that you can successfully go directly from a prospect to a customer. One of the reasons that this can be so successful is that your partner already has an established relationship with everyone on their list. They have an established rapport with their customer base who values their opinion.

Let me show you an example of why endorsements work so well:

My wife's grandmother was in town (she lives in Bermuda) and had lunch with my wife at a local restaurant. When they returned, I asked them how their lunch was. Her grandmother said that her meal was "heaven," and that she'd just eaten some of the best ribs of her life. I love ribs, so the next time we went out for dinner, guess where we went? And guess what I ordered?

Now, if I received a flyer in the mail from Rob's Rib House advertising "Best Ribs You'll Ever Eat?" would I eat there? Maybe, maybe not.

You see the difference is, I know my grandma-in-law – we have an established relationship. I know that she is a very classy lady who has traveled the world many times over, and that she really appreciates good food. If she says something is "heaven" I know it's going to be excellent; and there's an excellent chance next time I have an opportunity to try it, I will.

When you receive a flyer in the mail from a restaurant advertising that they have the best ribs in town, why should you believe them? Isn't it possible that their opinion may be a little biased? And exactly whose opinion is it anyways?

Still on the topic of ribs, if you read an article written by a renowned restaurant critic, who rated the ribs at Rob's Rib House, number two in the entire country? If you enjoyed ribs as much as I do, might you possibly go a little out of your way to try them? Of course you would.

That's the power of using an endorsement in your marketing. Many large companies have paid celebrities millions to appear in their commercials and ads. Most people know Michael Jordan isn't going to put his name to a product that is crap, and risk harming his reputation; even if he is getting paid to do it. Just the fact that Michael Jordan supports something instantly communicates that the product is quality, and endorses (or gives credibility) to the ad.

Let's take a look at an example of an endorsed joint venture versus cold mailing:

Let's suppose that you are selling a $97 home study course on how to write a book and get it published. Since you don't have a mailing list of your own, you set up a JV with someone in a similar but non-competing business who has a 10,000 person list. If your mailing goes well, and you get an industry average 2% response rate, your total sales would be $19,400 (10,000 x 2% x $97). Why is your response rate only 2%? Because people don't know anything about you, your business or your product. You're a stranger. You haven't established a relationship with them, and they have no reason to believe what you have to say is true – why should they? Not to mention that they are afraid of being ripped off.

Now, what if you got the owner of the mailing list (who communicates regularly with his clients, and thus has established a relationship with them) to write an endorsement on top of your sales letter? They could let their customers know how great they believe your offer to be, how valuable your product or service is, and how it has positively affected their life. If you took the exact same product, mailing list and sales letter, and did everything else the same, except that now you have the owner of the list endorsing you, do you think that you might be a little more successful?

If your JV partner had most of the key factors in place such as a good relationship with a high quality list, instead of a 2% response rate, you might achieve a success rate of 10% or more. Let's do the math, that's (10,000 x 10% x $97) = $97,000. That's incredible! One short letter made you five times more money than even the most well written and powerful sales letter ever could. That my friends, is the power of endorsed joint venture marketing.

Perhaps the best part about JVM is that it creates a win – win – win situation. Your partner wins because they make money with little or no effort, you win because you get a lot more sales than you could get on your own, with little, or no advertising cost, and the customer wins because they get affordable access to a product or service that benefits them.

The benefits of forming a JV partnership really are limitless. Here are 10 of the more potent benefits you might expect:

1. You can increase your credibility by teaming up and getting endorsements from other reputable businesses or experts.

2. You can very cost effectively gain new leads, customers and/or newsletter subscribers.

3. JV's save time and money on marketing and advertising costs.

4. You can easily and conveniently increase your sales and profits.

5. You can offer your customers new products and services.

6. You can target other potential markets, and/or find hidden income streams.

7. You can expand and grow your business quickly.

8. You can spread/reduce risk.

9. You can develop new technology (ie. software).

10. You can increase product distribution.

There are risks involved with joint ventures, but they pale in comparison with the risk associated if you partook in the same activities alone; and the potential rewards far outweigh the risk. Some of the risk you would expect to shoulder may include any number of the following:

- Wasting your time
- Losing money
- Accomplishing nothing
- Reducing your credibility

As always it is important to completely evaluate the risks involved and do your homework before and during the process.

As we discussed in a previous chapter, JVM is also a good way to get started in building your email database. But it proposes a little difficulty, which needs to be overcome. If you are relatively unknown, how do you get someone to agree to let you send out an email to their database?

You do everything you can to make it as easy as possible for them, and make the offer as attractive as you can. Give them a large percentage of the sales that you do with their list. Heck, even if you give them 100% of the sales or profits you make it can still be well worth it in the long run for you on the back-end.

Initiating a JV Partnership

You always need to put the other person or company involved first. Show them how partnering with you can help their business grow. Explain exactly what you are proposing using plain English. Put emphasis on the benefits to them and their customers, and how simple and easy it will be to work with you.

Explain your proposed commission arrangement; they may want to negotiate. 50% is standard, and anything less will likely get a blind eye, unless it is a very high profile product or something that incurs a high production cost.

If you think a potential business partner with a large email list has the time to write even an endorsement for your product, you're going to be in for a wake up call. You need to provide absolutely all the marketing including email copy, graphical ads, a high conversion sales site, testimonials, product support, order processing. If they need to do anything more than push a few buttons, it's too much. The more simple and painless it is for them, the more likely they are to accept. **Make it so easy that all they have to do is take the check to the bank.**

Always provide a sample product upfront with your proposal and don't try and charge them for it. When you go to the ice cream shop, do they charge you to taste the different flavors? Of course they don't. It doesn't make any sense to charge someone for the opportunity to try and get their business. So always provide a free complimentary copy of your product for them to review.

To get action, you clearly need to demonstrate in the proposal that the time it takes them to form a partnership with you is far outweighed by the rewards they'll receive.

JV Initiation Tips

Network: Always keep a lookout for possible joint ventures partners. Newsgroups and forums are a good place to look for like-minded people. Any seminars or courses you participate in are also a good place to meet potential partners.

Clarity: When you're approaching potential joint venture partners, be clear and upfront about your goals in your relationship with them. Don't go into too much detail unless they ask for it, and don't add hype or fluff to written or verbal proposals - they'll most likely see through it.

Be sincere - build trust and relationships: Joint ventures are like any relationship, where trust is paramount. Be sincere, courteous, friendly and honest.

Think long-term: Build a relationship to last a lifetime, not just a one time partnership. Don't burn bridges; the most profitable JVs are ones that run continuously over a long period of time.

Never give up: Contact as many potential partners as you can, then follow-up with them until they give you an answer. Remember it takes on average seven contacts to get an answer. Not everybody will say yes, especially the big guys. You may only get one response in ten, but don't forsake the cause because of a few failures; you never know when you will hit the goldmine.

Get noticed: People that receive JV proposals don't just receive one now and then. They get multiple JV proposals daily, and with an average offer mailing frequency of every 2 weeks they can only choose one in that time period. In order to get selected, you need to get noticed, and to get noticed you need to do something different. One big thing you can do is personalize proposals as much as you can. A boilerplate template won't get you noticed. Give them something others are not offering.

Irresistibility: Make your offer irresistible. Make your offer so good they could not possible refuse it. Describe the benefits in terms they will appreciate. Do everything for them, write the email copy, provide the ads, testimonials, links etc. Make it so simple they don't need to do anything, except hit the "send email" button. Above all, really highlight the financial benefits.

JV Agreement

Once you have found a party that is willing to do a joint venture, you may want to consider putting an agreement in writing. Simply outline the terms, and which party is to bring which assets (both tangible and intangible) to the agreement. Include things like commissions, time frames, payment terms and any other variables of relevance. Depending on the money involved and type of agreement it may be advisable to have a lawyer draw up the agreement.

Questions to Qualify JV Partners

Here are some questions you should ask your potential JV partners:

Do you have a customer list or database, which includes at the very least the

names and email addresses of your customers?

This is the first question you should ask them. If they don't have a list, then you can't joint venture with them. If they do have one, then continue on with the other questions.

Is your list composed of buyers (customers) or visitors?

A list composed of buyers is always going to be much more profitable than one composed of visitors. For the purposes of JVM you generally want to use a list composed of buyers. Buyers already have a quality relationship established with the list owner, whereas visitors are just that - visitors. Also, if you send an email to just visitors, or a list with visitors on it, they may accuse you of sending them spam. Always make sure that you ask the list owner if everyone on the list opted in to be on it. If they say no, or are unsure, thank them for their time and move on.

How big is your mailing list?

Size does matter. However, don't be fooled by extremely large lists, the quality of the list is much more important than the quantity. You don't necessarily need a large list to make money, especially if it is a list of very high quality. As well, potential partners with smaller lists are probably more likely to agree to form a joint venture with you.

How often do you contact people on your list?

This is another important question to ask. Someone who sends mailings out too often may desensitize their list to future offerings and many people may automatically delete the emails because they don't have time to read all of them. On the other hand, if mailings aren't sent often enough, a strong relationship with the customer may not be established. I find that 2-4 times a month works best in most cases.

What kind of success have you had with past JV partners?

If their success rate has been low with past joint ventures find out why. It could be for several reasons; low quality mailing list, poorly written sales letter, product was priced incorrectly, product was not of good quality etc. Ask to see the sales letter, or any other material that was sent out. If the sales letter is good, the pricing appears to be correct and the product is solid, chances are that the mailing list may not be of the quality that you are looking for. The higher their previous success rates, the more $$$ you are likely to make.

Do the clients on your list buy from you, and if so, how often?

The more they buy the better. If customers are used to spending money with the owner of the list, they are more likely to feel comfortable trusting their recommendation and buying from you.

What percentage of clients have bought from you more than once in the past?

This is helpful in determining the relationship between the owner and his customers. Generally the larger the percentage, the better the relationship, and therefore the better the quality of the list and the more sales you'll do.

When was the last time they have bought a similar product to what you are offering?

The sooner the better, as long as it was not too soon. It is generally good to wait an absolute minimum of 2-4 weeks before trying to sell a similar product to the same mailing list.

How much have they paid on average for products in the past?

For instance, if the average amount that they have paid in the past is $100, and your product sells for $1500, this is probably not the list for you. However if your product sells for $175, and their average is $100, you may want to consider lowering your price a bit to get it closer to the average. You'll usually find that it is more profitable to lower your price, than to try and sell it at a higher regular price. On the other hand, if your product sells for $50 and their average is $100, you may want to consider increasing the price. If you don't think that your product is worthy of a higher price, see what you can do to increase the perceived value of it (add bonuses of some kind). You may also ask the owner of the list (who knows their customers) what they think about the price you have set, when compared to the product that you are offering.

How have your customers paid for their purchases in the past?

Since we're primarily dealing with information marketing over the internet, and we would primarily prefer our systems to be automated, credit card, including PayPal would be the best payment options. If you are using an email list where 90% of previous purchases have been paid for by check, you can either decide to add this option for this mailing only, or to find a different list. You can also offer multiple payment options. For instance if the item the customer is purchasing from you sells for $99, you could offer three interest free monthly payments of $33, and automatically charge their credit card for them. The reasons for doing this is simple, it makes the decision a lot easier for the customer, because the product is more affordable. $99 may be a lot of money to some people to spend unplanned all at once, but $33 may be more manageable. Remember, the easier you make it for the customers to buy, the more customers you'll have.

Do you have a money back guarantee and how many returns have you had?

If they don't have a money back guarantee find out why? If they stand 100% behind their products they should have a guarantee. If they do have a guarantee, the longer and stronger it is the better. Next find out how many returns they had. If they have a lot of returns this tells you that either their clients are cheap, that the list is of poor quality, or that the product that they sell is shoddy. Believe it or not there are people who buy a product knowing full well that they will make the most of the money back guarantee. Check out their product, make sure it is all that they say it is. The average rate of return for online marketing is 4%; if their rate of return is above this, and it's not because their product is crap, you probably don't want to be using their list. You want a list that has an average or below average rate of return.

What types of products have your clients bought before?

Hopefully you'll know the answer to this question from your previous research. You just need to be sure that their past purchases are in sync with what you are offering. For instance if you're trying to sell a home remedies ebook to a list of customers that subscribe to a car and truck newsletter you're not going to be very successful. Instead partner with a company that is in a similar field as you, maybe a homeopathic or naturopathic ezine, or something along those lines.

What is your conversion rate?

Again, you just need to confirm that this JV will be worth your time. The higher the conversion rate the better, and the more successful your JV will be.

What is you value per visitor (VPV)?

Remember this one from earlier on? The higher the VPV the better. This one will again help you determine whether you should JV with this person.

Do you have any testimonials from past JV partners that I can see?

If they don't, be wary and ask them to send you the phone numbers from some of their past JV partners, then check them out. Also watch out for vague testimonials, they may not be real. People rarely leave testimonials that say "you're the best," they are usually more specific like "Bob wrote us an amazing endorsement which I believe is largely responsible for the success rate of 12% that we achieved using his email list."

What is the most expensive product that you have tried to sell to your list? What is the cheapest? What kind of response did you get?

If the response rate to a highly priced item was low, look at the sales letter. If the sales letter is weak, perhaps you could have more success with a better sales letter. If the sales letter is good, perhaps it could be that the price was not affordable for the list. If the response rate to a cheap product was low, with a decent sales letter, and a good quality product, the list may not be a good one to use.

Above all, joint ventures are great for everybody. Everybody wins and there are no losers. JV's are one of the fastest ways to grow your business and is something that you should look into implementing immediately, if you haven't already. Always keep a lookout for qualified JV partners. If you're interested in forming a joint venture relationship, send me your proposal to jv@justinmichie.com. There is also a sample JV agreement for your viewing pleasure on the members website for this book.

Section 7

The Conclusion

37

What Now?

I know we've covered a lot and I hope by now you're excited about all things you can do to improve your online business. Some of what's in this book may come to you naturally, others things you may need to learn. Some things you will not agree with and will resist. These are the things you need to work on the most.

The internet is a great place to make money and it affords a very enjoyable lifestyle. If you pursue some of the techniques and strategies described in this book, you should have enough work to keep you and a couple of others busy for at least a few years.

The opportunity potential on the internet is much the same whether you are a small home based business or a mega corporation. Some people have started with nothing more than a small idea and turned it into thousands of dollars. Some have become millionaires. And a select few have become billionaires.

Some internet marketers achieve phenomenal results while others barely break even, and there's good reason why. The most important factors concern desire, commitment, and time management.

No major successes happen without desire. Successful people all know what they want and are willing to exert great amounts of energy, effort and money to achieve it. Their eagerness and enthusiasm translates into intense commitment and burning desire. If you want to succeed you must have desire. Work without desire is fruitless and will never get you to where you want to be.

Once you have desire, you must have commitment to that desire. Commitment means that you will persistently forge on until problems are resolved and solutions are found. Desire without commitment doesn't get you anywhere. You need to commit to your desire and turn it into an action plan and then act on that action plan. In order to act appropriately you need to manage your time, and create an action based time management plan.

Time is something that only happens once, and once it happens there is no going back. The 3 seconds that it will take you to read this sentence are gone forever. You can't go back and do it over. Make every second count.

The most significant investment in any business is the time you put into it. And like any monetary investment, you want to make sure you invest well, and that means using your time appropriately. Internet marketing is a business and must be treated and run as a business. Not as a website, or a product, or a hobby, or anything else but a business.

In most business you're supposed to sit down and come up with some sort of long term business plan. The internet is a little different. Long term business plans are useless. On the internet things change too quickly and your business and your way of thinking will be completely different twelve months from now. Long term might only be two-to-three months down the road. If you plan ahead any longer term than that, you're doing nothing more than giving yourself months of excuses.

Make a list of your immediate short-term goals and plan your days. Proper planning requires systematically thinking about your entire business. Develop a strategy to achieve your goals. The whole point of developing a strategy is to intensely focus on the right things that will achieve results.

I always make a to-do list the night before, and then work through it the next day, crossing things off as I do them. I know it seems trivial, but it feels good to cross things off my list, and motivates me to do the next item so I can cross it off.

Instead of starting your day with easy, brainless tasks you don't mind doing, start your day with the hard things that you dislike doing and like to put off. What you usually feel like doing is not usually the highest leverage activity in your business. That way, not only do you get the more difficult tasks completed and off the back of your mind, but it also staves off procrastination and them never getting done. And most often the things you dislike doing are the most important.

Make yourself a daily schedule. Don't get lost in your email or surfing the web. Email and the internet are very powerful business tools, but they can also inhibit your ability to earn. According to a new survey by America Online and Salary.com, the average adult worker admits to frittering away 2.09 hours per 8-hour workday, mostly on internet related activities.

Schedule your time; include free time, phone time for returning calls, email time, surfing time, research time and work (to-do list) time.

If you're busy working, there's no need to stop to answer the phone, let the voicemail get it – that's why voicemail was invented. Keep your email client closed when working, it will eliminate the sudden urge to check and see who the newest email is from when you get the ping. With a computer there are endless distractions, and it is important to keep on track and on time.

Furthermore, identify your key areas of profit, and concentrate on spending the bulk of your time, money and effort there. Practice the Pareto Principal. Find the 20% of your business or customers that produce 80% of the profit. Then focus on it. Devote 80% of your efforts to these key areas and leave the remaining 20% for the other things.

Continuing Education

The internet is enormous, and an entire book could be written on each individual chapter in this book. What I have tried to do is give you an overview of the main aspects of marketing on the internet. What worked yesterday may not work today. New technologies keep popping up and replacing old ones.

No matter how much you learn, there is always someone who knows something you don't. It could be something small, or it could be something big. It's the things you don't know, that you don't know, that can have the biggest impact on your life. That's why you need to try and learn as much as you can in the time you have.

I try to attend a business or personal growth seminar at least once every 3-4 weeks, read a book or two a week, and buy every internet marketing/business course I can get my hands on. Something, no matter how small, could literally change the way I do business and more importantly, the way I live my life. That's why continuing your education is so important.

Go to the members site for this book, login (www.ssim.biz, username: ssim, password: member), and click on the continuing education link. There you'll find some of the programs that I've tried, seminars I've attended and books I've read, and recommend that you try/attend/read as well. The more you put into your business, the more you'll get out of it and the more satisfied you'll feel.

If you've ever bought, or considered buying a get-rich-quick program, you likely think that they don't work. While that may be true in most cases, in some cases they do actually work, although most may never know. The reason they don't appear to work is that many people that buy them expect things to happen overnight, and when they don't, they give up. They expect to get something for nothing (or almost nothing) and just because you buy, read, listen to, or watch something doesn't mean things are going to happen automatically.

Although internet marketing and the content contained throughout this book is by no means a get rich quick scheme, some people expect to make a fortune on the net overnight. Trust me, it won't happen. Even though internet marketing by definition is much easier, cheaper and quicker than traditional marketing, it still requires a lot of hard work and a strong game plan – don't give up before you give it a chance.

If a lifestyle that affords you the ability to do what you want when you want, buy what you want when you want, and go where you want when you want seems attractive then what are you waiting for? You now have some of the best tools on this planet to create massive, passive income in only a few hours a day, a few days a week – but you need to invest the time and have the desire and the commitment to get there.

-- With a little hard work, in no time at all, you'll soon be checking your email from the beach in the middle of nowhere. --

38

Final Thoughts

Don't expect things to happen overnight. All I can do is give you advice; it's up to you to put it into action. Sit down, set your goals, and get started right away. Don't wait until tomorrow, or the next day to get started. Start right now. The sooner you start, the sooner you can start living the life you want.

You need to act on your thoughts and ideas immediately. Have you ever turned on the TV or opened a newspaper or magazine and seen someone else making millions with an idea that you had, but never acted on? That could have been you.

The longer it takes you to go from idea to fruition, the less likely you are to complete it and the more likely it is that someone else will. On the internet if you're not early, you're late. Take action now, and don't make excuses.

No matter what you do, always give 110%, 100% of the time. Find your burning desire, commit to that desire then devise an action plan and act on it. Proceed at your own pace. Embrace fear. Embrace life.

Once you make your first million, don't forget to share your newfound wealth with others. Give to charity, tip generously, and most of all believe in yourself. I know you can do it - - the only thing stopping you is you.

Glossary

Action tracking: The ability of a stat or ad tracker to track a visitor's actions on your website, such as making a sale or joining your mailing list.

ACV (*see* annual customer value)

Ad tracker: Software that tracks the response to an ad, including click-throughs, sales or any other qualifying action.

Affiliate fraud: Fraudulent activity by an affiliate in an attempt to generate illegitimate revenue.

Affiliate marketing: The process of marketing products or services on behalf of other companies and being paid a commission for each qualifying action such as a sale or opt-in sign up.

Affiliate/Associate management: Affiliate management software which allows you to take on new affiliates, manage and them, and give them access to promotional tools etc.

Alert boxes: Grey alert dialog box usually reserved for error messages.

Alt tags: Provide an alternative text when non-textual page elements (images or graphics) cannot be displayed.

Animation: A moving image, or series of moving images.

Annual customer value (ACV): How much, on average, each customer is worth to in sales in one year.

Autoresponder: An email software program that sends out an automatic response to an email. (*see* also Sequential autoresponders)

Back-end marketing: The products sold to customers after the initial sale. These products are usually much higher priced, with larger profit margins than the product sold in the initial sale.

Backlink: Links that are directed towards your website from other sites.

Backup systems: An alternative storage system that will automatically backup the information on a regular basis, as a failsafe in the case of electrical, hardware or software failure.

Bandwidth: The amount of data that can be transmitted in a fixed amount of time.

Banner ad: A graphical advertising unit commonly displayed on webpages, usually 468 x 60 pixels.

Bartering: The exchanging of goods or services between businesses; no money is involved.

Blog: An online journal or web log containing personal thoughts and opinions (also called blogging)

Bookmark: A link stored in a web browser for future reference.

Branding sites: A website designed to build the brand or identity of business or individual.

Browser hijacking: The use of browser tricks to keep a visitor captive at a particular website, often by disabling the "back" button or using repeated popup windows.

CAC (*see* customer acquisition cost)

Chat room: Chat rooms are similar to newsgroups and discussion forums but allow chat in real time.

Classified ad: A brief text listing of items for sale and/or services offered, usually arranged by category.

Click popularity: The measure of the number of clicks received a website in a search engine's results page.

Click-through rate (CTR): The average number of click-throughs per hundred ad impressions, expressed as a percentage.

Comment tags: A way for webmasters to make notes in their HTML code, not visible in the web browser.

Control panel: Part of your web hosting, shopping cart or affiliate software that allows you to configure and perform maintenance directly through your web browser.

Conversion rate: The percentage of website visitors who take the desired action.

Cookie: Information that is stored on a user's computer by a website for future reference.

Cost per action (CPA): The cost the advertiser pays to the site publisher each time a specific, visitor-initiated action occurs, like the completion of a sale or a newsletter signup.

Cost per click-through (CPC): The measurement of how much it costs on a per click basis when you're paying for ads based on impressions.

Cost per mila (CPM): The cost per 1,000 impressions or views.

Cost per sale (CPS): The amount on average, it costs you in advertising and other costs to make each individual sale.

Cost per visitor (CPV): The amount, on average, it costs to get each visitor to a website.

CPA (*see* cost per action)

CPC (*see* cost per click-through)

CPM (*see* cost per mila)

CPS (*see* cost per sale)

CPV (*see* cost per visitor)

Cross-sell: When a suggestion is made to a customer to buy a complimentary product to one they are already purchasing.

CTR (*see* click-through rate)

Crawlers (*see* robots)

Customer acquisition cost (CAC): The total cost associated with gaining a new customer.

Data transfer: The amount of data transferred between two or more computers.

Dedicated IP: An IP address dedicated to a single computer or website.

Dedicated hosting: A single web server that is dedicated to the use of one user or website.

Description meta tag: A HTML tag that controls a text summary which may be displayed when webpage appears in search engine's results.

Directory: A listing of websites organized alphabetically by category.

Discussion forums: Web based chat room where messages are posted, not in real time.

Domain name: The name that identifies a particular website, also referred to as the site's URL.

Doorway pages: A webpage that is designed to rank well in search engines, then automatically redirect visitor to desired website.

Driving traffic: The process of getting prospects to your website.

Ebook: An electronic form of a book usually in .pdf, or .exe format.

Email: A computer based text or HTML message sent over the internet.

Email database: A list of email addresses, usually for the purpose of sending out marketing material.

Entry page: The page that a visitor arrives at on your website.

Exit page: The last page your visitor views before leaving your site.

Ezine: Regular occurring email communication, usually entertainment or news related.

FFA (*see* free for all sites)

Flash: A multimedia technology developed by Macromedia to allow interactivity (animation, audio and video) to fit in a small file size and be cross browser compatible.

Frames: A structure that allows a webpage to divide into two or more independent parts (or webpages).

Free for all sites (FFA): Sites that display a mass of backlinks in return for the poster's email address.

Front-end marketing: Focusing marketing and promotional efforts on acquiring new customers, usually by offering a low priced item where money is sometimes lost (loss leader).

Fulfillment house: A company that is designed to take orders, process payments and ship products for you.

Full site tracking: A stat tracker that can tell you everything a visitor does once they arrive at your website.

Google AdSense: A Google service that allows website owners to place Google syndicated ads on their site, for the purpose of creating advertising revenue.

Google AdWords: A paid search engine ad program that allows advertisers to bid on keywords and have their ads displayed with the search results.

Header tags: A HTML tag that contains information about the web document including its title and meta tags.

Hit: A single request for a file from a web server.

HTML (*see* hypertext markup language)

HTTP (*see* hypertext transfer protocol)

Hybrid search engines: Search engines that combine a directory and a search engine to give visitors the most relevant results to their queries.

Hyper text markup language (HTML): The authoring software language used to create webpages on the internet.

Hyper text transfer protocol (HTTP): The communications protocol that enables communication between a web server and surfer's computer.

Impression: A single instance of an ad being displayed on a webpage.

Inbound link: A link to your site from another site.

Internet protocol (IP) address: An identifying address where each computer connects to the internet.

Internet service provider (ISP): A company which provides internet access.

Interstitial ads: Ads that are shown in the transition between two pages of a website.

ISP (*see* internet service provider)

Joint venture: A cooperative arrangement or partnership that will mutually benefit two or more companies that have complimentary products and/or services.

Keyword: Words that are typed into search engines to find websites of a particular interest.

Keyword density: The percentage of keywords in relation to other words used in a specific text.

Keyword frequency: How often a keyword appears on a webpage.

Keyword proximity: How close two or more keywords are to each other.

Keyword spamming: Repeating the same keyword many times or using inappropriate keywords that are unrelated to the content of your webpage, for the purpose of gaining a higher ranking in search engines.

Link popularity: A measure of the number of backlinks and their relevance to a website.

Link exchanges: Where one website exchanges backlinks with another site.

Loss leader: A product that is sold at a loss to gain a new customer, which can be sold to on the back-end for a profit.

Macromedia Dreamweaver: Software developed by Macromedia to design and publish webpages.

Marketing plan: Part of a business plan geared toward the marketing strategy for a product, service or business.

Merchant accounts: An internet service that enables processing of credit cards online.

Meta tags: HTML tags that describe contents and/or characteristics of a webpage.

Microsoft Frontpage: Microsoft developed software for designing and publishing webpages.

Mousetrapping (*see* browser hijacking)

Navigation: The ability to move from one webpage to another through the use of links.

Negative keywords: The opposite of keywords. If someone performs a search that includes a negative keyword, the ad will not be displayed.

Newsgroups: These are places on the internet where people go to discuss various topics.

One tier commissions: A system in which commissions are paid on only one level in an affiliate marketing program.

Opt-in email: Where visitors actively opt-in to join an email list.

Opt-out: Where someone on an email list unsubscribes or opts-out from an email list.

Outbound link: A link from your site to another outside website.

Page view: A request to load a single webpage.

Paid search engine inclusion: Where a website owner pays a fee to have their webpages crawled for possible submission into a search engine.

Payment per action (PPA): An online advertising payment model where payment is based on qualifying actions such as sales or registrations.

Payment per click-through (PPC): Payment based on click-throughs, where you only pay for each instance of an ad being clicked on.

Payment per sale (PPS): An advertising model where you only pay when a sale is made.

Pop-over: A DHTML layer that appears as a popup in your web browser, but does not actually open a new window.

Pop-under: Pops up a new window underneath your browser window.

Popup: Opens a new browser window on top of the one being used.

Power squeeze page (*see* squeeze page)

PPA (*see* payment per action)

PPC (*see* payment per click-through)

PPC search engine: A paid search engine ad program that allows advertisers to bid on keywords and have their ads displayed with the search results.

PPS (*see* payment per sale)

Press kit: A marketing package put together to distribute to the media including a press release, introduction letter, business card and any other relevant information.

Press release: A news article intended to let the media know about something newsworthy to do with your company or products.

Reciprocal link: A link between two websites, often because of an agreement by the site owners.

Refresh page (*see* relay page)

Relay page: A webpage that redirects the visitor to another webpage, often used for tracking purposes.

Remote site tracking: The ability of a stat/ad tracker to monitor your visitors after they leave your site.

Return on investment (ROI): The money gained or lost on an investment.

Robots: Software used by search engines to index websites. They work by following links from one site to another and indexing everything as they go.

Robots.txt: A text file that lets search engine crawlers know which pages of your site you do or do not want indexed.

ROI (*see* return on investment)

Sales page: A webpage intended to sell a product or service.

Sales site: A website intended to sell a product or service.

Search engine optimization (SEO): The practice of optimizing a website to rank well in search engines.

Search engines: A program that indexes web documents, then matches documents relevant to search requests.

SEO (*see* search engine optimization)

Sequential autoresponders: An autoresponder than can send out multiple pre-scheduled emails.

Shared hosting: Multiple websites that are hosted on a single web server.

Shopping cart: Software used to allow visitors to shop on your website. Also integrates the sales process with your merchant account.

Shy yes page (*see* squeeze page)

SIG file: A short identifying block of text at the end of a message which provides information about the sender.

Simple autoresponders: An automatic email response to an incoming message.

Spam: Unsolicited bulk email, or in other words – junk email.

Spam filter: Filters out emails that appear to be spam.

Spider (*see* robots)

Squeeze page: A webpage designed to squeeze the name and email address from the visitor, usually by offering them a free gift or ethical bribe.

Statistics tracking: A software program allowing one to track website statistics.

Stickiness: A measure of the amount of time a user spends at a website.

Target market: Your primary market – the customers you want to sell to most.

Testing: Trying different variables in any marketing medium, such as headlines, email subjects or offers to determine which yields the best results.

Text ad: A text-only advertisement usually containing a text-based hyperlink.

Third party merchant accounts: The use of a third parties merchant account to process your credit card transactions.

Tracking: The ability to track or monitor what happens on your website.

Two tier commissions: A system in which commissions are paid on two levels for an affiliate marketing program.

Unique visitor: A visitors who has visited a website at least once in during a fixed time frame.

Up-sell: The practice of suggesting higher priced products to a customer who is considering a purchase.

Uptime: The amount of time a website is available, usually expressed as a percentage.

URL: The location of a resource (webpage) on the internet, also referred to as a domain name.

URL tracking: A tracking method in which special code is added to your URL, for the purpose of tracking ads.

Value per visitor (VPV): How much, on average, each visitor to your website is worth in sales.

Viewing time: The amount of time a visitor spends on an individual website or webpage.

Viral marketing: Marketing that encourages people to pass along a marketing message to others.

VPV (*see* value per visitor)

Web browser: A software application that allows for browsing on the World Wide Web.

Web host: A business that provides the storage, connectivity and services necessary to serve files for a website.

Web log (*see* blog)

Webpage: A specifically formatted document available for viewing on the internet.

Whois: Is a utility that gives ownership information about domains (www.who.is).

World Wide Web (WWW): The entire internet and everything it encompasses.

WWW: (*see* world wide web)

Index